COMMUNISM IN EASTERN EUROPE

Communism in Eastern Europe is a groundbreaking new survey of the history of Eastern Europe since 1945. It examines how Communist governments came to Eastern Europe, how they changed their societies and the legacies that persisted after their fall. Written from the perspective of the 21st century, this book shows how Eastern Europe's trajectory since 1989 fits into the longer history of its Communist past.

Rather than focusing on high politics, *Communism in Eastern Europe* concentrates on the politics of daily life, melding political history with social, cultural and gender history. It tells the history of this complicated era through the voices and experiences of ordinary people. By focusing on the complex interactions of everyday life, *Communism in Eastern Europe* illuminates the world Communism made in Eastern Europe, its politics and culture, values and dreams, successes and failures.

This book is an engaging introduction to the history of Communist Eastern Europe for any reader. It is ideal for adoption in a wide array of undergraduate and graduate courses in 20th-century European history.

Melissa Feinberg is Professor of History at Rutgers University. She is the author of *Curtain of Lies: The Battle over Truth in Stalinist Eastern Europe* and *Elusive Equality: Gender, Citizenship and the Limits of Democracy in Czechoslovakia, 1918–1950*.

COMMUNISM IN EASTERN EUROPE

Melissa Feinberg

Routledge
Taylor & Francis Group

NEW YORK AND LONDON

Cover image: © Sueddeutsche Zeitung Photo / Alamy Stock Photo RMJYP4

First published 2022
by Routledge
605 Third Avenue, New York, NY 10158

and by Routledge
2 Park Square, Milton Park, Abingdon, Oxon, OX14 4RN

Routledge is an imprint of the Taylor & Francis Group, an informa business

© 2022 Melissa Feinberg

Library of Congress Cataloging-in-Publication Data
Names: Feinberg, Melissa, author.
Title: Communism in Eastern Europe/Melissa Feinberg.
Description: New York; Abingdon: Routledge, 2022. |
Includes bibliographical references and index. |
Identifiers: LCCN 2021031810 | ISBN 9780367086091 (hardback) |
ISBN 9780813348179 (paperback) | ISBN 9780813348186 (ebook) |
ISBN 0367086093 (hardback) | ISBN 0813348188 (paperback)
Subjects: LCSH: Communism—Europe, Eastern—History—20th
century. | Communism—Social aspects—Europe, Eastern—
History—20th century. | Political culture—Europe, Eastern—
History—20th century. | Communist countries—Social life and
customs—History—20th century.
Classification: LCC HX240.7.A6 F45 2022 | DDC 335.430947—dc23
LC record available at https://lccn.loc.gov/2021031810

ISBN: 978-0-367-08609-1 (hbk)
ISBN: 978-0-8133-4817-9 (pbk)
ISBN: 978-0-8133-4818-6 (ebk)

DOI: 10.4324/9780813348186

Typeset in Bembo
by codeMantra

CONTENTS

MAPS

FIGURES

PREFACE

One day, more years ago than I care to admit, I was contacted out of the blue by an editor looking to put together a new list of books for college courses. She asked me if there were any books related to classes I taught that I particularly wanted to see in print. I immediately responded that I wished there was a new survey of the history of Eastern Europe since 1945. Most of the existing options had been originally written during the Cold War. They emphasized high politics and Soviet–East European relations. While these books provided a useful political narrative, my students found them boring and hard to read. They had trouble seeing the point in books that seemed like an endless procession of unfamiliar names and dates. During the Cold War, the events these books described were still recent, and understanding them was crucial to understanding contemporary geopolitics. In the 21st century, however, this was no longer the case. Of course, I said to the editor, politics was important to the history of Communist Eastern Europe, but it needed to be conceived differently. I wanted to see a book that put less emphasis on who was in power when and more on what it meant to live in a Communist society. Instead of high politics and foreign affairs, I wanted to see a survey that concentrated on the politics of everyday life, melding political history with social, cultural and gender history.

This book eventually came out of that conversation. While it was conceived with undergraduate students in mind, I hope it will be a useful introduction to the recent history of Eastern Europe for a wide variety of audiences. In composing the narrative, I have not jettisoned the key events of Eastern Europe's political history, but I have endeavored to put them into a new framework, one that relies on the voices and experiences of ordinary people. I could never have done this without having the benefit of the vast amount of excellent new research that has been published on Eastern Europe since 1989, including work by historians, anthropologists, sociologists, political scientists and journalists from all over the world. This book rests this research, which has revolutionized our understanding of how people lived during Communism and after its fall. In the notes, I have emphasized accessible work in English for the benefit of nonspecialist readers. But what is in the notes is only a small fraction of the pathbreaking research in this vibrant field.

One of my goals in this book was to reframe the narrative of the Communist era from the position of the present day. In the immediate aftermath of the Cold War, many people saw the events of 1989 as a victory for freedom. From today's perspective, we can see that nothing was that simple. Democracy can no longer be taken for granted in Eastern Europe, despite the fall of Communism. This book places 1989 within a longer trajectory and also shows how the events of the 1990s, as well as the concerns of the Communist era itself, are connected to the rise of populism in Eastern Europe today.

When I initially agreed to write this book, I foolishly thought it would be easy. I was wrong. Luckily, I had some help along the way. I would like to thank the many people who read and commented on parts of the manuscript as it developed. My first readers were the participants in the Philadelphia area modern German history workshop and the Monday seminar at the Imre Kertész Kolleg in Jena. Thanks to both groups for their constructive comments and their enthusiasm! A special thank you to Joachim von Puttkamer, Raphael Utz and Daniela Gruber for making my stay in Jena in spring 2019 possible. Many thanks also to the students in Paola Tartakoff's European history seminar and my own colloquium on modern East European history for their comments on Chapters 5 and 6. Several colleagues graciously read drafts of multiple chapters and gave me excellent feedback: very heartfelt thanks to James Bjork, Theodora Dragostinova, Malgorzata Fidelis, Benjamin Frommer and Eagle Glassheim.

As always, my biggest thanks go to Paul Hanebrink. Paul has read every chapter many times, made countless useful suggestions and done his best to make sure I got the Hungarian diacriticals right (any errors are definitely all mine). Paul is there when I need to talk and when I need to stay silent. He kept me focused during a pandemic and helped me to see when I really did need a break. He is not only my best reader, he is just the best.

INTRODUCTION

The Communist World of Eastern Europe

This book examines the long history of Communism in Eastern Europe. It considers not only the period when Communist parties ruled in Eastern Europe but the circumstances that led to their arrival and the legacies that persisted after their fall. When Communist rulers took power in Eastern Europe in the years after World War II, they sought to transform the societies they found there into something new. They aimed to create new industries, new cities and even new people. Things did not always turn out as planned, but Communism did nonetheless transform Eastern Europe. The goal of this book is to illuminate the world that Communism created in all of its complexity.

The Communists came out of the international socialist movement of the late 19th century.[1] Like all socialists, the Communists were motivated by a sense of injustice. They were appalled by a world in which wealth seemed to be ever concentrated in fewer and fewer hands, while the masses suffered from poverty and want. Influenced by the work of the thinker Karl Marx, Communists believed that the problem lay with the capitalist economic system itself. Communists saw capitalism as characterized by the struggle between two opposing classes: those who owned the means of production (the capitalists or the bourgeoisie) and those who actually did the work (the working class or the proletariat). In a capitalist system, there was no way for the working class to ever really get ahead. They would always be at the mercy of the bourgeoisie. For Communists, the only way to fundamentally change this exploitative system was to end it via a revolution that would bring the working class to power.

As both an ideology and a movement, Communism was forged out of the Russian Revolution of 1917. In 1917, a small group of revolutionary socialists led by Vladimir Lenin seized power in Russia. They were known as the Bolsheviks, but soon took the name Communist. Resistance to Communist

DOI: 10.4324/9780813348186-1

rule sparked a bloody civil war. After years of fighting, the Bolsheviks claimed victory. They began to transform the territories of the Russian empire into a new socialist state: the Soviet Union. Elsewhere in the world, Communist parties formed in solidarity with what was happening in the USSR, hoping to bring the revolution to their own countries. The Soviets became the leading force in a global Communist movement.

Under Lenin, and later under his successor, Joseph Stalin, Soviet Communists would create their own ideology, merging theory with practice as they tried to create the world's first socialist state. Marxist ideas—known as dialectical materialism—gave the Communists a basic set of principles for analyzing the world and predicting its future. For Communists, dialectical materialism was not a philosophy but a science based on the rational and objective observation of the world. Using this kind of analysis, Communists felt they had the key to understanding both the past and the present. As British Communist Eric Hobsbawm described it,

> "Dialectical materialism" provided, if not a "theory of everything," then at least a "framework of everything," linking inorganic and organic nature with human affairs, collective and individual, and providing a guide to the nature of all interactions in a world in constant flux.[2]

This gave Communists a sense of purpose and feeling of absolute certainty. Communists were convinced that they were on the right side of history and that their work would bring about a better world for everyone.

This conviction allowed Lenin and his comrades to create a dictatorship in which the opposition was outlawed and the power to create policy was centralized in the Communist leadership. The Soviet system would become even more authoritarian under Stalin. Many Communists came to see those who disagreed with the party line as enemies. Those who opposed party orthodoxy were not simply wrong; they were a danger to the continued existence of socialism and a threat to its goals. Good Communists were supposed to quell their doubts, align themselves with the party and dedicate themselves to building the new socialist world. Their heroic efforts would be what would bring that new world forth.[3]

When they first seized power in Russia, Communists believed that a worldwide socialist revolution was inevitable. When revolutionary uprisings elsewhere in Europe fizzled out and it became clear that a global revolution was not in the offing, Soviet leaders changed their focus, turning their attention to domestic transformation. Marx had imagined that socialist revolution would break out under the conditions of advanced industrial capitalism. The Russian empire had, in contrast, been largely rural with a small working class. A Communist society, therefore, could not come into being only through revolution. It would need to be created via a process of modernization, carried out through socialist rather than capitalist auspices. Communism became intertwined with the project of creating a modern industrial economy and a modern society. When Communism came to Eastern Europe, it would come not only as a set of ideas about how to achieve social equality, but as a set of plans for turning "backward" societies into modern ones.

Today, Communist regimes are often simplistically equated with tyranny. This view of Communism imagines an all-powerful state that ruled through fear. In this model, Communist states were static entities that existed primarily to oppress their people and quell dissent. The people naturally opposed their despotic rulers but were powerless to resist them. They lived their lives in miserable fear. Such a picture suggests that the only thing we need to know to understand Communist societies was that they lacked political freedoms.

This book shows that this one-sided picture does not adequately reflect the realities of life under Communism. The Communist regimes of Eastern Europe were dictatorships, but the ways power operated in these systems were complicated, not straightforward. Under Communism, East Europeans did not have the same political freedoms that people had in democratic societies, but they nonetheless felt entitled to make demands of their leaders and their leaders were compelled to take those demands seriously. Under Communism, most people did not live all their lives in fear. They went to school and pursued careers, made friends and had romantic relationships, moved into new apartments and raised families, took vacations and constructed weekend cottages. The Communist system constrained their opportunities, but at the same time it also enabled paths to flourishing.

The Communist world was a world of seeming contradictions. It censored books but also ended illiteracy. It put some people in jail for their political beliefs but gave women legal equality with men and access to a wide range of new careers. It was a world where bananas were almost impossible to find in the stores, but where on average people had more to eat than ever before. The following chapters provide a window into this world, its politics and culture, values and dreams, successes and failures.

The Impenetrable East

This book defines Eastern Europe as those countries that had Communist governments beginning in the years after World War II but were not part of the Soviet Union. This includes Albania, Bulgaria, Czechoslovakia, East Germany, Hungary, Poland, Romania, Yugoslavia and their successor states. With the exception of Yugoslavia (and, after 1961, Albania), these countries were militarily and economically allied to the Soviet Union and to each other. In addition to these economic and military ties, these countries were bound together by a common set of experiences. They were all part of a shared Communist world.

While the idea of a region called Eastern Europe gained a new coherence during the Communist period, the concept of "Eastern Europe" dates to the

Enlightenment of the 18th century. Before the Enlightenment, the most important regional distinctions in Europe were between the cultured South, the inheritor of the traditions of ancient Greece and Rome, and the more barbarian, Germanic North. During the Enlightenment, the writers and thinkers known as the philosophes began to imagine a different Europe, one divided along an East/West rather than a North/South axis. Their new mental map of the continent, however, continued to picture Europe as defined by a cultured center and a more savage periphery. As they envisioned it, the West was the home of civilization, while the East was a land of barbarism and backwardness.[4]

For the 18th-century philosophes, Eastern Europe was defined not by its latitude and longitude but by its level of civilization. Eighteenth-century Western travelers knew they had entered Eastern Europe not by consulting a map but just by looking at their environs. When Count Louis-Philippe de Ségur, newly assigned as the French ambassador to the court of Catherine the Great, traveled from Prussia into Poland in 1784, he immediately felt he had left civilization behind. Poland, said de Ségur, was poor and dirty; even the trees were sad. The German-speaker Georg Forster had similar thoughts when he took up a position at the University of Vilnius that same year. Poland, he said, was dilapidated and filthy, "half-wild" and "half-civilized." Overcome by the sight of his new home, he wrote, "I wept a lonely hour for myself—and then, as I gradually came to myself, for the so deeply sunken people."[5]

If one measure of Eastern Europe's backwardness was its poverty, another was its strangeness. Educated Europeans in the 18th century defined civilization according to what they deemed normal in their own lives. Civilized people, they believed, would have dress, manners, customs and values similar to their own. Yet what they found in Eastern Europe was decidedly alien to them. For the writer Johann Pezzl, East Europeans stood out easily on the streets of Vienna because of their exotic costumes. He described a colorful cast of characters, including

> the Hungarian striding stiffly, with his fur-lined dolman [a Turkish robe], his close-fitting trousers reaching almost to his ankles, and his long pigtail ... the round-headed Pole with his monkish haircut and flowing sleeves ... Serbians with their twisted mustaches ... Polish Jews, all swathed in black, their faces bearded and their hair all twisted in knots ... Bohemian peasants with their long boots

and more. The exotic appearance and manners of East Europeans made them seem a breed apart to Western observers. The Englishman William Coxe, who visited Poland in 1778, was convinced that "the Poles, in their features, look, customs, dress, and general appearance, resemble Asiatics rather than Europeans; and they are unquestionably descended from Tatar ancestors."[6]

One prominent feature of Eastern Europe's strangeness was its languages. Once Western travelers left Berlin or Vienna and headed East, they began to find themselves surrounded by people whose languages they found incomprehensible. While urban elites in 18th-century Eastern Europe usually spoke Western languages like German and French, Western travelers were not trained in Russian, Polish or Hungarian, adding to the sense of distance they felt from the people they observed in their travels. Language became an essential component of what separated the East from the West, adding to the perception of Eastern Europe as an unfathomable place outside of Western norms. In 1787, the composer Wolfgang Amadeus Mozart playfully marked his journey from Austrian Vienna to Bohemian Prague by giving himself and his friends ridiculous, supposedly Slavic sounding names like Hikkiti Horky and Punkititi to use while they were there.[7] Over 130 years later, the English crime writer Agatha Christie showed how Western perceptions of Slavic languages had only hardened in the intervening decades. In her 1925 novel, *The Secret of Chimneys*, Christie invented the Slavic country of Herzoslovakia, peopled by assassins and brigands, whose language sounded like "a cross between gargling and barking like a dog" and was unpronounceable by English throats.[8]

The conceptual division of Europe into a civilized West and a backward, poor and incomprehensible East did reflect the social and economic realities of the 18th and 19th centuries. On the whole, Eastern Europe was poorer and less industrialized than the West, with lower levels of literacy, particularly among the rural masses. However, neither region was actually as monolithic as imagined. The East had its pockets of wealth and industrialization, while many rural areas in the West were just as poor and isolated as their East European counterparts. As late as the 1880s, French officials complained that peasants in their own country were "like those of countries where civilization has never penetrated: savage, dirty, and don't understand a word of the language."[9] Yet, the existence of endemic rural poverty and illiteracy in the supposedly civilized West did nothing to disturb the mental map that by the 19th century firmly located backwardness in the East. The idea of Eastern Europe's backwardness became fixed, inextricably tied to the West's conception of itself as the center of civilization.

After World War II, the invisible line that divided Western and Eastern Europe turned into the Iron Curtain. The Cold War added new elements to the imagined division between East and West, but Eastern Europe remained the West's essential complement. In Western eyes, Communist Eastern Europe was still characterized by backwardness and poverty. In addition, it became a place of fear, slavery and oppression. During the Cold War, describing Eastern Europe's misery and grayness was a way to emphasize the West's freedom, prosperity and vibrancy. This did not only happen in the West itself. For East Europeans who were disappointed with Communism, the West took on the status of a mythical place that magically erased all the faults of their own system.

This long tradition of envisioning Europe partitioned along an East/West divide has made it difficult to conceive of Eastern Europe without measuring it against some imagined Western ideal. This book, however, tries to do just that. While it does occasionally compare Eastern Europe to its Western counterpart, its goal is to move away from stereotypes about the region and to present the recent history of Eastern Europe on its own terms.

Before the onset of the Cold War, there was little that bound the countries of Eastern Europe together, other than the space they shared on the mental map of Europe. The region encompassed myriad different political systems, economic conditions, cultures and languages. Communism gave this diverse region a larger degree of unity than it had ever known before. Under Communism, the countries of Eastern Europe had similar forms of government and similar economic systems. They shared some of the same vacation spots, consumer goods and television programs. Even more significantly, they were joined by the same guiding ideology and set of values. While not all people—or even all Communists—believed equally in Communist ideas or shared the same sense of social justice, this common ideology nonetheless gave East Europeans a similar intellectual background that framed their ways of looking at the world.

During the Cold War, Westerners often imagined that all the Communist countries of Europe were exactly the same. Yet, while Communism brought Eastern Europe together in new ways, it did not erase its diversity. Particularly after 1953, East European governments sometimes pursued quite divergent policies. In the past few decades, the trend among historians has been to emphasize these differences, showing how the countries of Eastern Europe were unique. This book strikes a middle road, illustrating how Communism created a set of shared systems, values and experiences that bound Eastern Europe together, while also pointing out the ways in which the various countries of Eastern Europe created their own distinctive paths, both during and after Communism.

A Note on Terminology

After 1948, each country in Eastern Europe had one ruling political party that was Communist in its ideology and orientation. These parties were commonly referred to as the Communist party. Yet they frequently had different official names. The Communist Party of Poland, for example, was formally called the Polish United Workers' Party. To make it even more complicated, many of Eastern Europe's putative Communist parties went through multiple name changes, particularly during the 1940s, when they merged with other socialist parties. To create greater readability and make the text more comprehensible to the nonspecialist reader, I have referred to all of Eastern Europe's ruling parties as the "Communist party" of their country, using their formal names only when the context explicitly required it.[10]

Eastern Europe's Communists often referred to their goal as building socialism and called their policies and values socialist. In this book, I have used the adjective "Communist" to refer to anything specifically tied to one of the region's Communist parties, such as its members, policies or organizations. When referring to motivating ideals, systems or even the state itself, I have used "Communist" and "socialist" interchangeably. My use of the word "socialist" reflects how the word was used in Communist Eastern Europe. It does not indicate something that all socialists would believe or support.

Notes

The references in the notes are accessible works in English that are good sources for further reading on all of the topics covered in this book.

1 Geoff Eley, "Marxism and Socialist Revolution," in *The Cambridge History of Communism*, Vol. 1: *World Revolution and Socialism in One Country, 1917–1941*, ed. Silvio Pons and Stephen A. Smith (Cambridge: Cambridge University Press, 2017), 49–73.
2 Brigitte Studer, "Communism as Existential Choice," in Pons and Smith, *World Revolution and Socialism in One Country*, 514.
3 Jochen Hellbeck, *Revolution on My Mind: Writing a Diary under Stalin* (Cambridge, MA: Harvard University Press, 2006).
4 Larry Wolff, *Inventing Eastern Europe: The Map of Civilization on the Mind of the Enlightenment* (Stanford, CA: Stanford University Press, 1994), 1–5.
5 Wolff, *Inventing Eastern Europe*, 17–19, 336–337.
6 Wolff, *Inventing Eastern Europe*, 29, 114.
7 Wolff, *Inventing Eastern Europe*, 107.
8 Agatha Christie, *The Secret of Chimneys* (New York: Dell, 1971), 36.
9 Eugen Weber, *Peasants into Frenchmen: The Modernization of Rural France, 1870–1914* (Stanford, CA: Stanford University Press, 1976), 4.
10 For similar reasons, I have kept to the lower case (Communist party or Communist parties) except when referring to a specific party, i.e., the Polish Communist Party.

1

COMMUNISM COMES TO EASTERN EUROPE

The first half of the 20th century was a tumultuous period in the history of Eastern Europe. For much of the 19th century, the region of Eastern Europe was governed by large, multinational empires. By 1918, the empires had dissolved, turning Eastern Europe into a land of democratic nation-states. These new countries struggled to successfully integrate their ethnically and religiously diverse populations and to create prosperous economies. During the 1920s and 1930s, the region was rocked by economic crisis and political turmoil. By 1938, democratic governments across Eastern Europe had failed and been replaced by rightist authoritarian regimes.

With the outbreak of World War II, Eastern Europe became a battlefield. Some East Europeans fought on the side of Nazi Germany, while others faced the German occupation of their countries. The war had devastating consequences for Eastern Europe. By the time it was over, millions of East Europeans had lost their lives. Much of the region lay in ruins.

As the Germans retreated, the victorious Soviet Red Army occupied Eastern Europe. After a few years, the Soviets engineered the creation of Communist governments in the region, which were modeled after the socialist system in the Soviet Union. While Communist regimes would not have been established in Eastern Europe without Soviet influence, the region's prewar history of nationalist conflict and its wartime experience played a crucial role in enabling the Communist path to power.

From Empires to Nation-States

The map of Eastern Europe has changed many times during the past 150 years. At the beginning of the 19th century, the region of Eastern Europe was divided

DOI: 10.4324/9780813348186-2

among four multinational empires: the Ottoman empire, the Russian empire, the Habsburg empire and the German empire. These empires encompassed a variety of peoples who spoke different languages, adhered to different religions and had their own distinctive cultural practices. At the beginning of the 20th century, all four empires still functioned effectively. However, the intense demands of World War I (1914–1918) strained their ability to serve the needs of their citizens, undermining popular faith in imperial leadership. As the war ended, all four empires were roiled by revolutionary unrest. As a consequence of its revolution, the Russian empire became the world's first Communist state: the Union of Soviet Socialist Republics (USSR). The German empire became a republic and the Ottoman and Habsburg empires disintegrated.

After the Habsburg and Ottoman empires collapsed, the victorious Allies (France, Great Britain and the United States) met in Paris to decide what would replace them. Nationalist activists from Eastern Europe wanted the former empires to be replaced with so-called nation-states: countries dedicated to the interests of one particular nation or ethnic group. Many of these activists went to Paris to lobby the Allies to recognize the right of their peoples to independence. They advocated the principle of national self-determination, or the idea that all nations deserved to govern themselves. Allied leaders, particularly the American president, Woodrow Wilson, were sympathetic to many of their appeals.

However, the realities of East European geography made it impossible to simply apply the principle of national self-determination to the European map. The different peoples of Eastern Europe did not live in neatly defined areas. As the residents of multinational empires, East Europeans often resided in mixed communities where several languages were used and multiple religions were practiced. Nor did all East Europeans see themselves as members of an ethnically based nation. Some people in mixed areas were bilingual and did not identify with one nation over another. These kinds of communities defied the desire of nationalists to create ethnically homogeneous populations.[1]

To make matters even more complicated, the Allies had geopolitical concerns that outweighed any commitment to abstract ideals like national self-determination. Replacing the Habsburg and Ottoman empires with a patchwork of small countries, they worried, might allow their defeated enemy, Germany, to gain an outsize influence in the region. The Allies were also concerned about the threat of socialist revolution emanating from the new Soviet Union. In redrawing the map, they placed a priority on establishing states they believed would be large and strong enough to maintain their independence against a resurgent Germany and the new threat of Soviet Communism. As a result, they created new countries that were ostensibly nation-states, devoted to the interests of one particular people. But in reality, each of these new states was multinational, just like the empires that had preceded them.[2] In recognition of this, the Allies forced the new governments of Eastern Europe to sign treaties

MAP 1.1 Eastern Europe after World War I.

that compelled them to respect the rights of their minority populations. East European leaders resented these treaties, noting that West European states were not required to provide similar guarantees.

The new state of Yugoslavia was emblematic of Eastern Europe's diversity, combining many different peoples under one government. Yugoslavia united three groups that saw themselves as separate nations: the Serbs, the Croats and the Slovenes. The Slovenes, who spoke their own language, were the smallest of these groups, forming about 8 percent of the population. The Serbs and the Croats spoke variants of the same language, referred to as Serbo-Croatian, but the Serbs wrote in the Cyrillic alphabet, while the Croats used Latin characters. These two groups had very different histories and practiced different religions: Serbs were largely Eastern Orthodox, while Croats were Catholic. Serbs were more numerous, comprising over one-third of the Yugoslav population, while Croats were just under 20 percent of the total. Yugoslavia was also home to several groups of Serbo-Croatian speakers who did not identify as either Serb or Croat, such as the Bosnian Muslims. In addition, Yugoslavia contained sizable communities of Albanian, German and Hungarian speakers.[3]

Yugoslavia's complicated mix of peoples was mirrored in all of the countries of Eastern Europe. While they were ostensibly unitary nation-states, they were actually multinational. Like Yugoslavia, Czechoslovakia united two groups that saw themselves as separate peoples: the Czechs and the Slovaks. In addition, the country contained a large German-speaking minority and smaller groups of Polish, Hungarian and Ukrainian (Ruthenian) speakers. Romania had a large Hungarian minority. Bulgaria had minorities of Turks and Bulgarian-speaking Muslims. The Roma, a frequently persecuted group with its own language (Romani), lived in every country in Eastern Europe. The numbers of Roma were particularly large in Romania and Hungary. Like the Roma, Jews lived throughout Eastern Europe. Hungary, which had lost much of its territory in 1918 and saw many Hungarian-speakers relegated to living in other countries, had relatively few national minorities but a very large Jewish population. Poland also had a large number of Jewish citizens, as well as substantial Ukrainian, German and Byelorussian minorities. East European Jews were a very diverse group. Some primarily spoke their own language, known as Yiddish, while others grew up speaking the language of the surrounding community, such as German, Hungarian or Czech. Some Jews considered themselves to be part of the same nation as their gentile neighbors, while others saw themselves a separate minority. Yet, regardless of how Jews saw themselves, antisemitic prejudice meant that others might see them as outsiders.[4]

During the 1920s, all the countries of Eastern Europe had some form of parliamentary government. Poland and Czechoslovakia were republics, while Bulgaria, Yugoslavia, Romania, Albania and Hungary were constitutional monarchies. But each had problems developing the political consensus necessary for maintaining a stable democratic government. National conflict played a significant role in this. Because each of these countries was ostensibly a nation-state, those outside of the majority nation sometimes felt excluded and threatened. Many of these minorities fought against the state rather than trying to work within it. Some German-speakers in Czechoslovakia, for example, began to agitate for autonomy or the right to unite with Germany. In some countries, there was also conflict among the different national groups the state was supposed to represent. In Yugoslavia, Serb and Croat politicians battled over who should have greater influence.

Soon, the democratic governments of interwar Eastern Europe began to crack under the strain. In Poland, the military leader and politician Józef Piłsudski staged a coup in 1926 and created an authoritarian government. In

Hungary, the institution of the open ballot in the countryside in 1922 allowed elites to completely dominate the electoral system. In Yugoslavia, the King, Alexander, proclaimed a royal dictatorship in 1929. Bulgaria's King Boris took power into his own hands in 1935, while Romania's King Carol did the same in 1938. Finally, Czechoslovakia's democracy wilted after the Munich conference in 1938, leaving it with only a truncated set of two political parties.[5]

Nazi Germany and Eastern Europe during World War II

In 1933, Nazi leader Adolf Hitler became the chancellor of Germany. Hitler and his followers dreamed of creating a new German empire that would incorporate much of Eastern Europe. Within a few years, Germany's drive for *Lebensraum* or "living space" to the East would drag most of the continent into a devastating war. Germany's quest for territory began under the banner of national self-determination. In March 1938, German forces moved to annex the country of Austria, where most of the population identified as ethnically German, in the name of national unity. In a time of heightened national tensions and growing support for fascism all over Europe, a large majority of Austrians supported unification with Germany.

Germany then took up the cause of Czechoslovakia's discontented German-speaking minority. Hitler argued that Czechoslovakia's Germans had been unfairly oppressed, and therefore, Germany should be allowed to annex the parts of Czechoslovakia where most of them lived, a region referred to as the Sudetenland. At a conference in Munich in September 1938, British, Italian and French leaders agreed to Hitler's demands. Left without allies, the Czechoslovak government agreed to comply, even though this meant losing a third of its territory and population, most of its military defenses and a sizable portion of its industry.[6]

British Prime Minister Neville Chamberlain argued at Munich that giving in to German demands would make war unnecessary. Instead, Munich only convinced Hitler that Germany could easily take more of the East. Only a few months later, on March 15, 1939, he demanded that the Czechs place all of their territory under German "protection." Czechoslovakia was divided into pieces: Slovakia became an independent state allied with Germany, while the western portion of the country was turned into a German satellite called the Protectorate of Bohemia and Moravia. The Czechs initially retained some local autonomy, but the ultimate authority in the Protectorate came from Berlin.[7]

In September 1939, Germany continued its plan of eastward expansion by declaring war on Poland. Within five weeks, the Polish army had been defeated and Poland once again disappeared from the map. A few days prior to the invasion, the Germans signed a nonaggression pact with the Soviet Union, the Molotov-Ribbentrop Pact, guaranteeing that the Soviets would not interfere. In return, the two countries secretly agreed that the Soviet Union would annex

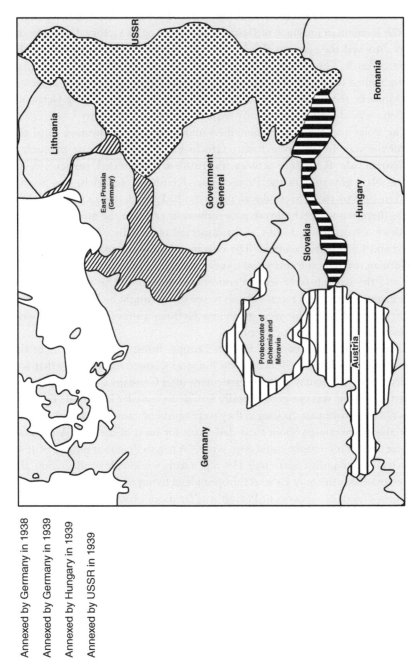

Annexed by Germany in 1938

Annexed by Germany in 1939

Annexed by Hungary in 1939

Annexed by USSR in 1939

MAP 1.2 East–Central Europe in 1939.

the eastern third of Poland. The Soviet would later also take the Baltic states and the Romanian province of Bessarabia. Following its victory, Germany directly annexed the western third of Poland, making it formally part of the German Reich. The remainder was turned into what was effectively a German colony named the General Government. Unlike the Protectorate of Bohemia and Moravia, the General Government would be ruled directly by Germans; the Poles would not be allowed any semblance of local autonomy.[8]

The Poles and the Czechs remained under German occupation until the end of the war. In the Protectorate, Czechs had to accommodate themselves to German rule. Resistance activity was ruthlessly suppressed, particularly after the Nazi governor of the Protectorate, Reinhard Heydrich, was assassinated in 1942 by two Czechoslovak men who had parachuted in from London, where there was a Czechoslovak government in exile. In the aftermath of the Heydrich assassination, 3,188 Czechs suspected of resistance activity were arrested and 1,357 were executed. The village of Lidice was made into a symbol of German revenge: the entire town was leveled, the adult male residents were shot and the women were sent to concentration camps. The town's children were examined by Nazi racial officials to see if they might be "Germanizable." The few judged acceptable were given new German names and sent to live with German families; the rest perished.[9]

Compared to other parts of Eastern Europe, however, Nazi terror in the Protectorate was limited. Bohemia was home to a large arms industry that was needed for the German war effort. Particularly after Germany attacked the Soviet Union in 1941, it was not economically feasible to consider large-scale deportations of Czech nationals. As long as they were obedient, most non-Jewish Czechs were able to quietly go about their daily lives for most of the war. A German traveler to the Protectorate could even write, "A trip to Prague at the end of 1942 was a trip to tranquility. Surrounded by war, a truly worldwide conflagration, the Protectorate was the only Central European land living in peace."[10]

The German occupation of Poland was far more brutal. As in the Protectorate, most of Polish public life was shut down: universities were closed, civic associations were outlawed and political activity was banned. In Poland, however, the intelligentsia—teachers, doctors, lawyers, clergy and others with at least a secondary school education—was targeted for destruction. Hans Frank, the Nazi governor of the General Government, noted in his dairy that Hitler had told him, "Poles may have only one master—a German. Two masters cannot exist side by side, and this is why the members of the Polish intelligentsia must be killed. It sounds cruel, but such is the law of life."[11] In the first weeks of the occupation, special killing squads known as *Einsatzgruppen* murdered approximately 50,000 Polish civilians. In just one of the regions that would be directly incorporated into Germany, the Warthegau, 10,000 noncombatants were killed in two months.[12] Arbitrary and unpredictable violence remained common throughout the period of occupation.

Throughout the German-occupied territories, Poles faced restrictions on their movements and were forced to show deference to their occupiers. They were required to give up seats on trains and buses to Germans and to salute those in uniform. The justice system was put completely in German hands. German police were granted the authority to sentence any Pole who acted against Germany to death.[13] Decrees obligated Poles to work for Germany if needed. During the war, between 1.3 and 1.5 million people were sent from the General Government to work in Germany. While some went willingly, wrongly believing they would at least be able to earn a living wage, a majority were simply gathered off the street in mass roundups and forced to work on German farms and in German factories.[14]

The brutality of the German occupation fueled a vast underground resistance movement that spanned both civilian and military activities. It included organizations devoted to a wide array of functions, including education, culture, social welfare and politics. The Polish underground press was the largest in Europe; it published hundreds of newspapers and periodicals, some in editions that ran to tens of thousands of copies, as well as more ephemeral flyers. Armed resistance was gradually centralized around one group, the Home Army (*Armia Krajowa* or AK). By 1943, it had an estimated 350,000 members.[15]

In the eastern third of Poland, Soviet officials set about incorporating the region into the rest of the Soviet Union. Unlike the Nazis, the Soviets did not consider the Poles to be a lesser race. But Soviet officials did want to depose and replace local elites, who they considered to be enemies of socialism. During the 21 months that the Soviets ruled what had been eastern Poland, they arrested over 100,000 people. Of these, 30,000 were executed and the remainder were sent to prisons and labor camps in the Soviet interior. Many of the dead were Polish army officers taken as prisoners of war. In the most infamous incident, over 4,000 Polish officers were killed and buried in the Katyń forest. Soviet officials denied responsibility for the murders until 1990. A further 315,000 people, including many of the families of those who had been arrested, were deported and sent to Siberia or Kazakhstan, where they were dumped on collective farms to fend for themselves.[16]

When Soviet leader Joseph Stalin agreed to the nonaggression pact with Nazi Germany in 1939, he knew he was striking a deal with an enemy. Yet he believed that making common cause with Hitler would protect Soviet security, at least in the short term. He was wrong. Hitler and his Nazi followers were convinced that Soviet Communism was an evil plot created by Jews to destroy Western civilization. They aimed to wipe it from their earth. On June 22, 1941, Germany launched Operation Barbarossa, a massive attack on the Soviet Union.[17]

While the biggest battles of the German-Soviet war would be fought on Soviet territory, Barbarossa would mark a massive escalation of violence across Eastern Europe. This was particularly true for the region's Jews. Beginning with the invasion of Poland, Jewish civilians in territories taken by the Germans were subject to arbitrary violence and special restrictions, including the expropriation of their property, deportation and murder. In occupied Eastern Europe, Nazi officials felt free to experiment with anti-Jewish laws that would have been seen as too radical at home in Germany. It was in occupied Poland that Jews were first required to mark themselves with a yellow star (Jews in Germany itself would not have to do this until September 1941). It was also in occupied Poland that Nazi officials began to systematically segregate Jews from the rest of the population, forcing them to move to specially marked and sealed areas within cities or towns known as ghettos. In March 1941, the Warsaw ghetto alone contained 460,000 people, tightly packed into an area that had been home to only 80,000 before the war.[18]

After the war against the Soviet Union began, Nazi anti-Jewish policies moved from discrimination and deportation to genocide. As the Wehrmacht advanced into Soviet territory, special killing squads were tasked with shooting the Jewish population. In one single action, over 30,000 Jews from the Ukrainian city of Kiev were killed at the site known as Babi Yar. After being ordered to appear before German authorities, the Jews were led outside of town where they were required to hand over their valuables and remove their clothes. They were then forced to the edge of a ravine and shot. A very few survived to tell their stories by playing dead inside the mound of bodies until night fell and they could escape.[19] Approximately two million Soviet Jews would be murdered in a similar fashion.

As these mass murders were being carried out on Soviet territory, Nazi leaders began to plan the extermination of all European Jewry. Young and healthy people would be selected for forced labor, while the rest of the Jewish population would be killed. In the fall of 1941, officials from the Reich Security Main Office (RSHA) began to establish a network of special camps in the General Government where victims could be killed more easily and efficiently with poison gas. The first to be sent to these extermination camps were Polish Jews from the ghettos in the General Government. As the war continued, Jews from throughout Europe were put into cattle cars and deported to the camps. Only a tiny minority of those who were deported survived the war.[20]

While Poland and the Czech lands spent the war under German occupation, Hungary, Romania, Slovakia and Bulgaria were German allies. Each agreed to join the Axis in exchange for realizing its own territorial ambitions. Slovakia received its independence, Hungary got back some of the territory it had lost in the Treaty of Trianon at the end of World War I, Bulgaria took over territories it had coveted since the Balkan Wars of 1912–1913 and Romania was given part of Ukraine and took back Bessarabia. Bulgaria was able to remain neutral in the German-Soviet war, but Hungary, Slovakia and Romania each contributed substantial numbers of soldiers to Operation Barbarossa.

Germany's East European allies shared many aspects of the Nazi worldview, including the conviction that Communism was a devious Jewish plot bent on destroying European civilization. These countries had their own history of antisemitism. Hungary had introduced a law to limit the number of Jewish students at Hungarian universities already in 1920. In March 1939, the Hungarian government conscripted Jewish men into a special labor service. In Romania, the country's fascist dictator, General Ion Antonescu, mounted his own campaign of vicious anti-Jewish violence in the Romanian provinces of Bukovina and Bessarabia and in Romanian-occupied Ukraine (Transnistria), leading to the deaths of 280,000–300,000 people. Romanian forces slaughtered at least 25,000 Jews in the Ukrainian city of Odessa alone, throwing their bodies into the Black Sea. Yet, Hungary resisted Germany's demands to deport its Jewish citizens to the camps. Hungarian Jews would only be sent to Auschwitz after Germany occupied the country in March 1944. Romania similarly refused to deport Jews from central Romania. Romania's actions were more out of a concern for its own national interests than for the Jews themselves—realizing that Germany might lose the war, Romania hoped to court the Allies, who had promised to prosecute those who had persecuted Jews. Even if these governments were not acting from disinterested motives, the result was that about half of Romanian Jews and one-third of Hungarian Jews survived the war.[21]

The genocide of Eastern Europe's Jewish population was planned and carried out by Nazi Germany. But local communities throughout the region often condoned and even participated in anti-Jewish violence. Many East Europeans took the opportunity provided by the deportation and murder of the Jewish population to enrich themselves. While the Germans took the greatest spoils, plenty was left for local people. When Jews were deported, their neighbors rushed to lay claim to their houses and apartments. Looters scooped up even the most prosaic possessions, including bedding, clothes and kitchen equipment. Dr. Zygmunt Klukowski, a Polish doctor from the town of Szczebrzeszyn, witnessed the widespread theft of Jewish property in his community. As he wrote in his diary in October 1942, "The population grabs from opened Jewish houses anything they can get hold of. People shamelessly carry big bundles with Jewish belongings or merchandise from small Jewish shops."[22]

Some East Europeans nobly risked their lives to hide their Jewish neighbors from German authorities. More commonly, however, people agreed to hide Jews in exchange for payment, charging them exorbitant prices for food and shelter and threatening to turn them into the police if they did not pay. Jews who tried to hide among the Aryan population might find themselves accosted by blackmailers. Emanuel Ringelblum, a Polish-Jewish historian who lived in hiding for a time in Warsaw, wrote that these blackmailers "are a real plague of locusts, descending in their hundreds or maybe even thousands on the Jews on the Aryan side and stripping them of their money and valuables and often of their clothing as well."[23] The profits did not need to be high for some to willingly partake in exploitation and murder. In the Polish countryside, some peasants helped local police and German officers look for Jews hiding in the forest in return for no more than a few pounds of sugar or their victims' clothes.[24]

Heda Margolius Kovály, a Czech Jew, was in a German forced labor camp as the war started coming to an end. As Soviet soldiers drew closer, German soldiers evacuated the camp and marched the starving inmates westward, shooting any who failed to keep the pace. Heda Kovály and her friend Hanka were able to escape and make their way back to Prague thanks to the help of strangers. A fugitive in the city, which was still in German hands, Kovály turned to her friend Jenda for a place to hide. Before Heda and her family were deported, Jenda had said, "Whatever happens, I'll be your anchor ... I'll never stop waiting for you to come back. You'll always have somewhere to come back to." Yet when Heda rang his doorbell, Jenda looked horrified and exclaimed, "For God's sake, what brings you here?" Other friends reacted in a similar fashion, turning her back into the street. She contemplated throwing herself into the Vltava river before finally finding a friend willing to help conceal her until the Germans retreated from the city.[25]

Like many Jewish survivors, Kovály discovered that those who had profited from Jewish property during the war were reluctant to return what they had taken. Some who had taken the possessions of Jewish families for safekeeping pretended they had never done so. Others openly refused to give things back. Some months after the war ended, Kovály worked up the courage to go see about her family's summer house. When she knocked, "a fat unshaven man opened the door, stared at me for a moment and then yelled, 'So you've come back! Oh no! That's all we needed.'" Rather than fighting for her family's property, she turned and left. Yet, Kovály said, for every former acquaintance who refused to acknowledge her, there was another who reacted with kindness. This latter group included her mother's old dressmaker, who ran into Heda on the street and immediately took her home and made her a dress on the spot out of fabric remnants she had saved during the war, crying all the while.[26]

Liberators or Occupiers? The Red Army Enters Eastern Europe

In early 1943, the Soviets stopped the German advance at the Battle of Stalingrad, turning the tide of the war in favor of the Allies (the USSR, Great Britain and the United States). Once it became apparent that Germany might be defeated, Hungary and Romania began to consider abandoning their erstwhile ally. Romania was able to do so in August 1944, when the country's young king, Michael, led a coup that removed General Antonescu from power. In Hungary, regent Admiral Miklós Horthy also entered into secret talks with the Allies. To forestall Hungary's defection, Germany militarily occupied Hungary in March 1944. In October, the Germans set up a friendlier government led by the Arrow Cross, a group of Hungarian fascists. In Slovakia, partisans led an uprising in August 1944, also hoping to take the country out of the war. German troops briefly occupied Slovakia and defeated them.

In the summer of 1944, the front lines of the war began to move into Eastern Europe, as the Red Army pushed the retreating Wehrmacht back toward Germany. Some East Europeans would greet the Soviet soldiers as liberators. Others would see them as the enemy. Both groups, however, would be exposed to wartime violence as soldiers moved through their communities.

In Hungary, the capital city of Budapest was engulfed in a siege that lasted 102 days. A majority of the city's residents lived through these three months of warfare. Without running water or electricity, starving people crammed into unheated basements to avoid the bombs, watching helplessly as the city was destroyed around them. Civilians faced many kinds of violence. Arrow Cross paramilitaries shot thousands of Hungarian Jews during the siege, claiming they were a danger to the city's defenses. As they advanced through the city, Soviet soldiers looted private homes, taking, as one woman remembered, "our clothes, household linen, food, drink, everything." They also carried out mass rapes of Hungarian women and girls. Their crimes were so extensive that Hungarian Communists pleaded with Soviet commanders to stop the violence, arguing that the Red Army's actions would turn Hungarians against the party forever.[27]

As the Red Army advanced on Hungary, Alaine Polcz fled her native Transylvania to stay with her mother-in-law on a rural estate about 40 miles outside of Budapest. Instead of finding safety, she wound up in the middle of the fighting as the front stalled around her for months. Russian soldiers ransacked the place

FIGURE 1.1   A Soviet soldier communicates with his superiors in war-torn Budapest, 1945. © Photo by TASS via Getty Images.

where she was staying, confiscated most of their possessions and took her husband away; in the following nights, she was raped repeatedly by different groups of soldiers. For many years afterward she had a nightmare in which she was pursued by Russians. Just as one was finally about to catch her, she would wake up, panting and sweating, with "her heart throbbing in the corners of her eyes."[28]

As bombs fell overhead, Polcz took shelter in a filthy, lice-infested cellar with 80 other people. Her days blurred into a procession of forced labor, sexual violation and hunger. At one point, a Soviet soldier raped her in the cellar as those around her said nothing. Trying to care for her sick, elderly mother-in-law, she was forced to offer her body to one soldier for some bedding and to another for a cup of milk. In desperation, she contemplated suicide and looked unsuccessfully for a large rock to bash her own head in. Yet, like Heda Kovály, Alaine Polcz was also sustained by the occasional kindness of strangers, both Hungarian and Russian, who took her in or gave her food or helped to care for her mother-in-law. Eventually the Russians evacuated the villages and she was able to walk to Budapest where she reunited with her mother, whose apartment was miraculously intact, even though half of the building had burned down.[29]

To the north, the Polish Home Army was concerned about Soviet power after the Germans were defeated. Home Army commanders hoped they could liberate the capital city of Warsaw themselves and greet the Red Army as equals rather than captives. On August 1, 1944, as the Soviets approached Warsaw, the Home Army began a massive uprising in the city. Things did not go as they planned. The Soviet advance stalled just outside the center of the city, allowing the Germans to regroup and send in reinforcements. The Home Army would find itself facing the full force of the Wehrmacht alone.

Nazi leaders saw the uprising as an excuse to destroy the city and kill its population. Even if Germany lost the current war, they reasoned, the demolition of Warsaw would neutralize Poland for future generations. SS Commander Heinrich Himmler ordered his troops to slaughter Polish civilians. On August 5 and 6, SS troops brutally gunned down tens of thousands of noncombatants in the neighborhood of Wola, including women and children.[30] By the time the Home Army surrendered in October, at least 150,000 Polish civilians had been killed. After the surrender, the Germans sent many of the survivors to concentration camps and proceeded to systematically blow up the city, house by house, block by block. By the time the Red Army finally arrived in January 1945, Warsaw was no more than a smoldering ruin.[31]

Events in the multinational state of Yugoslavia followed a different trajectory from the other countries of Eastern Europe, ending in civil war. Under German pressure, Yugoslavia had finally agreed to formally join the Axis in March 1941. Serbs opposed to this German alliance then toppled the government in a coup, convincing Hitler to attack Yugoslavia. After a brief offensive, Axis allies Germany and Italy occupied and dismembered the country. They created a nominally independent Croatian state, while Serbia was occupied by

Germany and Italy established a protectorate over Montenegro. The rest of the country was divided up by Germany, Italy, Hungary, Bulgaria and Albania (itself under an Italian protectorate).

The new state of Croatia was led by the fascist Ante Pavelić and his Ustaše party. Ustaše leaders hoped to create an ethnically pure nation-state, by violence if necessary. As Croatia's new Minister of Justice, Mirko Puk, declared,

> Besides the Jews and Communists in our country, there is another enemy, and that is the Serbs ... The Serbs came to our lands with the Turkish detachments as thieves, as dregs, and as garbage from the Balkans ... Let those who came to our homeland 200–300 years ago return to where they came from. Either leave our homeland willingly, or we will drive you out by force.[32]

The Ustaše began a violent campaign of ethnic cleansing. One hundred and eighty thousand Croatian Serbs were uprooted and deported to Serbia, but even more were simply murdered. By 1943, the Ustaše had killed approximately 400,000 people. In addition to Serbs, Jews, Roma and Bosnian Muslims were among the victims.[33]

Yugoslavia had several large armed resistance groups. The first was the Chetniks, led by the Serb military officer Draža Mihailović. The Chetniks were Serb nationalists who wanted to restore the former Yugoslav state. While they initially concentrated on fighting the Germans, the Chetniks were soon consumed with fighting the Ustaše. In revenge for Ustaše attacks on Serb civilians, the Chetniks slaughtered Croats and Bosnian Muslims (who they identified as Croat allies). The second resistance movement in occupied Yugoslavia was the Communist Partisans, led by Josip Broz Tito. The Partisans were not motivated by racial ideologies or ethnic rivalries, but they did want to supplant the former monarchy with a socialist state. In part because of their very different postwar goals, attempts to create an alliance between the Chetniks and the Partisans failed. Soon, the Chetniks, the Partisans and the Ustaše were all fighting each other.

The experience of Kata Pejnović exemplifies the brutality of this conflict. Pejnović was a Serb peasant woman from the Lika region in Croatia. Although she had little formal education, she read widely and joined the Communist Party of Yugoslavia in 1938. As a known Communist as well as a Serb, she was targeted by the Croatian fascist regime. Her husband and three sons, aged 19, 13 and 3, were arrested and killed by the Ustaše in July 1941.[34] Describing her emotions after this devastating loss in the Partisan press, she said, "My heart collapsed out of sadness and grief. But one needed to avenge my golden apples and [the] thousands ... who had perished. I clenched my heart and my fist."[35] Pejnović dedicated herself to advancing the Partisan cause by mobilizing peasant women of all ethnicities to assist in the fight. By the end of the war, approximately two million women had joined the Partisan movement, and tens of thousands had enlisted in the Partisan army. Most were assigned to administrative or medical positions, but, as in the Soviet Union, some women did serve in combat.[36]

The Partisans eventually emerged as the victors in the Yugoslav civil war, albeit only after a massive loss of life on all sides. The Allies had initially supported Mihailović and the Chetniks. But when the Partisans had more success against the Germans, they began to offer aid and assistance to Tito. At the Tehran conference in November 1943, the Allies formally agreed to support the Partisans, helping them to draw more recruits. Tito's forces joined the Red Army to liberate Belgrade in the autumn of 1944 and moved on to liberate the rest of the country from the retreating Germans themselves. Unlike other parts of Eastern Europe, there would not be a significant Soviet military presence in Yugoslavia.

In 1939, Germany had hoped to create an empire in Eastern Europe. In 1945, Germany was defeated, but its goals had been achieved by another power: the Soviet Union. At the end of the war, the Red Army occupied most of the region. As they emerged from the violence of the war, East Europeans would have to contend with this new reality.

The Uprooted and Transplanted Multitudes

In Europe, World War II ended on May 8, 1945. But the end of hostilities did not mean life returned to normal. The extent of the destruction varied from place to place, but, with the exception of Bulgaria, the loss of life was far greater in Eastern Europe than in Western Europe. It is impossible to accurately count the numbers of the dead, particularly given that such a large percentage were civilians. Estimates can vary widely depending on the methodology used to create them. As a whole, however, Eastern Europe lost roughly 10 percent of its population in the war. The losses were heaviest in Poland, which lost approximately 15 percent of its interwar population, including 90 percent of its Jewish population. Yugoslavia lost about 10 percent of its population, many killed by their neighbors as the civil war divided communities. The death tolls in other countries were smaller but still devastating.[37]

The survivors faced great challenges. Thousands of towns and villages lay in ruins. The war had decimated the region's industry and infrastructure, particularly in Poland, Hungary and Yugoslavia. Factories were ruined, machinery damaged or taken by Soviet occupiers, railways and bridges blown up, and telephone and telegraph networks destroyed. Agriculture was disrupted and livestock decimated, creating constant food shortages in the immediate post-war years. Millions lacked basic shelter. In Yugoslavia, a quarter of the population was homeless at end of the war, while in the city of Warsaw, 85 percent of the housing stock had been destroyed.[38] Even in the Czechoslovak capital

FIGURE 1.2 People walk through ruined Warsaw, 1946. © Photo by Bettman via Getty Images.

of Prague, which had been saved from heavy bombing, Holocaust survivor Heda Kovály remained homeless for months. She finally got a place to live only by marching into the chairman of the Housing Authority's office with all her belongings and telling him she would sleep there until he found her an apartment.[39]

Hungarian Alaine Polcz recalled that when the war ended,

> It seemed as if the entire country lay in ruins and some sort of migration had begun. Everyone was going somewhere with wheelbarrows, backpacks, half-wrecked bicycles, sleds, tottering wagons which people pulled with their hands or by harnessing themselves to them—they crawled along here and there ... Houses were collapsing and being gutted by fire—they had to move on, and now everyone was searching for a place."[40]

In the months after the German surrender, Europe was flooded with these displaced persons. Some, like Polcz, had fled in the wake of the Red Army. Others had been sent to Germany as forced laborers or had survived the concentration camps. Still others were prisoners of war. By September of 1945, more than ten million displaced people had journeyed home, some by walking hundreds of miles.[41]

During the war, Nazi Germany had subjected much of Eastern Europe to a brutal occupation. With Germany's defeat, Eastern Europe's ethnic Germans faced retaliation. In the newly reconstituted Czechoslovakia, Czech leaders blamed the Sudeten Germans for the dismemberment and occupation of the country. They insisted that there would be no real peace if the Sudeten Germans were allowed to stay in Czechoslovakia. The Allies agreed to what would be euphemistically called the "transfer" of the Sudeten Germans to Germany or Austria. Over a period of roughly 18 months, some three million Sudeten Germans were expelled from their homes and transported over the border. The expelled were allowed to take only limited amounts of luggage and money; all other property had to be left behind. The Allies mandated that the expulsions be carried out in an "orderly and humane" manner, but this was not always the case. In the weeks or months before they were loaded onto trains bound for Germany, the Sudeten Germans were frequently subjected to the kinds of discriminatory policies Jews had endured under Nazism, such as wearing armbands marked with the letter "N" (for *Němec*, or "German" in Czech). Some were put into camps or forced to work repairing roads or cleaning the streets. Others faced acts of random violence, including rape and murder.[42]

Additional population transfers followed postwar territorial changes. Most of the land taken by Germany or its allies during the war was returned to its prewar owners, but the Soviet Union demanded some spoils. The formerly independent Baltic states of Lithuania, Latvia and Estonia; the territories of Subcarpathian Rus; northern Bukovina; Bessarabia and the part of eastern Poland the Soviets had annexed in 1939 all became part of the Soviet Union. Poland was compensated for this loss with territory that had been part of prewar Germany, effectively moving the entire country of Poland approximately 125 miles to the west. The Germans who had been living there were forced to move to make way for Polish settlers. Between 1945 and 1950, 3.5 million Germans were expelled from this region (millions more had fled earlier as the Red Army advanced on Germany and never returned).[43] Many of the new settlers came from the part of eastern Poland that had been given to the Soviet Union. 1.46 million Poles left that region rather than live under Soviet rule. They were exchanged for half a million Ukrainians, Byelorussians and Lithuanians who had been living in Poland.[44]

These population movements were part of a larger phenomenon of ethnically based migration across Eastern Europe in the aftermath of World War II. After the end of World War I, the Allies created a series of states in Eastern Europe that all contained large national minorities. They required the governments of those states to agree to respect the rights of those minorities. Nonetheless, resentments persisted on all sides. Now, in the wake of an even deadlier conflict motivated at least in part by nationalist animosities, many believed that a lasting peace depended on national homogeneity, even if that homogeneity could only be achieved by the mass movement of peoples. In other population transfers, Germans were expelled from Hungary, Romania and Yugoslavia. There were

MAP 1.3 Eastern Europe in the aftermath of World War II.

population exchanges between Hungary and Czechoslovakia, Hungary and Yugoslavia, and Yugoslavia and Italy. Many Jewish survivors decided to leave Europe; most emigrated to North America or to Palestine (after 1948 the state of Israel).[45]

The end result was an Eastern Europe that was much more ethnically homogeneous than it had ever been. National minorities still existed, but their numbers were greatly reduced. The dream that earlier nationalist activists had of creating countries devoted to the interests of one nation (or a group of related nations) had now come much closer to being realized, but only at the cost of an extraordinarily bloody war, genocide and forced population exchanges.

These population movements spurred internal migration as well. The Czechoslovak and Polish governments promoted the rapid settlement of the land that had been populated by expelled Germans, both to prevent the possibility of a German return and to limit the economic damage caused by the expulsion of millions of workers. In Poland, the Central Resettlement Committee issued an announcement in May 1945 telling Poles,

> You want bread? There's bread in the west! You want land? There's land in the west! ... city dwellers will find workshops and stores left by the Germans and for educated workers there are office jobs and administrative positions... To the West!"[46]

Millions flocked to this Polish "Wild West" in search of opportunity. Some went simply to try to take what they could, not intending to stay for long. Others, particularly those who had been forced to leave their homes in eastern Poland, hoped to build new lives. Many, however, found it difficult to develop ties to their new home. The Polish writer Maria Dąbrowska considered moving to the city of Wrocław (formerly the German Breslau) after the war but decided against it. She wrote,

> One reason I always felt so awful in Wrocław is the inconsolable nostalgia that pervades the atmosphere there ... As if all the desires of those uprooted and transplanted multitudes were emanating from them, saturating the air with excruciating melancholy.[47]

The millions of apartments, farms and businesses abandoned by their former German owners left many opportunities for corruption. German property was supposed to become state property, but many helped themselves. In Czechoslovakia, as well as in Poland, so-called gold-diggers streamed to the borderlands looking for loot. Some hoped to take charge of farms or homes, while others went merely to fill bags or suitcases with whatever they could find, from clothes to radios to paintings. Many properties went to those who arrived first, not necessarily to those who would operate them most effectively. This led to disputes with later settlers over who should be allowed to take over expropriated property. State officials had pushed the rapid migration of settlers to the border regions, but in practice the chaos this created made it more difficult to create lasting stability there.[48]

The expropriation of the property of expelled populations, and the kinds of activities it encouraged, shows one of the many continuities that existed between World War II and the postwar years. During the war, the expropriation of property was commonplace; it occurred at the level of policy, but also within the realm of mass individual experience. Millions helped themselves to the objects left by the dead and deported, just as they also experienced their own pain of loss. The weight of these experiences served to normalize both property confiscation as an official state policy and the practice of opportunistic theft. In Czechoslovakia, those who were caught pilfering the property of expellees often justified their actions by noting that everyone was doing it, an attitude that would persist into the socialist period.[49]

Moving Forward: Postwar Coalition Governments

The Soviet Union won the war, but at great cost. As the Wehrmacht advanced into Soviet territory, it leveled villages and slaughtered civilians. To defeat them, the Red Army incurred massive losses. Approximately 10 percent of the Soviet population died in the conflict, far exceeding British and American casualties. Given this bloody reality, Stalin's primary postwar concern was neutralizing the possibility of a future German threat. Since most of Eastern Europe had either actively supported Hitler or quickly been conquered by the German army, Stalin saw the future of Eastern Europe as a matter of Soviet security.

At a meeting with Soviet leader Joseph Stalin in Moscow in October 1944, British Prime Minister Winston Churchill agreed that the USSR could create a sphere of influence in Eastern Europe. A few months later, in the Soviet resort town of Yalta, Stalin, Churchill and US President Franklin Roosevelt agreed that any future governments in Eastern Europe should be friendly to the Soviet Union, but also that elections would be held in all countries liberated from the Nazis. As the Soviets saw it in early 1945, "friendly" governments would be antifascist and would include Communist involvement. They would not necessarily be one-party states.[50]

As the Red Army swept through Eastern Europe, the Soviets deposed occupation or fascist governments and sponsored the creation of what they called "people's democracies." These new people's democracies would be ruled by coalition governments that would govern until elections could be held. These coalitions brought Communist parties together with their opponents in a joint administration called a national front. While these coalition governments included a range of political parties, they excluded former fascists and parties that had actively cooperated with the Germans, which meant that the right end of the political spectrum was not represented.

The postwar coalition governments in Eastern Europe were all formed along the same national front model, but they functioned differently in different countries. In Yugoslavia and Albania, where Communists had achieved power without Soviet assistance, what began ostensibly as multiparty coalitions quickly devolved to de facto Communist party control of the state. In Bulgaria and Romania, coalitions functioned more in name than in reality, although opposition parties were able to complete in elections in 1946. In Hungary and Czechoslovakia, power was at least initially more truly shared among the members of the coalition.[51]

In Poland, the transition from wartime to postwar coalition government was particularly contentious. There was a long history of Russian-Polish animosity, and Stalin was especially concerned with having a Polish government that was friendly to the Soviet Union. During the war, a group of non-Communist Polish politicians who had escaped to London were recognized as the official

Polish government in exile. But as the Soviet army moved into Polish territory, it recognized a different group of Polish leftist politicians who had spent the war in exile in the USSR as the real provisional government of a liberated Poland. The Polish government in London refused to acknowledge the authority of this Soviet-backed provisional government.

A civil war broke out between the Soviet-supported provisional government and the Home Army, the Polish resistance group that had been loyal to the Polish government in London during the war. Eventually, a segment of the London exile government, most prominently Peasant Party leader Stanisław Mikołajczyk, agreed to join the Soviet-backed provisional government, and Stalin agreed to hold free elections in Poland. The Allies recognized this new coalition government that included Mikołajczyk and the Polish Peasant Party as the legitimate government in postwar Poland. Nonetheless, Home Army partisans continued to wage guerrilla warfare in Poland for several more years.[52]

Following its defeat, Germany was administered by the victorious Allies. The country was divided into four occupation zones, each governed by one of the Allies. (Although France had been quickly defeated in the war, it was allowed to act as a full partner, along with Great Britain, the United States and the Soviet Union.) Austria, which had been united with Germany from 1938 to 1945, was also divided into four zones, as were the capital cities of Berlin and Vienna. The Soviet occupation administration controlled the eastern zone of Germany. While the French, Americans and British placed more of an effort on the economic reconstruction of their zones, the Soviets demanded reparations to help offset their enormous economic losses. They extracted as much as they could from their zone, including disassembling entire factories and sending them to the USSR.[53]

The first question that all of Eastern Europe's postwar governments faced was how to approach the enormous task of postwar reconstruction. Across Europe, in the West as well as in the East, there was widespread popular support for state-led solutions to economic regeneration, including centralized planning and the nationalization of key industries such as mining, telecommunications and transportation. This was one of the legacies of the war. In the 1930s, millions of Europeans suffering from the economic dislocations of the Great Depression had looked to fascism as an alternative to liberal democracy. Although fascism had been defeated and largely discredited, many believed that Europe needed to find a new way forward, one that would be more effective at managing the inequities of the capitalist system. In Great Britain, this conviction enabled the Labour Party to achieve victory in the country's 1946 elections, despite the fact that it was the conservative Tory Party that had led the country to victory over the Nazis. The new Labour government then laid the foundations for the postwar British welfare state; it established a national health care system, introduced new taxes on the wealthy and nationalized the steel and railway industries.[54]

In Eastern Europe, there was also a general consensus in favor of a greater state role in the economy and policies that increased economic equality. This was in part because right-leaning political parties had been banned, but it also reflected large-scale support for postwar change. Hungary, Czechoslovakia, Poland and Bulgaria all nationalized a large percentage of their industry between 1946 and 1947. Countries across the region also promoted land reform in these years, confiscating large agricultural estates with the goal of redistributing the land to small farmers. Lands that had devolved to the state as a result of postwar expulsions or population exchanges were also used for this purpose. Not surprisingly, land reform was popular with peasant farmers and agricultural laborers who hoped to have their own farms.[55]

Broad support for these kinds of economic policies had the effect of bringing people closer to their country's Communist party. Outside of Czechoslovakia, Communist parties had been banned throughout Eastern Europe in the 1930s. They survived underground, but their members were always under the threat of arrest. This meant that their numbers had been quite small; in most cases, this number would shrink further during the war (the exception to this was Yugoslavia, where hundreds of thousands joined Tito's Partisans in the context of the civil war). Known Communists were persecuted by the Nazis and their fascist allies; many were arrested or killed. Those who avoided arrest often fled to the Soviet Union or joined partisan resistance groups. Despite their small size, Eastern Europe's Communist parties entered power as partners in the postwar coalition governments because they had Soviet support.

In the immediate postwar period, Eastern Europe's Communist parties made it a priority to gain new members. While the specific results varied by country, Communists were astoundingly successful in gaining new adherents. The Hungarian Communist Party had only 3,000 members in December 1944 but over 600,000 in January 1946. The Romanian party had only 1,000 members during the war, but it had grown to 800,000 in October 1945. The most spectacular growth of all was in Czechoslovakia, where the Communists went from 28,000 members at the end of the war to over a million in March 1946, giving the Communist Party of Czechoslovakia the distinction of being the largest political party in Czechoslovak history.[56]

What drew people to the Communist party? The reasons spanned a wide spectrum. Some saw the Communists as an alternative to the failed policies of the past. Communists argued that because they had not been in government before 1945, they could not be held responsible for their country's previous failures. Others were captivated by the Communists' sense of purpose. While the Communist parties of Eastern Europe had somewhat different platforms that were dependent on the particular circumstances of their respective countries, they all had a compelling vision for a new society based on social justice and alleviating inequality. The Communists had a message of change and a set of clear plans for carrying it out. Other parties were often reduced to responding to the Communists rather than articulating their own visions for a postwar future.

The Communists promoted themselves as representing the forces of anti-fascism. While the USSR's decision to sign the nonaggression pact with Germany was a black mark on its record, after 1941 East European Communists had been active in wartime resistance to Nazism. While other political parties might be seen as morally tainted by their collaboration with the Germans, the Communists proudly claimed that they had stood firm against Hitler. Finally, while they were clearly tied to the victorious Soviet Union, local Communists in Eastern Europe emphatically declared that they would not be tied to Soviet models of development. Each country, they insisted, would be able to follow its own road to socialism and a better life, according to whatever policies most suited its circumstances.

While some were attracted to Communism because of its idealism and its concrete policies for postwar reconstruction, others became party members because they saw it as a good opportunity to gain power or wealth. In 1945, Eastern Europe's Communist parties had few members, but as partners in the postwar coalition governments, they had plenty of jobs to give away. Heda Kovály, who became a party member herself, remembered being disgusted by those who had become Communists purely for financial gain. Some, she said, hoped to conceal their wartime profiteering or collaboration. Others hoped that party loyalty would reward them with a career. "A Party card," she recalled, "soon became an essential credential for the large number of men jockeying for positions as the managers of nationalized companies, farms and factories or as custodians of property left behind by evicted German and Czechoslovak émigrés."[57]

By 1947, Communists all over Eastern Europe had managed to build a large base of popular support. In Czechoslovakia, the Czechoslovak Communist Party even gained the highest vote total of all the parties in the first postwar elections held in May 1946. But even here, the Communists won only 38 percent of the vote. A majority still preferred to vote for political alternatives. Soon, Communists would turn to means other than the ballot box to consolidate their hold on power.

The International Situation Intensifies

In March 1946, former British Prime Minister Winston Churchill gave a speech in Fulton, Missouri. Churchill warned that the Soviet Union was encouraging the establishment of Communist dictatorships in Eastern Europe. To make his point, he used the image of an "Iron Curtain" that had fallen across the European continent, irreparably dividing the East from the West. When

Churchill spoke, this Iron Curtain did not actually exist. Travel still flowed freely from the East to the West, and coalition governments still functioned in much of Eastern Europe. But within the next few years, Churchill's prediction that Communist governments would control Eastern Europe would come true.

During the war, the Soviet Union and the United States had been allies, united in their desire to defeat the Germans. As soon as the war was over, however, the relationship between the two countries, now both recognized as global superpowers, began to sour. Stalin started to suspect the United States and its Western allies did not respect Soviet security goals. The United States and its allies in turn suspected that the Soviets wanted to create their own European empire. Churchill's speech in Missouri was itself a manifestation of this increased tension between the two sides.

Things came to a head in 1947. In March, US President Harry S. Truman, worried that the Soviet Union was supporting Communist revolutionaries in Greece and Turkey, announced what would become known as the Truman doctrine. Truman committed the United States to fighting Communism all over the world, declaring that Communism was a threat to the American way of life. According to Truman, the essence of the United States—and the West more generally—was freedom. Communism, he charged, destroyed freedom. Communist regimes were dictatorships because no one would willingly choose to live in an unfree society. Communists, Truman claimed, ruled by fear, terror and misinformation, feeding their subjects lies that kept them in chains and preventing them from discovering the truth.[58]

Six months later, representatives from nine European Communist parties met in the Polish town of Szklarska Poręba where they agreed to create the Communist Information Agency or Cominform. The Soviet representative at the meeting, Andrei Zhdanov, observed that the world was dividing into two warring ideological camps: the Communist and the capitalist. For Zhdanov, however, the force behind this split was American aggression. It was the Americans, he said, who had embarked on a course of imperialist expansion. The United States was the enemy of social justice; it offered economic assistance to other countries just to bring them into economic bondage. American capitalists kept American workers from revolt only by telling them malicious lies about the Soviet Union, pretending socialism would bring darkness when it would really bring liberation.[59]

Truman and Zhdanov disagreed about everything but this: the world had been divided into two opposing camps. Each side in this conflict believed it had the right values, while its opponent was morally bankrupt. Each side was convinced that the other wanted to control the world and that it had to be prevented from doing so. This animosity formed the basis for the Cold War: the state of tension between the United States and the Soviet Union that lasted for over four decades. While they never declared war on each other, the Soviets and the Americans saw each other as adversaries, and they demanded that their allies also take sides.

The establishment of Communist regimes in Eastern Europe took place against the backdrop of the nascent Cold War. As tensions with the United States increased, Stalin gradually became convinced that only way to be sure of friendly governments in Eastern Europe was for those governments to be controlled by Communists. The message given to East European Communists at Szklarska Poręba was that the time for coalition was over. Communists could trust no one but themselves. Stalin began to push Eastern Europe's Communist leaders to gather power in their hands and to neutralize their opponents.

While historians sometimes write of Communist "takeovers" in Eastern Europe, these seizures of power happened gradually. With the exception of Yugoslavia and Albania, East European Communists did not take power via military means. Rather, they used a combination of fear, intimidation and voter fraud to put them into a position where they controlled all the branches of government. With the power of parliaments and presidencies behind them, they had free rein to socialize the economy and jail any remaining enemies. They could use what were technically legal means to make sure that they re-tained this power in perpetuity. For example, they could rewrite their country's constitution to give a leading role to the Communist party and pass laws that made it a crime to slander the state.

The case of Hungary is one example of how this worked. In the immediate postwar period, the Hungarian Communist Party was not particularly popular. Hungary was more agricultural than industrial, and it did not have a very large working class. The behavior of Soviet soldiers in occupied Hungary also turned many people against anything associated with the Soviet Union. For these rea-sons, the Hungarian Communists performed poorly in the first postwar elec-tions held in November 1945. The Communists earned only 17 percent of the vote, while the peasant-oriented Smallholder's Party won 57 percent. In the following elections, held in August 1947, the Communists hoped to capitalize on scandals they had helped to create within the Smallholder Party. But even after working to disenfranchise over 400,000 voters, they still earned only 22 percent of the vote. This was the largest total of any single party, but it was far from meeting their expectations.

Although they were not very successful at gaining votes, the Hungarian Communists were quite skilled at undermining their political opponents and exploiting their divisions to their own advantage. Their road to power was not through the ballot box but via a policy of divide and conquer, a policy that Hungarian Communist leader Matyás Rákosi referred to as "salami tactics": slicing off each opponent from the rest as one would cut slices from a salami. Initially, they concentrated on neutralizing the Smallholder's Party, putting one of its leaders under house arrest (ostensibly for being involved in an anti-state conspiracy) and forcing another to resign. They were assisted in this by their control of the police force, something that Communist parties working in national front coalitions across Eastern Europe always insisted be part of their portfolio. The Communists also developed a network of sympathizers and informers within other political parties who would help them to weaken their opponents from within.

At first, the Hungarian Communists were assisted in their attacks on rightist parties by their leftist allies, the Social Democrats. Eventually, they turned on them as well. The Social Democrats were forced to merge with the Communists, creating a single socialist party, the Hungarian Workers Party (HWP). This effectively neutralized the Social Democrats as an independent political force. The new HWP then turned to intimidating the remaining opposition parties, forcing them to join the HWP in a new national front that would run only one combined slate of candidates in the next election. This gave the HWP control over all candidates and ensured they would completely control the parliament. By the end of 1949, it was the only political force left in the country. The Hungarian Communists had succeeded because their opponents were never able to cooperate and unite against them. Instead, they let themselves be picked off one by one, until there was no one left to oppose Communist power.[60]

As Communists were moving into power throughout Eastern Europe, tensions mounted between the former Allies, who still jointly occupied defeated Germany. The Western zones were allowed to take part in the US Marshall plan, which helped to integrate Western Germany into a larger trans-Atlantic capitalist economy. The Soviets saw the Marshall plan as an instrument of US imperialism and refused to allow the Soviet occupation zone (and all of Eastern Europe) to take part. The tension building between the two sides erupted in June 1948 when the British, French and Americans moved to carry out a joint currency reform in their zones and insisted that the new currency also circulate in the German capital of Berlin, which was located inside the Soviet zone but divided among the four former allies. In response, Stalin ordered a blockade of the city, shutting down entrance into the Western-controlled zones.[61]

Stalin had hoped to force the Western allies out of Berlin. This did not happen. Berlin would remain a divided city, its geography a symbol of Cold War conflict. But when the Berlin Blockade finally ended almost a year later, the division of Germany into two separate states—one Communist and one capitalist—was a foregone conclusion. The new German Democratic Republic (GDR, popularly known as East Germany) officially came into being in October 1949.

By the end of 1949, there were effectively one-party Communist governments in Albania, Bulgaria, Czechoslovakia, East Germany, Hungary, Poland,

Romania and Yugoslavia. Now that they had attained power, the Communists were able to proceed with their larger goal: to institute a socialist revolution that would work its way into all corners of life.

Notes

1 Tara Zahra, *Kidnapped Souls: National Indifference and the Battle for Children in the Bohemian Lands, 1900–1948* (Ithaca, NY: Cornell University Press, 2008).
2 Pieter Judson, *The Habsburg Empire: A New History* (Cambridge, MA: Belknap Press, 2016), 442–454.
3 Paul Robert Magocsi, *Historical Atlas of Central Europe* (Seattle: University of Washington Press, 2002), 153–158. Statistics are from the 1981 census (interwar data lumps all "Serbo-Croatians" together).
4 Magocsi, *Historical Atlas of Central Europe*, 140–173.
5 John Connelly, *From Peoples to Nations: A History of Eastern Europe* (Princeton, NJ: Princeton University Press, 2020), 362–389.
6 Mark Mazower, *Hitler's Empire: How the Nazis Ruled Europe* (New York: Penguin, 2008), 53–56.
7 Chad Bryant, *Prague in Black: Nazi Rule and Czech Nationalism* (Cambridge, MA: Harvard University Press, 2007), 22–30.
8 Mazower, *Hitler's Empire*, 67–77.
9 Bryant, *Prague in Black*, 170–172.
10 Bryant, *Prague in Black*, 179.
11 quoted in Jan T. Gross, *Polish Society Under German Occupation: The Generalgouvernement, 1939–1944* (Princeton, NJ: Princeton University Press, 1979), 75.
12 Catherine Epstein, *Model Nazi: Arthur Greiser and the Occupation of Western Poland* (New York: Oxford University Press, 2010), 129.
13 Timothy Snyder, *Bloodlands: Europe Between Hitler and Stalin* (New York: Basic Books, 2010), 128.
14 Gross, *Polish Society under German Occupation*, 78–81.
15 Gross, *Polish Society under German Occupation*, 281.
16 Snyder, *Bloodlands*, 135–138, 151.
17 Paul Hanebrink, *A Specter Haunting Europe: The Myth of Judeo-Bolshevism* (Cambridge, MA: Harvard University Press, 2018).
18 Mazower, *Hitler's Empire*, 95.
19 Snyder, *Bloodlands*, 203.
20 For a readable overview, Doris L. Bergen, *War and Genocide: A Concise History of the Holocaust*, 2nd ed. (Latham, MD: Rowman and Littlefield, 2008).
21 Mazower, *Hitler's Empire*, 330–340; Hanebrink, *A Specter Haunting Europe*, 137–138; Connelly, *Peoples Into Nations*, 485–497.
22 Jan T. Gross, *Golden Harvest: Events at the Periphery of the Holocaust* (New York: Oxford University Press, 2012), 43.
23 Quoted in Gross, *Golden Harvest*, 93.
24 Gross, *Golden Harvest*, 85.
25 Heda Margolius Kovály, *Under a Cruel Star: A Life in Prague 1941–1946*, trans. Franci Epstein and Helen Epstein (New York: Holmes and Meier, 1997), 26–38 (quote on 26).
26 Kovály, *Under a Cruel Star*, 47.
27 Krisztián Ungváry, *Battle for Budapest: One Hundred Days in World War II*, trans. Ladislaus Löb (London: I.B. Taurus, 2003), 224–252, 285–291 (quote on p. 287).

28 Alaine Polcz, *One Woman in the War, Hungary, 1944–1945*, trans. Albert Tezla (Budapest: Central European University Press, 2002), 112.

29 Polcz, *One Woman in the War, Hungary*, 94–121.

30 Mazower, *Hitler's Empire*, 515.

31 Snyder, *Bloodlands*, 303–309.

32 Max Bergholz, *Violence as a Generative Force: Identity, Nationalism and Memory in a Balkan Community* (Ithaca, NY: Cornell University Press, 2016), 65.

33 Mazower, *Hitler's Empire*, 347.

34 Maja Brkljačić, "Kata Pejnović," in *Biographical Dictionary of Women's Movements and Feminisms in Central, Eastern, and Southeastern Europe: 19th and 20th Centuries*, ed. Francisca de Haan, Krassimira Daskalova and Anna Loutfi (Budapest: Central European University Press, 2005), 420–422.

35 Jelena Batinić, *Woman and Yugoslav Partisans: A History of World War II Resistance* (Cambridge: Cambridge University Press, 2015), quote on 55, also 96–97.

36 Batinić, *Women and Yugoslav Partisans*, 2.

37 The figures here are from Bradley Abrams, "The Second World War and the East European Revolution," *East European Politics and Societies* 16, no. 3 (2002): 631.

38 Abrams, "The Second World War and the East European Revolution," 634–635.

39 Kovály, *Under a Cruel Star*, 53–54.

40 Polcz, *One Woman in the War*, 123.

41 Tara Zahra, *The Lost Children: Reconstructing Europe's Families after World War II* (Cambridge, MA: Harvard University Press, 2011), 8.

42 David Gerlach, *The Economy of Ethnic Cleansing: The Transformation of the German-Czech Borderlands after World War II* (New York: Cambridge University Press, 2017), 27–64.

43 Gregor Thum, *Uprooted: How Breslau Became Wrocław during the Century of Expulsions*, trans. Tom Lampert and Alison Brown (Princeton, NJ: Princeton University Press, 2011), 77.

44 Magocsi, *Historical Atlas of Central Europe*, 192.

45 Magocsi, *Historical Atlas of Central Europe*, 192–193; Theodora Dragostinova and David Gerlach, "Demography and Population Movements," in *The Routledge History of East Central Europe Since 1700*, ed. Irina Livezeanu and Árpád von Klimó (New York: Routledge, 2017), 154–158.

46 Quoted in Thum, *Uprooted*, 79.

47 Quoted in Thum, *Uprooted*, 165.

48 Gerlach, *The Economy of Ethnic Cleansing*, 104–151.

49 Gerlach, *The Economy of Ethnic Cleansing*, 104–151.

50 Norman M. Naimark, *Stalin and the Fate of Europe: The Postwar Struggle for Sovereignty* (Cambridge: Belknap, 2018).

51 For a good summary of the complicated politics involved in these coalition governments, see Geoffrey Swain and Nigel Swain, *Eastern Europe Since 1945*, 4th ed. (New York: Palgrave, 2009): 18–56.

52 Molly Pucci, *Security Empire: The Secret Police in Communist Eastern Europe, 1945–1953* (New Haven, CT: Yale University Press, 2020), 29–76.

53 Norman Naimark, *The Russians in Germany: A History of the Soviet Zone of Occupation, 1945–1949* (Cambridge, MA: Belknap, 1995).

54 Mark Mazower, *Dark Continent: Europe's Twentieth Century* (New York: Vintage, 2000), 182–191.

55 Tony Judt, *Postwar: A History of Europe Since 1945* (New York: Penguin, 2005), 63–99; Abrams, "The Second World War and East European Revolution," 639–642.

56 Abrams, "The Second World War and East European Revolution," 662–663.

57 Kovály, *Under a Cruel Star*, 68–70.

58 Denise M. Bostdorff, *Proclaiming the Truman Doctrine: The Cold War Call to Arms* (College Station: Texas A&M University Press, 2008), 1–9.
59 Andrei Zhdanov, "The International Situation," *For a Lasting Peace, For a People's Democracy*, November 10, 1947, 1–2.
60 Laszlo Borhi, *Hungary in the Cold War, 1945-1956: Between the United States and the Soviet Union* (Budapest: Central European University Press, 2004), 47–139.
61 Paul Steege, *Black Market, Cold War: Everyday Life in Berlin, 1946–1949* (New York: Cambridge University Press, 2007).

2
CREATING A STALINIST SOCIETY

By 1948, the antagonism between the Soviet Union and the United States had reached the level of open conflict. At the time, many expected that war would soon break out between the world's two superpowers. The threat of war increased the pressure on other countries to declare their allegiance to one side or the other. It also helped convince Joseph Stalin that Soviet security required compliant Communist regimes in the countries of Eastern Europe. Having pushed the Communist parties of Eastern Europe to establish themselves as the sole political force in their countries, Stalin demanded that they show the Soviet Union their loyalty. Instead of allowing the Communist governments in Eastern Europe to develop their own policies for establishing socialism in their countries, Stalin pressed them to adopt the path he had taken in the Soviet Union beginning in the late 1920s.

In the USSR, Stalin had instituted the first centralized economic plans, abruptly turned the economy toward rapid industrialization and forced the collectivization of agriculture. Opponents of these policies were arrested and charged with treason. Stalin created a cult of personality around himself and consolidated loyalty via terror. The policies and practices that characterized Stalin's rule in the Soviet Union are referred to as *Stalinism*. After 1948, the Communist governments of Eastern Europe began to adopt similar policies. They moved swiftly to create planned economies, to shift resources toward rapid industrialization and to collectivize agriculture. They also used terror to silence their opponents, labeling them enemies and saboteurs.

For some East Europeans, Stalinism meant repression. East Europe's Stalinist governments arrested hundreds of thousands of people for their opposition to Communism. Many lived in fear that the same would happen to them. Others, however, were enthusiastic about the changes they saw happening around

DOI: 10.4324/9780813348186-3

them. Many young people were excited about the chance to fundamentally reshape their world and were hopeful that their new Communist governments would lead them toward a more prosperous and equitable society.

Closing Off the National Road to Socialism

Communist parties gained power in Eastern Europe through the support of the Soviet Union. Before World War II, Communist parties had little influence in the region, with the exception of Germany and Czechoslovakia. After the end of the war, the Soviets helped Eastern Europe's Communist parties gain power despite their lack of popular support. Nonetheless, as they tried to win the votes of their countrymen in the years between 1945 and 1948, East European Communists emphasized their independence from the Soviet Union. They insisted they would adopt policies suited to their own countries and that they would not blindly follow the Soviet Union's way of creating socialism. Bulgarian Communist leader Georgi Dimitrov, a party elder with strong ties to Moscow, declared in February 1946, "Not every party will follow the same road to socialism. They will not follow the Soviet model exactly, but each will act in their own way."[1] In a similar fashion, Czechoslovak Communist Party leader Klement Gottwald told a plenum of leading party members in September 1946, "this path, our path, is our own—special, longer, more roundabout."[2]

This changed with the coming of the Cold War. After 1948, Stalin demanded that the countries of Eastern Europe adopt domestic and foreign policies that adhered to the Soviet line. With one exception, the men who headed Eastern Europe's Communist parties complied. Most of them had spent the war years in Moscow. They knew Stalin, perhaps even feared him, and many of them owed their positions to his support.

The exception was in Yugoslavia. Tito had not spent the war in Moscow, but at home, building his own army. When Tito showed a propensity to act without consulting Moscow, Stalin turned on him and the Yugoslav Communists. In a letter from March 27, 1948, Stalin claimed that Yugoslav Communist leaders had turned away from the true path toward socialism and were acting in a way that could not be considered Marxist-Leninist. He compared the Yugoslavs to Trotsky and Bukharin, Soviet leaders who had opposed Stalin and had been branded as traitors as a result.[3]

Stalin expected that once the Yugoslav Communists became aware of the depth of his displeasure, they would replace Tito with someone more amenable to following Soviet orders.[4] But Yugoslav leaders refused to be cowed. In a reply to Stalin, Tito reiterated Yugoslavia's commitment to building socialism along Soviet lines. Yet, he wrote, "no matter how much each of us loves the land of socialism, the USSR, he can, in no case, love his own country less."[5] Unwilling to countenance such insubordination, Stalin broke off relations with Yugoslavia and had the country expelled from the Cominform, effectively

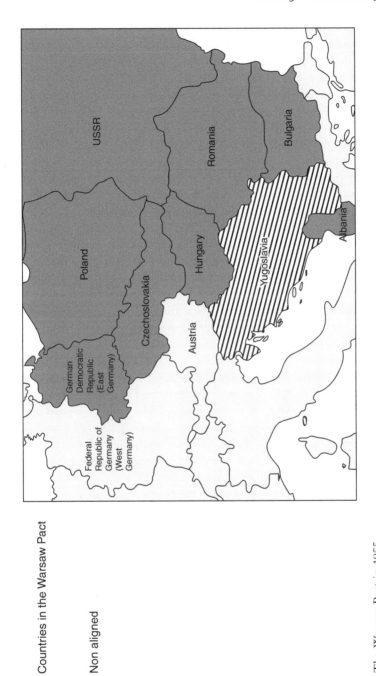

Countries in the Warsaw Pact

Non aligned

MAP 2.1 The Warsaw Pact in 1955.

excommunicating Yugoslavia from the rest of the socialist world. Even Albania, whose partisan leaders had been tightly connected to Tito's regime, opted to cut its ties to Yugoslavia and stay within the Soviet orbit.

To the other Communist leaders of Eastern Europe, Tito was a traitor. At home, standing up to Stalin increased Tito's popularity. From this point forward, Yugoslavia would set its own trajectory; it would never rejoin the Soviet bloc. Until its demise in the 1990s, Yugoslavia remained a socialist state, and it retained many similarities to the other countries of Eastern Europe. There were some key differences: the Yugoslav economy would be somewhat less centralized, according to the principle known as worker self-management. Its people would also inhabit a different space. Cut off from the Soviet Union and its allies, Yugoslavia had to develop economic ties to the West. Yugoslavia was not aligned to any bloc, but its people moved more freely to the West than to the East.

The Yugoslav Communists were able to survive the split with the Soviet Union because, as the victors in Yugoslavia's civil war, they had substantial popular support and had eliminated their domestic rivals. By 1948, Tito's regime had firmly established itself as the legitimate power in the country. Other East European Communist leaders knew they did not have these advantages. For them, the Yugoslav–Soviet split served as a cautionary tale, reminding them that staying in power depended on maintaining good relations with Stalin and the Soviet Union.

The close relationship between the Soviet Union and the rest of Eastern Europe would be formalized in two organizations. The Council for Mutual Economic Assistance (CMEA, also referred to as Comecon) was created in 1949 to promote economic ties between the Soviet-allied countries of Eastern Europe and the USSR. By the early 1950s, most of Eastern Europe's foreign trade was with other Comecon members. The Warsaw Treaty Organization or Warsaw Pact was a political and military alliance established in 1955 in response to North Atlantic Treaty Organization (NATO), the North American–European alliance created in 1949. As with NATO, the Warsaw Pact signatories pledged to defend each other if attacked and to coordinate military affairs. Together, these two organizations created the institutional framework that would bind the countries of Eastern Europe not only to the USSR but to each other.

Stepping into the Sunny Realm of Socialism

After they took power, Eastern Europe's Communist governments committed themselves to rapidly building socialism along the Soviet model. From the perspective of the West, this meant crushing freedom and creating oppressive dictatorships. Eastern Europe's Communist regimes did swiftly eliminate all formal political opposition. Elections continued to occur under socialism, but their results were of little import. Communist leaders, not elected assemblies, held the real power. Once a decision had been made by the party's Central Committee, citizens had no way to overturn it. Because each country's Communist party unofficially controlled all state institutions, the countries of socialist Eastern Europe are often referred to as "party-states."

Like the Soviet Union, the Communist regimes of Eastern Europe followed the *nomenklatura* system. Under this system, key positions in all areas of life, including government, public administration, the economy and education, could only be filled by candidates who had been nominated from within the Communist party and who were party members. In this way, the party controlled who could be a senior diplomat, run a large industrial enterprise or direct a major research institute. It was nearly impossible to reach an elite position in any field without being a member of the Communist party and having the approval of party leaders. Party leaders were thus assured that only party loyalists would gain positions of power and influence.

In Eastern Europe, just as in the Soviet Union, Communist parties were hierarchically organized. At the top of each party's hierarchy stood a group of officials elected into its Central Committee; this Central Committee approved and implemented all major policies. Executive authority was typically delegated to a smaller and select group of Central Committee members known as the Politburo. Each party also had a leader, whose power typically went well beyond his formal job description. This followed the model of the Soviet Union, where Joseph Stalin amassed enormous authority over both party members and state machinery. As the countries of Eastern Europe moved to adopt the Soviet model, their leaders also gained this kind of authority. Because so much power was concentrated in their hands, they were often referred to as the "little Stalins." Enver Hoxha in Albania, Georgi Dmitrov in Bulgaria, Klement Gottwald in Czechoslovakia, Walter Ulbricht in the German Democratic Republic (GDR or East Germany), Mátyás Rákosi in Hungary, Bolesław Bierut in Poland and Gheorghe Gheorghiu-Dej in Romania all exerted enormous power in their countries.

While they did establish dictatorships, Communists themselves did not equate building socialism with oppression. They claimed that taking power would allow them to create a better world. While many East Europeans did not agree, others, particularly young people, enthusiastically welcomed the chance to help make a more just and equitable society. The Czech Antonín Liehm was one of these young people. He later remembered,

> We felt that we knew how to solve human problems. We stepped from the darkness of Nazism straight into the sunny realm of freedom, friendship, happiness—in short, socialism. We considered anyone who failed to understand this as a reactionary bourgeois; people were neatly divided into good and bad; everything was clear and simple.[6]

Many young Communists in the years just after the establishment of Communist regimes in Eastern Europe shared Liehm's sense of certainty. They believed in the Marxist theory of history, which told them that the transition to socialism was the inevitable result of immutable historical laws. As they saw it, opposing socialism was like opposing the laws of physics; it was not a valid choice for anyone who was committed to reason over faith. Those who supported Communist goals were on the right side of history. Those who did not agree were not simply political opponents: they were enemies bent on turning mankind from its proper path.

In the years after they assumed power, Eastern Europe's Communist governments devoted considerable resources to convincing their citizens to share this worldview. One way was through the media. Media outlets, including radio, newspapers, magazines and books, were purged of voices opposing socialism. In 1951, Czech Auschwitz survivor Heda Margolius Kovály got a job in a scientific publishing house as an art director. All of the employees were Communist party members, most of them young and incredibly enthusiastic, with what Kovály described as a "naïve belief in the infallibility and virtual holiness of the Party." None of them, Kovály claimed, ever doubted a decision made by the Central Committee. When Kovály commented that a florid painting of Soviet leader Joseph Stalin with a tractor was bad art, the colleague who had showed it to her reported her to the editor-in-chief and demanded to no longer share an office with such a reactionary. Kovály believed that she kept her job only because her husband was Deputy Minister of Foreign Trade. She would be fired after his arrest the following year.[7]

Making sure that the media promoted the party line and extolled the virtues of socialism was only the beginning. Communist activists used a wide variety of means to bring their message to ordinary people. Propaganda posters promoting socialist policies decorated workplaces, schools and streets. Factories, hostels and dormitories established "red corners"—brightly decorated spaces where workers or residents could read newspapers and other literature or even play socialist-themed games.[8] In factory cafeterias, newspapers were read aloud as workers ate lunch. Loudspeakers on village greens blasted state radio broadcasts.

Under Stalinism, Communist propaganda around Eastern Europe became more similar in both content and vocabulary. Posters and slogans in different countries sounded many of the same themes, which were derived from Soviet sources. Americans, for example, were usually referred to as "war-mongering imperialists" who threatened nuclear war as a means of world domination. They were blood-thirsty, exploitative and racist, bent only on lining their own pockets. In contrast, socialism and the Soviet Union were represented by light, progress, friendship, civilization and modernization. The USSR was "the defender of peace, the builder of the radiant future, the caretaker of women and children."[9]

As Eastern Europe's Communist parties worked to transform themselves along the Soviet model, they also promoted the Soviet Union itself. In local media, the Soviet Union was constantly celebrated and East Europeans were urged to emulate its people and practices. Articles praising Soviet achievements were placed in newspapers or folded into radio broadcasts, Soviet novels were translated into local languages and sold in bookstores, Soviet movies played in theaters, exhibitions of Soviet art filled museums and reproductions of Soviet posters graced walls. One Albanian architect, Petraq Kolevica, remembered, "The radio never stopped informing us about the Soviet Union and broadcasting Russian songs."[10]

Part of this promotion of all things Soviet was the glorification of Stalin himself. Over the course of Stalin's rule, a cult was created around him inside the Soviet Union. He was publicly venerated as a great leader and as the source of Soviet achievements. Pictures and posters of Stalin were everywhere, from public offices to private homes. He was immortalized in films, songs, poems and paintings, where he was portrayed as a genius and the father of his people. This cult of Stalin did not develop spontaneously. It was quite consciously constructed, with Stalin's knowledge, as a means of legitimizing his regime and mobilizing the population. The Stalin cult was imported into Eastern Europe to serve the same purpose and also to underscore the pivotal relationship between the countries of Eastern Europe and their Soviet patron. Images of Stalin were soon ubiquitous throughout the Soviet bloc. Choirs sang songs praising him, poems were written in his honor and books of his writings were made available in enormous print runs. Streets, factories and even whole towns were named after him. Statues of Stalin appeared in many East European towns and

FIGURE 2.1   People carrying posters of Stalin at a May Day parade in Bucharest, 1950s. © Sovfoto/UIG/Bridgeman Images.

cities, none bigger than the one erected in Prague in 1955, which loomed over the city from its perch on Letná hill.[11]

The Stalin cult was linked to the creation of local leader cults. The "little Stalins" all had their own cults, which used their image as a means of connecting with the population. In Hungary, pictures of Hungarian leader Mátyás Rákosi could be seen in schools, shops, railway stations, public buildings and even doctor's offices. A butcher was so moved by the cult of Rákosi that he sculpted a bust of the leader out of lard and placed it in his shop window, hoping to boost sales. Unfortunately, when the temperature rose, the bust began to melt, bringing the attention of the police. To mark Polish leader Bolesław Bierut's sixtieth birthday in 1952, celebrations were organized in workplaces throughout the country, and workers promised to increase their output in his honor. When Bulgarian leader Georgi Dmitrov passed away in 1949, his embalmed body was laid to rest in a public mausoleum so that future generations could pay their respects to the great leader. The same happened to Czechoslovak Communist Party chief Klement Gottwald after his death in 1953. Legions of schoolchildren were taken to view his body in its memorial on Vítkov hill before it was finally removed in 1962.[12]

Like Stalin, the leaders of Communist Eastern Europe were portrayed as fathers and educators, leading their people to a better life under socialism. They were often pictured in landscapes that symbolized the prosperous future socialism would bring. One famous picture of Hungarian leader Mátyás Rákosi placed him in the middle of a field of wheat, indicating his deep ties to his native land and his success at coaxing plenty from its soil.[13] Leaders were also commonly photographed among crowds of children or with workers and peasants, indicating their connections to the common people and their concern with future generations.

Although they were dictatorships, Stalinist regimes were intent on getting their populations to actively participate in political life. Under Stalinism, silently going about your daily life and ignoring politics was seldom an option. Communist party activists, also known as cadres, pushed those around them to take part in an array of activities. Political meetings and rallies were common occurrences at workplaces, and employees were expected to attend—in their free time, not during work hours. Local activists arranged a steady stream of lectures, discussions, films or other performances in villages, towns and urban neighborhoods. They also organized courses in adult literacy or political education. People were strongly encouraged to join mass public associations, such as youth leagues, women's groups and trade unions. These organizations were not formally Communist, but they were controlled by Communist leaders. Their activities provided a way to mobilize people who were not in the Communist party itself.

The Czechoslovak Federation of Women (CFW) was one such organization. Its goal was to convince Czechoslovak women that capitalism brought only war and misery, while socialism was the way to peace. According to the CFW, any woman who wanted a safe and happy future for her children needed to commit herself to the socialist cause. CFW activists saw their job as "fighting over the soul of every woman who still isn't clear on what building socialism and defending peace means... refuting the lies and calumnies spread by enemies, convincing (them) daily of our truth." To spread this message, the CFW organized "agitation Sundays" where pairs of female activists went from house to house, visiting women and trying to convince them to join the CFW and to sign up for factory work in order to help build the socialist economy.[14]

When a Communist activist knocked on a door and asked the resident inside to join an organization, subscribe to a socialist newspaper or sign a petition advocating a ban on atomic weapons, what she was really asking was whether or not the resident supported their Communist government. This put those who were not enthusiastic Communists into an uncomfortable position. While there were rarely any immediate consequences for not signing a petition or subscribing to a newspaper, activists did usually note down the names of those who refused. One Hungarian housewife remembered that she and her neighbors tried to pretend they were not home to avoid having to speak with the activists who came around constantly wanting to talk with them about politics. When they were caught, however, they did what they could to seem like model citizens, knowing that what the activists really wanted to hear was agreement, not debate.[15] Like these Hungarian women, many East Europeans signed what was offered or agreed to take the paper, even if they did not intend to read it, rather than risk coming into open conflict with the state.

Anti-Communists who fled Eastern Europe for the West after 1948 often asserted that East Europeans only cooperated with the Communist state out of fear. A Bulgarian pharmacist who left his country in 1953 claimed that ordinary Bulgarians had decided it was useless to resist Communist attempts to get them to participate in politics. Instead of staying home, they went to rallies when they were asked and cheered on cue. They marched in parades and signed statements extolling socialism and decrying its enemies. Even children, the pharmacist said, "have learned, like all grownups, to say the correct thing at the right place."[16]

According to this Bulgarian pharmacist (the journalist who recorded his story did not reveal his name), anything that looked like enthusiasm for socialism in Stalinist Bulgaria was fake. Ardent young Communists like Antonín Liehm would have vehemently disagreed; these activists threw themselves into their work because they believed they were making a better world. Historians have argued over the extent to which people in the Stalinist period were motivated by fear or enthusiasm. Which was it? However, this very question may lead us to the wrong conclusions. Putting the situation in these terms compels us to divide people into two categories: those who supported Communism and those who resisted it. But this is a false dichotomy; it merely reproduces the ideological framework of the Cold War, in which people on both sides of the Iron Curtain were pressured to take sides and declare themselves to be either fervent Communists or committed capitalists. As this book will show, the reality was far more complicated.

You Are the Ones to Dig the First Foundations! Industrialization and the Planned Economy

What did it mean to adopt a Stalinist model? First and foremost, it meant moving to establish a socialist economy as quickly as possible. In a socialist economy, the state takes over the functions performed by private owners under capitalism. The state owns the means of production (such as factories or natural resources) and makes decisions about how best to use them for the good of society as a whole. Under capitalism, the market decides how much of an item should be produced and at what price it should be sold. Under state socialism, production targets are determined by the state. This is called a centrally planned economy.

Socialist economic plans were determined by planning professionals. These planners developed multiyear blueprints for the economy. These plans, usually done in increments of five years, determined what would be produced across the entire country and how these goods would be utilized. For example, a five-year plan might decree that in year one of the plan, five million tons of steel would be produced. If the planners hoped to increase steel production, they would set the production targets higher for each successive year of the plan. Planners also determined what would happen with that steel: for example, they might decide that one million tons would go to the automobile industry, two million tons to the machine tool industry, one million tons to build trains and lay track for the railways and so on.

Central planning was an attempt to conceive of a national economy in completely rational terms. Under the capitalist law of supply and demand, resources could easily be wasted on frivolities or on goods that would be consumed only by the wealthy. In an ideal centrally planned economy, those same resources would be used to feed, clothe and house the masses or to develop new industries that would lift the entire nation. Central plans did help to reduce income inequalities in Eastern Europe. But they could also easily go awry, creating the shortages that were endemic throughout the entire lifespan of socialism in Eastern Europe.

Central plans were very complicated documents; the first completed Five-Year Plan in Yugoslavia filled enough volumes to weigh over one and a half tons![17] Given this complexity, shortfalls in any one area could create ripple effects throughout the entire economy. To return to the example of the steel industry from above, to ensure that the steelworks could meet the first-year target of five million tons, planners needed to provide them with enough fuel, iron ore, labor and other inputs. If the promised fuel or ore failed to appear, plant managers had a problem; they would still be held responsible for meeting their targets. To avoid being caught short, managers often told planners they needed more supplies than they really did. If they wound up with more than they needed, they kept it, anticipating shortages in the future. This constant hoarding of supplies helped to create the shortages such hoarding was meant to forestall.[18]

Central planning affected the ways Eastern Europe's economies interacted with the rest of the world. East European currencies were not convertible, meaning they were not tied to world markets, just as the prices of East European goods were set by planners, not by markets. Under the socialist system, foreign trade was typically handled by special import and export companies which were detached from the rest of the economy. Most foreign trade in Comecon countries took place within the group. Because their currencies were not convertible, East European countries could find it difficult to import goods from the West. To do so, they had to either exchange goods they had produced for the goods they wanted or purchase the imports using a convertible, or hard, currency, such as US dollars or West German marks.[19]

One aspect of moving to central planning was increased nationalization. All of the countries of Eastern Europe had embarked on the process of nationalizing key industries in the immediate postwar period. In part because the state took over the property of expelled Germans (who had previously taken the property of deported Jews), over half of all industry in Poland and Czechoslovakia had been nationalized before 1948. In other countries, particularly Bulgaria, Romania and East Germany, most industries were still in private hands when the Communists came to power. Within a few years, however, almost all industrial production and distribution, as well as a majority of retail businesses and services like shops and restaurants, had been brought under state control.[20]

Under Stalinism, the primary goal was to rapidly build industrial capacity, as Stalin had done in the Soviet Union in the 1930s. The tense international situation of the early Cold War gave added urgency to these plans. Many believed that a war between the East and the West was almost inevitable. Eastern Europe would need to be ready for this possibility. With the exception of East Germany and the western part of Czechoslovakia, Eastern Europe was much less industrialized than Western Europe. At the time the Communists took power in Hungary, 52 percent of all workers were engaged in agriculture, while in Bulgaria 68 percent of the population made their living from farming, animal husbandry or forestry. In Romania, over 80 percent of the population lived in the countryside.[21] Socialist governments intended to change this imbalance within the space of only a few years.

Via their central plans, Eastern Europe's Stalinist regimes directed all available resources toward industrialization, prioritizing new factories and machines over the production of consumer goods. Communist leaders promised that socialism would eventually bring a better life for everyone, but they asked their citizens to defer their dreams of a higher standard of living until their plans for creating an industrial economy had been realized. Everyone would need to sacrifice for this future.

The centerpiece of Stalinist-era industrialization was heavy industry, such as steel, arms or machinery. Yet the ramifications reverberated through all sectors of the economy. Industrialization revolutionized the production of all kinds of goods, including everyday items like bread or beer, by centralizing the manufacturing process in factories. One example of how this worked was the Újpest Danube Shoe Factory in Hungary. Before the Stalinist period, shoes in this region of Hungary were made in small-scale workshops or factories where much of the work was done by hand. During Hungary's first Five-Year Plan, officials decided to centralize shoe production. As they nationalized the existing workshops, they closed them and moved their workers to the new Újpest Danube Shoe Factory. Within three years, the new shoe factory employed 2,513 people and had become the largest producer of shoes in the country.[22]

There were both economic and political imperatives behind these policies. Concentrating industrial production in large factories allowed for better use of existing resources and greater automation of work processes, making it possible to produce more for less. It also made it easier for the state to plan production and control distribution.

One hallmark of the Stalinist industrialization drive was the construction of entirely new socialist cities centered around heavy industry, such as the East German Stalinstadt, the Hungarian Sztálinváros or the Bulgarian Dimitrovgrad. The largest of these was the Polish steel town of Nowa Huta, the centerpiece of Poland's Six-Year Plan. The heart of Nowa Huta was the Lenin Steelworks, an enormous complex capable of producing 1.5 million tons of raw steel annually. The city built around it would house the plant's workers. Initially planned as a settlement for 100,000 people, Nowa Huta was built from the ground up in a period of only a few years.[23]

In the early 1950s, tens of thousands of young men and women streamed into Nowa Huta in search of opportunity. Most of them came from poor backgrounds and many were of peasant origin. In postwar Poland, like in much of Eastern Europe, a majority of the population was peasants—small-scale, subsistence farmers living in villages. Successfully achieving large industrialization projects like the building of Nowa Huta depended on taking people from peasant farms and making them into factory workers. While perhaps two-thirds of those who came to build Nowa Huta were men, women were well represented among the recruits. One of the goals of Stalinist industrialization across the region was to mobilize the labor power of women, bringing them permanently into the industrial workforce.[24]

Those drawn by mobilization campaigns to work in Nowa Huta imagined shining smokestacks and a new, modern city. When Szczepan Brzeziński arrived in 1950, however, he was greeted by a big red banner in the middle of empty fields. He realized that he would not be working in the city, but building it. The first volunteers to the site were told, "You are the first, the ones to dig the first foundations for the apartment buildings in which you and the first workers will live. So, be proud that this honor fell to you! History will write about you!" Only four years after he arrived, Brzeziński, who had now been trained as an electrician, climbed a construction crane and described a very different vista. Instead of muddy fields, an enormous steelworks lay before him. It was a hive of activity, bustling with trucks and cranes and almost 30,000 workers erecting some 500 buildings. Outside of the steelworks, the city sprang up rapidly; 14,885 new apartments were built in Nowa Huta between 1949 and 1958.[25]

Building a city out of nothing in such a short span of time demanded tremendous effort. Edmund Chmieliński, who excitedly left his home village to join a youth brigade in Nowa Huta, recalled, "I didn't know then that work building Nowa Huta would be still harder, more backbreaking and dangerous [than life in the village], and life in the brigade no bed of roses."[26] For Chmieliński, the effort was worth it. He described his days in the brigade as the happiest he had ever known. Others, however, were sorely disappointed by the backbreaking labor, tough living conditions, lack of proper training and the absence of much in the way of leisure.[27]

Building Nowa Huta required sacrifice and dedication on the part of its workers. Stalinist industrialization demanded similar efforts from workers everywhere. In this period, central plans called for the doubling or tripling of industrial output in the space of only a few years. To make this happen, all workers would have to perform extraordinary feats.

Stalinist governments instituted a variety of policies aimed at improving worker productivity. One technique was to tie a worker's pay to a norm or quota. Analysts determined how much they believed an ideal worker could complete in a standard shift. Those who completed the full amount were paid their full salary. Those who did less were paid less, while those who overfulfilled their quotas received bonuses. Most workers hated the quota system because they believed it set unrealistic targets, forcing them to work at an impossible rate and resulting in low wages for most workers. A worker at the Újpest Shoe Factory complained that her norm was set at "1600 pairs, which I just couldn't meet under any circumstances. My pay was very low. When I complained, they said my machine was bad."[28] To make matters worse, norms were not stable; managers periodically raised them, pushing their employees to work ever harder and faster.

Labor competition was another technique designed to build enthusiasm and encourage workers to do more in less time. In labor competitions, an individual or a work group volunteered to show they could complete an amount of work well above the usual norm. For example, a worker in the Újpest Shoe Factory might promise to complete 2,000 pairs of shoes in a single shift. Or an entire brigade might pledge to fulfill its plan targets two weeks ahead of schedule.

Those who were very successful in these feats of labor could become heroes of labor or *Stakhanovites*. The term "Stakhanovite" was Soviet in origin; it referred to a miner, Aleksei Stakhanov, who completed 14 times his quota in a single shift.[29] In reward for their extraordinary feats, Stakhanovites could earn status and material rewards. Hungarian coal miner Barnabás Varga boasted that his feats of labor had earned him an apartment, furnishings, a radio, paintings and a fur coat for his wife.[30] Others were rewarded mainly with recognition in the form of medals or articles detailing their results in the local press.

As part of the broader policy of labor competition, workers were encouraged to donate either their money or their labor for the good of the state or socialism more generally. Managers periodically organized special extra shifts (sometimes called the "Stalin shift" or the "Lenin Saturday") where workers worked for free, donating their time in support of a specific cause, which could be anything from Korean war orphans to the glory of socialism. The causes changed, but the extra, unpaid shifts sometimes became permanent. These special shifts were ostensibly voluntary but were often not actually so. Those who refused to participate risked consequences, such as being assigned to the worst equipment or most boring duties, not being promoted or even the loss of their job. Workers were also asked to contribute money from their wages to "peace loans" to help their governments work for peace by advancing socialism.

Some workers, particularly among the youth, embraced labor competition enthusiastically, at least at first. Leopold Sulkowski, a vocational instructor at the Lenin Steelworks in Nowa Huta, remembered seeing young heroes of labor honored at a rally. "I looked into the faces of these workers," he said. "They were convinced what they were doing was right; they were filled with the satisfaction that it gave them, and worked with unheard of self-sacrifice."[31] Other workers, however, resented the Stakhanovites because managers used their outsize results as justification for raising work quotas for everyone.

Many workers were willing to make sacrifices in the short term, with the expectation that their efforts would soon be rewarded with better wages and a higher standard of living. They became dissatisfied when they felt that their leaders asked only for more sacrifice without delivering on the promise of a better life. Hungarian coal miners were incensed that after several years of rising norms and lowered wages, they were asked to contribute substantial parts of their earnings to a peace loan. "Under the old system," one said in frustration, "I could buy one set of work clothes with one day's wages, now I have to work for a week before I can afford a set."[32]

Under Stalinism, trade unions had been taken over by Communist parties, and union officials did not oppose state directives. Nonetheless, disgruntled workers protested low wages, poor working conditions and the unavailability of basic consumer goods. In Poland, there were 432 unauthorized strikes between

1949 and 1952, and in Czechoslovakia, there were 218 such strikes between 1948 and 1953.[33] Less formal protests that did not involve work stoppages were even more common. In 1952, workers at a building site in the Czech town of Třnec protested price hikes in their workplace cafeteria. The workers were upset that they were only allowed to purchase meals at a subsidized rate if they had worked six full shifts per week and complained that the food was of poor quality and that the servings, especially of meat, were too small. The workers loudly demanded changes for several days. Their managers tried to appease them by appealing to the need to complete the current Five-Year Plan. This did not satisfy the protesters, but they were not willing to go on strike over the issue, so the matter was dropped.[34]

These kinds of protests show the difficulty Eastern Europe's Stalinist regimes had mobilizing workers. Workers may have supported Communist goals, but they expected a socialist government to improve their quality of life. When the opposite occurred, many workers began to suspect that their Communist governments did not really have their interests at heart.

Revolution in the Countryside

The Stalinist drive to rapidly create a socialist society was not limited to industry. Eastern Europe's Communist regimes also hoped to radically remake the agricultural sector. This meant changing the very foundations of rural life. At the time the Communists came to power, most rural residents were peasants who worked their own small plots of land, often no more than one or two hectares in size (a hectare is 2.47 acres). Earlier interwar governments had encouraged peasant land ownership. Land reform policies broke up the holdings of former aristocrats, putting more land into peasant hands. After the end of World War II, Communists helped to sponsor more land reform. By 1948, much of the rural landscape was dominated by small peasant proprietors.

Communist planners believed they had a better alternative to independent peasant cultivation: collectivization. Under collectivization, peasants would agree to pool their land together into cooperatives which they would work communally. There were economic arguments to be made in favor of collective farms. Just as in industry, creating larger production units enabled mechanization and allowed for more efficient use of both land and peasant labor. The result would be increased yields from less labor, enabling more rural people to leave their villages and join the growing industrial sector. The economic rationale behind collectivization echoed trends in agriculture in capitalist countries, where it was the market that pushed inefficient small proprietors off the land and encouraged the consolidation of large farms.

Collectivization was, however, not merely—or, some would charge, even primarily—about economic rationality. Collectivization, just like rapid industrialization, was ideologically motivated. Its goal was to restructure existing power relations in the countryside and replace them with a new socialist order. This would be a hard task: rural peasants had little sense of what a socialist order might be or why they would want to abandon their former ways of life to embrace it. Many of Eastern Europe's Communist leaders were wary of rushing to implement collectivization, but Soviet pressure persuaded them to set aside any doubts.[35]

Unlike the nationalization of industry, collectivization proceeded slowly and in waves. The first collectivization campaigns began in 1948 (in the GDR not until 1950), but results were mediocre outside of Czechoslovakia, where 45 percent of all arable land was in the hands of collective or state farms by 1953.[36] Yugoslavia, whose leaders were not bound to follow the Soviet model, abandoned collectivization altogether after only a few years. Following Stalin's death in 1953, the push to collectivize stalled and even went backward, as existing collectives failed due to poor management or recidivism. A second wave of

FIGURE 2.2 Czechoslovak poster urging farmers to fulfill their grain quotas, ca. 1947–1950. Photo © CCI/Bridgeman Images.

campaigns began with Soviet encouragement in 1955, to be interrupted by the events of 1956. The last wave commenced in 1957 and worked with renewed speed. By 1960, collectivization was nearly complete in much of the region; in 1962, Romania was the last of the Soviet bloc nations to declare collectivization accomplished.[37]

Unlike in the Soviet Union, land in Eastern Europe was not nationalized; peasants remained the owners of their plots. To create collective farms, local officials needed to persuade peasants to voluntarily agree to pool their land, livestock and other resources together into a joint enterprise. This went against the very core of how most peasants saw the world. Peasants, especially those with larger farms, valued land ownership, seeing it as a source of status, stability and autonomy. Land provided their livelihood and their place in their community. They simply did not see how their lives would function if they gave up the rights to their land. Many had also heard dire rumors about the violence and famine that accompanied collectivization in the Soviet Union, convincing them they needed to resist the kolkhoz (the Soviet term for collective farm) with all their might.[38]

Communist activists went to villages to educate the rural population about the benefits of socialism and collectivization. They tried to persuade peasants that capitalism exploited them by catching them in cycles of debt, leaving them prey to unscrupulous bankers and creditors. Collective farming, they said, would release them from this vicious cycle, allow for the mechanization of agricultural production and create more bountiful harvests. Newspapers, posters, songs, plays, radio programs and films aimed at the rural population extolled the benefits of collective farms. In the Balkans, a majority of the rural population was illiterate, so oral forms of propaganda were particularly important. One Romanian song about the joys of joining the collective painted a vivid picture of a happy, socialist countryside:

> Let's go to the Collective, to strive for Peace,
> Because the Party leads us.
> To improve ourselves, it called on us to go to school,
> So the capitalists can see how the collectivists work.
> They work happily, to get out of poverty,
> They work enthusiastically, to create socialism.[39]

One element of the campaign to promote collectivization was the demonization of capitalist exploiters. Socialism would remove these exploiters from the countryside, allowing the rest of the community to prosper. But who were these exploiters? Previous land reform measures had already confiscated the estates of the former nobility and other large landowners. Banks had been nationalized along with other businesses. Instead, activists pointed to the so-called *kulaks* or wealthier peasants. These kulaks, they said, were sabotaging the peaceful advance of socialism.

The term kulak, just like the impetus to begin collectivization itself, was brought into Eastern Europe from the Soviet Union. In Romania and in the GDR, local terms were used to indicate these "village rich" (*chiabur* in Romania and *Großbauer* in the GDR), while in the rest of the region, local governments adopted the Soviet word for their own use. As in the Soviet Union, the definition of a kulak was never precise. The Romanian leader Gheorghe Gheorgiu-Dej noted that

> the village bourgeois … is a type apart from others, who has formed his household working, sweating, exploiting and speculating … They aren't that much different from other peasants if you look at their clothing or the fact they work.[40]

Generally speaking, kulaks were peasants who owned larger farms, yet most so-called kulaks did not possess very large holdings: owning a farm of even 14 hectares—or in some regions even less—was enough.[41] Ultimately, local officials had the power to decide who was a kulak and who was not. As one Romanian villager remembered, "Whoever they wanted to destroy, they did; whoever not, they didn't."[42]

During the drive to collectivize in the Soviet Union (1929–1935), millions of people identified as kulaks were removed from their villages and deported to Siberia or Central Asia. In Eastern Europe, mass deportations were not the norm, although a minority did face this fate. Those identified as kulaks primarily faced economic harassment in the form of increased taxes or quotas of farm produce. During World War II, farmers in Germany, Bohemia, Hungary and Bulgaria had been required to make mandatory deliveries of grain, meat and/ or milk to local authorities. After the war, these policies continued and similar quota systems were implemented in Yugoslavia, Slovakia and Romania (and briefly in Poland) as a means of stabilizing food supplies and prices. After the campaign against the kulaks began, these quotas became a means of confiscating kulaks' land and livestock, eliminating their livelihood.

In Hungary, for example, in 1948 quotas for farmers with larger holdings were suddenly tripled or even quadrupled. Those who could not come up with enough grain to meet their delivery requirements had no choice but to sell land or other belongings in order to make up for the shortfall. Not meeting one's delivery obligations was grounds for criminal prosecution, which could result in imprisonment or a stint in a labor camp.[43] A Romanian farmer remembered,

> They imposed a very high quota. You received a small notebook in which every quantity—of meat, wheat, barley, corn—was listed. They knew that no one could possibly give that much, so then they could say you were engaged in sabotage, and they locked you up. There was no one we could ask why the amounts were so high.

Another recalled, "If you couldn't pay, they took bread right off the table ... and the clothes you were wearing, and whatever was in your house, they took it and sold it at auction, you couldn't recover it."[44]

In the early 1950s, those who had been identified as kulaks were forbidden from joining collectives or were expelled from them if they were discovered to have joined, forcing those who had lost their land to abandon the countryside altogether. This made ideological sense, as it prevented wealthier peasants from taking charge of the collectives by virtue of their status in the community. However, it also meant that new collectives lacked the expert knowledge of the most successful farmers, making it harder for them to prosper. After 1953, the campaigns against the kulaks lessened, and these farmers were allowed to join collective farms.[45]

The first to agree to join collectives—and the ones to do so most willingly—were usually those who did not possess land of their own or so-called new peasants who had only gotten their own land via land reform measures after 1945. These people tended to have only tiny plots, and they lacked the skill and resources to develop them. Those who had a bit more land tended to be skeptical of Communist claims about the superiority of collective farming. In Poland, for example, peasants worried that joining a collective would take away their independence and autonomy without giving much in return. As one said, "the cooperative will be governed by bureaucrats, while we will be doing all the work."[46]

Frustrated by peasant recalcitrance, local activists, who might themselves be facing pressure from their superiors to show success, turned to more coercive methods of persuasion. Common tactics included invading peasants' homes at all hours, threats of violence or retaliation, even locking people in rooms until they signed papers agreeing to join the collective. Sometimes actual violence was used, but more often activists just relentlessly pursued people until they were willing to sign. A Romanian villager remembered, "He [an activist] kept after you constantly, he'd come, sit around for an hour, come again: 'What've you been doing, have you changed your mind?' He'd sit some more ... anyway, he'd come three or four times a day. We'd hide, people would hide ... 'I'm not here!'"[47] Hiding and running away worked for a while, but eventually most gave in to the relentless pressure.

A Bulgarian woman from a mountain village that was finally collectivized in 1958 remembered a big group of men came to her family's house to persuade her father to join the collective. As she recalled, "Dad saw they were lots of people and there was nothing he could do. He signed up voluntarily to avoid being beaten up." Her father, she said, had joined a collective "voluntarily by force."[48] He signed the paper of his own volition, but only to prevent harm from coming to himself and his family. Like this man, many finally agreed to collectivization only because they felt they had no choice. In addition to the pressure they faced from local officials, private farmers were confronted with ever-increasing taxes and delivery quotas. Given these economic realities, most realized that in the long term there were only two viable options: to join a collective or to migrate to the city. Many did indeed leave the countryside; rural populations declined substantially during the period of collectivization.

Communist activists went into the countryside, imagining that they would show rural people how socialist ideals and practices would improve their lives. While some, particularly the poorest and most marginalized, were receptive to the idea of collectivization, many others were skeptical. Faced with stiff resistance, activists and local officials charged with forming collective farms began to coerce those they could not convince. Communist governments may have sincerely wanted to persuade peasants of the benefits of collectivization, but they did not see their failure to do as a reason to reevaluate their policies. If they could not achieve their goals with words, they would do so with violence.

Enemies of the People

By 1948, the Communist parties of Eastern Europe had eliminated formal political opposition and established themselves as the ruling forces in their countries. Having acquired power, they meant to keep it. Marxist ideology gave them the certainty that they were on the right side of history. In the end, they knew, socialism would be victorious. Nonetheless, the forces of capital would not give up their power easily. Capitalists, they believed, would work incessantly to undermine Communist regimes, both from within and from without.

Western actions during the early Cold War helped to crystallize this conviction. The Truman doctrine, the Marshall Plan, the Berlin blockade and the creation of NATO all provided concrete evidence that the United States was intent on mobilizing the world against the Soviet Union and its allies. Beginning with Truman and continuing throughout the entire Cold War, American politicians referred to the countries of Eastern Europe as "captive nations," clearly suggesting that the region's Communist regimes were illegitimate and welcoming their overthrow. The outbreak of the Korean War in June 1950 added enormously to the tension, providing proof that the West was willing to use violence to defend the interests of capitalist imperialism.

The specter—whether real or imagined—of possible capitalist aggression spurred Eastern Europe's Communist leaders to consolidate their position at home. In the Manichean environment of the Cold War, you were either in the socialist camp or its enemy. This meant that anyone who did not support socialist rule was a possible threat. During the years between 1948 and 1953, all of the countries of the Soviet bloc initiated campaigns to find and eliminate these enemies within. Soviet leaders, including Stalin himself, encouraged this turn to terror.

The most obvious threats were those who had been part of the privileged elite of the capitalist order, now labeled class enemies. These included members of the former bourgeoisie, kulaks, people who had been high-ranking members of political parties that had opposed the Communists and community leaders (such as clergy) who refused to publicly support Communist regimes after they took power. Those identified as class enemies were purged from public life. Many suffered the loss of assets (through nationalization or taxation), jobs and positions in community or voluntary organizations. It is impossible to determine the precise number of people affected by such measures, but it is clear that these policies affected wide swathes of the population, in both urban and rural areas.

The Czech Milada Horáková was one of those who abruptly found she had become an enemy of the people. Horáková was a lawyer and feminist activist who had been imprisoned by the Nazis for being part of a resistance group during World War II. After 1945, she was elected to the Czechoslovak parliament as a member of the National Socialist Party (a Czech political party that had no relationship to the German Nazi party). She was also the president of the Council of Czechoslovak Women, one of the most influential women's organizations in the country, and a vice president of the Czechoslovak Association of Former Political Prisoners. Yet to Czechoslovak Communist leaders, her long record of service meant little compared with her established record of opposition to Communist policies. Just days after the Communist seizure of power in 1948, Horáková was ejected from the civic organizations she had once led and fired from her job as a lawyer with the Social Office of the City of Prague. Her removal was reported in the press as a triumph for the new regime. The following month, she resigned her parliamentary seat in protest.[49]

Even after they had successfully removed opponents like Milada Horáková from their positions, Communist officials worried that enemies could be working secretly to sabotage their policies or preparing the ground for a violent overthrow of the socialist state. Their concerns were fueled by Soviet advisers to the region, who frequently suggested that their East European comrades needed to do more to find and neutralize potential opponents. These Soviet advisers played key roles in developing the state security services (also sometimes referred to as the "secret police" or "political police") in all of the countries of the Soviet bloc. In the first years of Communist rule, these security services grew rapidly—the Hungarian state security organization grew from 9,000 employees in 1949 to 28,000 in 1950.[50] One of their primary tasks was to monitor those suspected of working against Communist governments. To this end, the security services employed agents who read mail, listened to phone calls and created networks of informers who reported back on what they had observed others say or do.

Milada Horáková was arrested in 1949 on suspicion of espionage and treason. She was one of approximately 90,000 Czechoslovaks prosecuted for political crimes during the years between 1948 and 1954, although her case was exceptional.[51] Horáková was accused of leading a ring of spies who were working with the West to bring about a war that would overthrow Czecho-slovakia's Communist regime. At their public trial, she and her co-defendants all admitted to these crimes. Horáková herself stated during the trial that she realized her treasonous work with the West might bring atomic bombs down on the city of Prague, killing millions, including her own daughter. Citing her extreme callousness to human life, the judge sentenced her and three of her co-defendants to death (the other nine received prison sentences). Even though many in the West, including Eleanor Roosevelt, Winston Churchill and Albert Einstein, petitioned for clemency on her behalf, Horáková was hanged in the courtyard of the Pankrác prison in June 1950.[52]

The crimes Horáková had admitted in court had never occurred. Her true offenses were merely corresponding with Czechoslovak opposition politicians who had fled the country and meeting with others who opposed Communist rule to discuss the situation. During their trial, Horáková and her co-defendants were coerced into repeating statements that had been written for them by state security agents, like actors in a play. The Horáková trial was what is called *show trial*: a legal proceeding where all of the testimony had been written out in advance. The participants were forced, often via torture, to memorize their parts and repeat them in court. Show trials had taken place in the Soviet Union in the 1930s, and it was Soviet advisors who brought the show trial to Eastern Europe. Show trials occurred in all of the countries of the Soviet bloc between 1948 and 1954.[53]

Only a tiny minority of those accused of political offenses wound up in show trials. These trials were carefully constructed media events, designed to engage the whole population. The Horáková trial, which was the biggest show trial of the political opposition in Czechoslovakia, was broadcast live on the radio, and the transcripts were printed daily in all of the major newspapers. The show trials served a pedagogical purpose; they were meant to educate the population about the enemies of socialism. The prosecutor in the Horáková trial was quite open about this. In his closing statement, he presented the trial as guide for recognizing further traitors and urged working people to be on the lookout for new enemies. He concluded with a rousing warning to any who might threaten socialism, declaring,

> We advise the traitors at home and abroad: keep your hands off the re-public. The people of our republic are not only building paradise on earth; they will also defend this paradise against the forces of the old, mean world which is condemned to destruction.[54]

Show trials transformed theoretical threats to socialism into a concrete real-ity. Their defendants embodied the many faces of socialism's enemies. In some show trials, like in the Horáková trial, the accused were former politicians who supposedly worked with Western intelligence or Yugoslav agents to bring about regime change. In others, they were members of the old capitalist elite who tried to sabotage the new planned economy or to thwart collectivization. This allowed Communist officials to blame problems with meeting plan targets on outside forces. One Hungarian show trial involved managers from the Standard Electric plant, who were alleged to have worked with American and British agents to sabotage Hungarian industry. One of the defendants, Imre Geiger, claimed he had purposely directed the production of shoddy goods and hoarded crucial raw materials to prevent other enterprises from fulfilling their plan targets. Under his watch, he said, Standard Electric sent poorly made equipment to the Soviet Union, Bulgaria and Romania so that their communications networks would not function in a possible war with the West.[55]

Show trials taught East Europeans to recognize potential enemies of socialism and mobilized the population in the fight to stop them. As part of the publicity campaigns around the trials, ordinary people were pressed to declare their disgust for the traitors. Millions signed petitions in their workplaces, schools or community meetings condemning the accused and asking for the most severe punishment. During the Horáková trial alone, over 6,300 such petitions were submitted to the court. Because the accused had confessed the charges, to not publicly renounce their actions made it seem as if you condoned their treason, perhaps indicating you also were an enemy of socialism.[56]

The duty to be vigilant did not end once a trial was over. Communist leaders exhorted their citizens to be on guard and to report any suspicious activity, effectively enlisting them to watch each other. In the atmosphere of heightened tension that the trials helped to create, many feared not showing enthusiastic support for the Communist state would bring them under suspicion. Stalinist regimes gave the public many opportunities to show this support, with constant rallies and meetings, either in support of the plan, or against nuclear war, or to condemn enemies of the regime. Attending these kinds of events was one way to show that you were not an enemy.

Communists themselves were not insulated from this terror. The search for hidden enemies extended even into their ranks. This was instigated by Stalin himself, just as he had initiated a similar search for traitors within the Soviet Communist Party in the mid-1930s. Thousands of East European Communists were investigated as possible spies or enemies, and the trail soon reached into the highest levels of each country's Communist party. The biggest show trials of the period were those of leading Communists. The first such trial was that of the Hungarian László Rajk in 1949. At the time of his arrest, Rajk was a member of the Politburo and Hungary's Foreign Minister. His trial was designed to highlight the threat of Yugoslavia, which had recently been expelled from the Cominform. Rajk claimed to have cleverly hidden his true agenda, acting as a loyal Communist when he was really the mastermind of an enormous spy ring in cahoots with Tito to overthrow the Hungarian Communist regime.

Communist leaders of Rajk's stature were arrested in all of the countries of the Soviet bloc, although not all faced the ignominy of a public trial. The trial of the Czechoslovak Rudolf Slánský was one of the most significant. Slánský had been Czechoslovakia's Minister of the Interior, responsible for overseeing the security service itself. After his arrest, he went from being the instigator of Stalinist terror to its victim. The case against Slánský was overtly antisemitic. The trial took place in 1952, a few years after Stalin had reversed his earlier support of Israel. Eleven of the 14 defendants, including Slánský himself, were of Jewish origin, and they were alleged to have created a Zionist conspiracy. Their goal, in the words of the prosecutor, was for "Czechoslovakia to become again a land dependent on imperialists, where the Czechoslovak people were once again subjugated by imperialist exploitation, ruled over by industrialists, bankers and estate owners."[57]

Rajk and Slánský were actually loyal Communists who had given their lives to the cause. Each fell under suspicion as state security agents were being pressed, often by Soviet advisors, to find more traitors. Their downfall illustrates how the search for enemies took on a frenzied life of its own. Those who were arrested were presumed to be guilty; the role of interrogating agents was to prove their guilt, no matter how unlikely. Agents ignored exculpating evidence and instead insisted that innocent and ordinary events, like meetings with colleagues, were really instances of espionage. Under the pressure of intensive interrogations that could last for months, suspects confessed. Their supposed accomplices would then be arrested and interrogated until they confessed and named further suspects. The fevered search for more enemies only stopped after the death of Stalin in March 1953.[58]

Show trials were specifically constructed to create fear in their audiences, and they successfully sparked very different varieties of this emotion. The spectacle of once powerful men and women confessing that they had worked with foreign powers undetected for decades exacerbated Cold War tensions and fed fears of another world war, this time between East and West. For those who supported socialism, this might inspire them to work harder to ensure its survival. To those who opposed their Communist governments, show trials signaled the ability of these regimes to neutralize their adversaries and underscored their power. No matter what they might have privately thought of a trial's veracity, few were willing to publicly challenge their results, knowing that doing so might mean they would be placed under suspicion themselves.

To observers in the West, show trials were simply fake spectacles that made a mockery of the idea of justice. Yet this misses the point of these trials. Their goal was not to adhere to Western notions of criminal procedure but to bring a Stalinist worldview to life. This was a world in which the West menaced the East, where enemies constantly threatened socialism, but where socialism nonetheless emerged victorious. Whether or not they agreed with this worldview, East Europeans needed to live by it or face the consequences. In this way, show trials created their own forms of truth, whether or not they adhered to the facts.

These Women Do Not Pay Attention to the Police

Scholars can only create rough estimates of how many people were imprisoned during the Stalinist period. Taking into account only those arrested for political offenses, the numbers are highest in Hungary, where approximately 750,000 people were convicted of political crimes between 1948 and 1953, and in Poland, where 350,000–400,000 people were arrested for such offenses between 1948 and 1956. Albania arrested 80,000 people during that period. In East Germany, recent research indicates that around 200,000–250,000 people were arrested between 1949 and 1971. The numbers are smaller elsewhere: in Romania, 40,000 people were arrested between 1948 and 1953. In Czechoslovakia during the same period, 90,000 were put on trial, while in Bulgaria, 40,000 were imprisoned. Yugoslavia had left the Soviet alliance in 1948, but it nonetheless persecuted tens of thousands as enemies of the state. In all cases, most of those arrested were class enemies or anti-Communists; party members like Rajk or Slánský were a small minority. The vast majority of those convicted received jail terms or sentences in labor camps. A very small percentage shared Milada Horáková's fate.[59]

These numbers are sobering. However, the number of people affected by Stalinist terror is far larger. Family members and even friends might face consequences from a person's arrest, such as the loss of a job or expulsion from university. But arrests had ramifications that went far beyond those directly affected. Every person arrested was a symbol of the power of the state to attack its opponents. Fear of that power led many to censor their actions and even to monitor what they said to friends and neighbors. J.Z., a Czech in his mid-twenties who fled illegally to the West in 1951, recalled, "since the Communists came to power in Czechoslovakia friendship has become very superficial and people grew distrustful in their mutual relations." For J.Z., the problem sprang from the Gottwald regime's determination to vanquish all opposition to Communist rule. To foil any possible resistance, he said, the Communists coerced people into providing them with information. As he put it, "they use human weakness or hardship to know all their opponents and learn what everybody is thinking."[60]

Yet while such fears were quite prevalent, they did not encapsulate the entirety of everyday experience, even for those who were anti-Communists. Zygmunt Ostrowski worked as an assistant in a butcher shop in Poland in 1951. Because of shortages, people stood for hours in line in front of the shop every day, hoping to be able to purchase some of the small amount of meat that was delivered each day. They lined up as early as 3:00 a.m. and stood waiting until the day's delivery arrived, which might not be until after 11:00 a.m. As they waited, Ostrowski remembered, "they talk in the lines (especially) the women, they talk. And these women do not pay attention to the police, but talk about what poverty (there is). How bad (it is) in Poland, how life is good in America."

While they might seem contradictory at first, the accounts of J.Z. and Zygmunt Ostrowski indicate that people's response to Stalinist terror was complicated and situational. Fear of arrest might provoke caution, but people ignored that caution when it suited them.[61]

Individuals could even mobilize aspects of terror to their own advantage. A Romanian woman described how this worked in the context of black market transactions in Bucharest. Peasants came to the city's Hala Obor market hoping to illegally sell meat or other scare commodities. Police frequently patrolled the market to foil these transactions and sometimes arrested both buyers and sellers. The woman went to the market in June 1952 to buy a black market chicken. She observed several people trying to surreptitiously sell chickens for three times the daily wage of an average worker (and more than twice the official price of a chicken). For each illicit chicken on offer, there were multiple housewives angling for the opportunity to buy one. Faced with limited supply and excessive demand, the buyers began to threaten each other with arrest. The woman said that when she tried to buy a chicken, other potential buyers threatened her, saying, "Don't buy it; if you do we will call a [police] agent!" The woman was scared at first, but then decided to use the same tactics herself, telling another potential buyer she would denounce her to the police if she bought a chicken. Her ruse worked and she was able to purchase the bird herself.[62]

This account shows how fear it did not simply emanate from Communist governments to their subjects. It could also be mobilized by ordinary individuals in pursuit of the own ends. The woman in the market was not silenced by fear, nor did she abandon her fear to express community solidarity, like the women in the butcher shop line. Instead, she used the institutions of state repression herself, purely for her own advantage, and by doing this she even extended their reach. Whether or not this woman was a Communist, the Communist system was, at least in part, created and sustained by the actions of ordinary people like her.

Notes

1 Ben Fowkes, *Eastern Europe 1945–1969: Stalinism to Stagnation* (Harlow: Pearson Education, 2000), 33.
2 Kevin McDermott, *Communist Czechoslovakia, 1945–1989* (New York: Palgrave Macmillan, 2015), 39.
3 *The Soviet-Yugoslav Dispute: Text of the Published Correspondence* (London: Royal Institute of International Affairs, 1948), 14–17.
4 John R. Lampe, *Yugoslavia as History: Twice There Was a Country*, 2nd ed. (New York: Cambridge University Press, 2000), 249.
5 *The Soviet-Yugoslav Dispute: Text of the Published Correspondence*, 19.
6 Kevin McDermott, *Communist Czechoslovakia, 1945–1989: A Political and Social History* (New York: Palgrave, 2015), 27.
7 Heda Margolius Kovály, *Under a Cruel Star: A Life in Prague 1941–1946*, trans. Franci Epstein and Helen Epstein (New York: Holmes and Meier, 1997), 97–99 (quote on p. 97).

8 Katherine Lebow, *Unfinished Utopia: Nowa Huta, Stalinism and Polish Society, 1949–1956* (Ithaca, NY: Cornell University Press, 2013), 129–133.

9 Rachel Applebaum, "The Friendship Project: Socialist Internationalism in the Soviet Union and Czechoslovakia in the 1950s and 1960s," *Slavic Review* 74, no. 3 (2015): 488.

10 Elidor Mëhilli, *From Stalin to Mao: Albania and the Socialist World* (Ithaca, NY: Cornell University Press, 2017), 51.

11 The Prague statue was one of the last to appear in Eastern Europe and one of the latest to remain; it was demolished in 1962. Hana Pichová, "The Lineup for Meat: The Stalin Statue in Prague." *PMLA* 12, no. 3 (2008): 614–630.

12 Balázs Apor, *The Invisible Shining: The Cult of Mátyás Rákosi in Stalinist Hungary, 1945–1956* (Budapest: Central European University Press, 2017), 165–166; Izabella Main, "President of Poland or 'Stalin's Most Faithful Pupil'? The Cult of Bolesław Bierut in Stalinist Poland," in *The Leader Cult in Communist Dictatorships: Stalin and the Eastern Bloc*, ed. Balázs Apor, Jan C. Behrends, Polly Jones and E.A. Rees (New York: Palgrave Macmillan, 2004), 179–193; Markus Wien, "Georgi Dmitrov: Three Manifestations of His Cult," in Apor et al., *The Leader Cult*, 194–207; Cynthia Paces, *Prague Panoramas: National Memory and Sacred Space in the Twentieth Century* (Pittsburgh, PA: University of Pittsburgh Press, 2009), 182–187.

13 Apor, *The Invisible Shining*, 156–157.

14 Melissa Feinberg, "Battling for Peace: The Transformation of the Women's Movement in Cold War Czechoslovakia and Eastern Europe," in *Women and Gender in Postwar Europe*, ed. Joanna Regulska and Bonnie G. Smith (London: Routledge, 2012), 23.

15 Melissa Feinberg, *Curtain of Lies: The Battle over Truth in Stalinist Eastern Europe* (New York: Oxford University Press, 2017), 100.

16 "Refugees give assorted interpretations of life in Communist Bulgaria," Open Society Archive, Budapest, fond 300-7-4-7.

17 Lampe, *Yugoslavia as History*, 242. After this first plan, Yugoslavia would move to the more decentralized system of worker self-management.

18 Katherine Verdery, *What Was Socialism and What Comes Next?* (Princeton, NJ: Princeton University Press, 1996): 20–23.

19 Marcin R. Wyczalkowski, "Communist Economics and Currency Convertibility (Economie Communiste Et Convertibilité Des Monnaies) (La Economía Política Comunista Y La Convertibilidad Monetaria)," *Staff Papers (International Monetary Fund)* 13, no. 2 (1966): 155–197.

20 Mark Pittaway, *Eastern Europe 1939–2000* (London: Arnold, 2000), 55.

21 Jozsef Ö. Kovács, "The Forced Collectivization of Agriculture in Hungary, 1948–1961," in *The Collectivization of Agriculture in Communist Eastern Europe: Comparison and Entanglements*, ed. Constantin Iordachi and Arnd Bauerkämper (Budapest: Central European University Press, 2014), 213; Constantin Iordachi and Dorin Dobrincu, "The Collectivization of Agriculture in Romania, 1949–1962," in Iordachi and Bauerkämper, *Collectivization of Agriculture*, 251; Mihail Gruev, "Collectivization and Social Change in Bulgaria, 1940s–1950s," in Iordachi and Bauerkämper, *Collectivization of Agriculture*, 331.

22 Mark Pittaway, *The Workers' State: Industrial Labor and the Making of Socialist Hungary, 1944–1958* (Pittsburgh, PA: University of Pittsburgh Press, 2012), 115.

23 Katherine Lebow, *Unfinished Utopia: Nowa Huta, Stalinism and Polish Society, 1949–1956* (Ithaca, NY: Cornell University Press, 2013), 3.

24 Lebow, *Unfinished Utopia*, 2.

25 Lebow, *Unfinished Utopia*, 44–73, quote on p. 54.

26 Lebow, *Unfinished Utopia*, 51.

27 Lebow, *Unfinished Utopia*, 55.

28 Pittaway, *The Workers' State*, 120.
29 Lewis Siegelbaum, *Stakhanovism and the Politics of Productivity in the USSR, 1935–1941* (Cambridge: Cambridge University Press, 1988), 2.
30 Pittaway, *The Workers' State*, 134.
31 Lebow, *Unfinished Utopia*, 87.
32 Pittaway, *The Workers' State*, 137.
33 Malgorzata Fidelis, *Women, Communism and Industrialization in Postwar Poland* (Cambridge: Cambridge University Press, 2010), 83; Kevin McDermott, "Popular Resistance in Communist Czechoslovakia: The Plzeň Uprising, June 1953," *Contemporary European History* 19, no. 4 (2010): 291.
34 Feinberg, *Curtain of Lies*, 171
35 Gail Kligman and Katherine Verdery, *Peasants Under Siege: The Collectivization of Romanian Agriculture, 1949–1962* (Princeton, NJ: Princeton University Press, 2011), 2–7.
36 Jan Rychlík, "Collectivization in Czechoslovakia in Comparative Perspective, 1949–1960," in Iordachi and Bauerkämper, *The Collectivization of Agriculture*, 192.
37 Nigel Swain, "Eastern European Collectivization Campaigns Compared, 1945–1962," in Iordachi and Bauerkämper, *Collectivization of Agriculture*, 497–534.
38 Kligman and Verdery, *Peasants Under Siege*, 88–149.
39 Kligman and Verdery, *Peasants Under Siege*, 242–243.
40 Kligman and Verdery, *Peasants Under Siege*, 327.
41 Nigel Swain, "Eastern European Collectivization Campaigns," 516–517.
42 Kligman and Verdery, *Peasants Under Siege*, 331.
43 Swain, "Eastern European Collectivization Campaigns," 518–519.
44 Kligman and Verdery, *Peasants Under Siege*, 333.
45 Swain, "Eastern European Collectivization Campaigns," 505–508.
46 Dariusz Jarosz, "The Collectivization of Agriculture in Poland: Causes of Defeat," in Iordachi, *Collectivization of Agriculture*, 122.
47 Kligman and Verdery, *Peasants Under Siege*, 310.
48 Yana Georgieva Yancheva, "Self-Identification Through Narrative: Reflection on the Collectivisation of Agriculture in Bulgaria," *European Review of History* 19, no. 5 (2012): 801.
49 Melissa Feinberg, *Elusive Equality: Gender, Citizenship and the Limits of Democracy in Czechoslovakia, 1918–1950* (Pittsburgh, PA: University of Pittsburgh Press, 2006), 211–222.
50 Mark Pittaway, *Eastern Europe 1939–2000* (London: Arnold, 2004), 50.
51 Kevin McDermott, "Stalinist Terror in Czechoslovakia," in *Stalinist Terror in Eastern Europe*, ed. Kevin McDermott and Matthew Stibbe (Manchester: Manchester University Press, 2010), 100.
52 Wilam Iggers, *Women of Prague* (New York: Berghahn Books, 1995), 287–312.
53 Feinberg, *Curtain of Lies*, 1–11.
54 Iggers, *Women of Prague*, 301.
55 Feinberg, *Curtain of Lies*, 16–18.
56 Feinberg, *Curtain of Lies*, 22–26.
57 *Proces s vedením protistátního spikleneckého centra v čele Rudolfem Slánským* (Prague: Ministerstvo Spravedlnosti, 1953), 8, 62.
58 Igor Lukes, *Rudolf Slánský: His Trials and Trial*, Cold War International History Project Working Paper #50.
59 Kevin McDermott and Matthew Stibbe, "Stalinist Terror in Eastern Europe: Problems, Perspectives and Interpretations," in McDermott and Stibbe, *Stalinist Terror in Eastern Europe*, 13–14.
60 Feinberg, *Curtain of Lies*, 109.
61 Feinberg, *Curtain of Lies*, 114.
62 Feinberg, *Curtain of Lies*, 169–170

3

SOCIALIST MODERNITY IN THE 1950s AND 1960s

Once they seized power, Eastern Europe's Communist regimes initiated a wave of revolutionary changes using the Stalinist model. Their goal was the total economic and social transformation of their countries. They would take societies that had largely been capitalist, rural and traditional and make them modern, industrial, urban and socialist. They set about this enormous task with great zeal. Then, on March 5, 1953, Joseph Stalin died unexpectedly. In the aftermath of his death, some elements of the Stalinist system began to change. New leaders in the Soviet Union promoted a shift away from Stalinist terror. Campaigns against class enemies and supposed spies gradually ceased, and the fear they had caused lessened.

While the changes prompted by Stalin's death were significant, they did not fundamentally alter the larger project of social and economic transformation that had begun in 1948. During the 1950s and 1960s, the economies of Eastern Europe grew at a tremendous rate, matching Western Europe's postwar economic boom. On average, East Europeans achieved a higher standard of living and a longer lifespan; they became more educated and had more social mobility, regardless of gender or economic background. While the pace of change was never smooth or uniform, many East Europeans felt their quality of life improved during these decades.

These transformations occurred in other modernizing societies during the same period, including capitalist Western Europe. The Communist regimes of Eastern Europe, however, saw themselves as creating a distinctly socialist form of modernity. Socialist modernity would be dedicated to creating a society that was not only more industrialized but more egalitarian. It would serve the needs of the collective, not the individual, and it would be rationally planned and directed from above, not left to the whims of the market. As it developed,

DOI: 10.4324/9780813348186-4

however, socialist modernity created its own unique problems. Flaws in the centrally planned economy meant that East Europeans needed to learn to live in an economy of shortages. Shortage, in turn, cemented new hierarchies of privilege that worked against Communism's stated goals of equality.

A Piece of Bacon and a Piece of Butter

Under Stalinism, East European governments directed vast amounts of capital and labor toward industrialization, hoping to close the long-standing economic gap between Eastern and Western Europe. The available macroeconomic data shows that they were quite successful. Before World War II, Eastern Europe had been in economic decline relative to Western Europe. During the decades after 1950, Communist governments managed not only to reverse this decline but to narrow the gap with the West, even though the West was experiencing massive economic growth during this period. In 1938, the aggregate gross national product (GNP) of Eastern Europe was roughly 61 percent of Western Europe; by 1973, it had risen to 82 percent.[1]

This was a great achievement, but it was not always felt by the working population. Particularly in the years before 1953, East Europeans experienced a scarcity of consumer goods and a falling standard of living. During the first years of Stalinism, the wages of Hungarian workers went down by 16.6 percent. In Czechoslovakia, real wages in 1951 were lower than they had been in 1937.[2] People all over the region complained that it was difficult to buy basic foodstuffs, particularly meat, milk, sugar, coffee, eggs and butter, either due to shortages or because of high prices. New clothing was in short supply. A Czechoslovak mining supervisor was disgusted that his countrymen worked so hard to find so little in the stores, remarking "They constantly write about our filling standards [production quotas] up to 500 or 800 percent but if I need some pants I can't get them. To get shoes you need a purchase voucher." A young Pole who worked at a meat processing plant in Kraków was similarly incensed that after saving for two years he still did not have enough money to buy a new suit: his economic dissatisfaction pushed him to risk illegal emigration.[3]

In the aftermath of Stalin's death, surviving members of the Soviet Politburo began to reevaluate his policies. They worried that their East European colleagues had gone too far in their rush to industrialize and had allowed living standards to deteriorate precipitously, causing worker unrest. Workers did take to the streets in Czechoslovakia at the beginning of June 1953. The instigating event was a currency reform that was suddenly announced at the end of May. In this reform, any savings over the amount of 300 Czechoslovak crowns would be converted to the new currency at a rate of 50 to 1, effectively demolishing private savings. At the same time, retail prices for food doubled. Worker protest was centered around the industrial city of Plzeň, where thousands walked off the job and some even stormed the city hall. Police were required to restore order and hundreds were wounded in the fray. A few of the Plzeň demonstrators made anti-Communist statements, but most were primarily motivated by concerns over wages and living standards. While the largest protests were in Plzeň, the currency reform sparked strikes or protests at 129 factories around the country.[4]

The situation in the German Democratic Republic (GDR or East Germany) was even more grave. East German leader Walter Ulbricht had zealously pursued Stalinist economic goals, ignoring their impact on the everyday lives of East German workers. The East German situation reached a nadir in 1953. A coercive collectivization campaign pushed thousands of farmers to flee to West Germany, disrupting agricultural production. Basic items like coal, bread, butter and potatoes were in short supply. Some of the food that was available was of poor quality; cookies for sale in Potsdam in early 1953 reportedly smelled of gasoline, sickening consumers.[5] At the same time, officials called for even more sacrifice, announcing a 10 percent increase in work norms would take effect for all industrial workers at the end of June. Coming just as prices for public transportation and medical care increased, these measures would decrease the real wages of workers by as much as 25–30 percent.[6]

In the months after Stalin's death, Soviet leaders Beria, Malenkov and Molotov pushed the East Germans to moderate their policies. Under Soviet pressure, the East German Politburo announced a "New Course" on June 10–11, promising to increase supplies of consumer goods and to lift restrictions on the self-employed (such as farmers and shopkeepers). Yet, ambivalent about the idea of reform, they did not revoke the plan to increase work norms. On June 16, angry construction workers in East Berlin marched in protest from their construction sites to the government buildings on the Potsdamer Platz. As they walked, they were spontaneously joined by thousands of other Berliners, shouting slogans demanding change.

This protest was followed on June 17 by strikes and demonstrations in at least 700 locations around the country. Demonstrators called for a reversal of the new norms, lower prices on consumer goods, and, more radically, demanded free elections. Most of the protests were peaceful, but some were accompanied by attacks on jails, police stations and other government or party offices. The East German government was at first seemingly unable to comprehend the gravity of the situation. Seeing a crowd of demonstrators, the mayor of the city of Leipzig thought they had gathered to show support for the Rosenbergs, the American couple sentenced to death for being Soviet spies, when they were actually marching against their own government. Ill-prepared East German leaders were unable to restore order; Soviet troops came to their rescue. By evening, Soviet soldiers had dispersed the demonstrators and cleared the streets.[7] Shaken by the events, East German leaders agreed to restore the older work norms; increase funding for pensions, health care and social welfare programs and put more resources into the construction of new housing.[8]

The Soviet Union pushed other Communist leaders across Eastern Europe to implement similar policies. Soviet leader Nikita Khrushchev, who eventually emerged as Stalin's successor, believed that socialism should provide its citizens with a better standard of living, even one equivalent to that enjoyed by residents of the capitalist West. As he said in 1958, "It is not bad if in improving the theory of Marxism one throws in also a piece of bacon and a piece of butter."[9] Yet even though he put more resources into the production of consumer goods and sponsored a massive campaign to build apartments, Khrushchev did not think that the Soviet Union—or its East European allies—should mimic the West's unbridled materialism. He wanted the Soviet population to be able to live without want and even to enjoy occasional luxuries. But Khrushchev still believed that socialism was about the pursuit of social justice and global equality, not personal luxury.

Following the Soviet path, East European governments began to take personal consumption and worker satisfaction more seriously. Progress was uneven, but, on average, per capita consumption increased by 40–50 percent during the 1960s and by 20–50 percent in the 1970s. The effects of this can be seen in changing dietary patterns. Under Stalinism, people complained of being able to find basic foodstuffs. With de-Stalinization, diets began to improve. By the 1960s, East Europeans ate substantially less bread and potatoes (the traditional staples of the poor) and substantially more meat, eggs and sugar. Hungarian per capita meat consumption more than doubled between 1950 and 1989, while in Czechoslovakia it tripled. By the 1980s, East European diets were statistically no different from those in the West. At the same time, spending on food declined, leaving the population with more money to spend on clothes, leisure or, after 1960, new consumer durables like televisions.[10]

Communist governments also began to devote more resources toward social welfare provision, creating a substantial social safety net that added considerably to East Europeans' economic security. Before the Communist era, many East Europeans faced destitution if they could no longer work due to old age or illness. Communist regimes had instituted new social welfare provisions, such as healthcare and retirement benefits, already under Stalinism. These systems initially applied only to workers, but gradually spread to other sectors of the population, such as collective farm workers, independent farmers and the self-employed. By the 1970s, healthcare and retirement benefits were seen as rights and were available to all. A typical pension ranged from 50 to 70 percent of previous wages. Most men could retire by age 60 and women by 55; retirement ages were even earlier in Bulgaria and Albania. Those who were or became disabled could also receive state support.[11]

For those of working age, the Communist state effectively guaranteed full employment and made it difficult to be fired from a job.[12] The hours in the typical work week declined from their Stalinist highs and settled around the 40-hour mark. Work was considered a right of all socialist citizens, but it was also a duty. Able-bodied adults were expected to have jobs and could even be prosecuted for continued unemployment under the charge of parasitism. Work, particularly work in the state sector, offered benefits beyond wages, including generous sick leave, maternity leave and paid vacation time. Many enterprises offered their workers special perks, such as apartments, childcare facilities, subsidized meals in workplace cafeterias, access to vacation properties, athletic and cultural facilities and dedicated medical clinics.[13]

Khrushchev repeatedly declared that by the 1980s living standards in Communist countries would overtake those in the West. That never happened. Nonetheless, after 1953 East Europeans did find that their lives began to improve. Within two decades, they had achieved an unprecedented level of economic security. This success, however, did not eradicate people's desires for an even better quality of life. For the next few decades, Communist governments would struggle to fulfill at least a portion of those desires.

An Economy of Shortage

Gradually, the privations of the Stalinist period became a thing of the past. While this new prosperity was not uniform, in the 1960s many East Europeans began to earn more money and found more in the stores to spend it on. Compared with the scarcity of the war and postwar years, it was a remarkable change. As a Romanian woman remembered,

> In 1963 ... until 1970–72, it was a time of blossoming. One began to find everything. One even found black caviar in the grocery stores. You found it by the kilogram. You found everything that you had: whiskey, gin, bitters, everything that was over there [the West] was over here.[14]

All kinds of new goods became available, from elegant clothes and modern furniture to vacuum cleaners and televisions. While many of these goods were not easy to acquire (televisions were about three times more expensive in Eastern Europe than in West Germany), their presence in department store windows was a tangible reminder of socialism's promise to deliver a better life.[15]

Yet even as the average standard of living improved dramatically, consumers continued to face periodic shortages of all types of goods. Some shortages were unpredictable, as when something that was usually obtainable inexplicably disappeared from store shelves for a while. Others were long-standing and well known, such as the fact that oranges were typically available only around Christmastime. Some major purchases—like apartments or automobiles—were in such short supply that they required potential buyers to spend years on waiting lists. The reasons for these shortages varied. Some goods might not be available because central planners had not thought to include them in their plan or had not calculated for sufficient quantities; sanitary products for women were often in this category. Some shortages resulted from an unforeseen problem in production or distribution, which could result in an excess of a particular item in one area, but a shortage in another. With some luxury goods, planners purposely kept production low and set high prices to moderate demand. Some items—like oranges or coffee—could not be produced locally and were therefore subject to fluctuations in the global marketplace and the availability of hard currency to pay for them.

East European governments tried to eliminate the problem of shortage, but they repeatedly failed. The particular goods subject to shortage varied by time and place, but shortage itself remained a fact of life throughout the entire Communist period, uniting all the countries of the region. The Yugoslav writer Slavenka Drakulić found what she described as "museum of communist shortages" when she cleaned out her grandmother's house after her death in the 1970s. One large oak cupboard was full of carefully preserved old clothes and shoes, some almost never worn. Another was packed with a huge variety of everyday items. The lower shelves held nonperishable foodstuffs like flour, sugar, salt, coffee, tea, beans, pasta and tomato paste. The upper shelves contained what seemed like an entire drug store, including detergent, soap, shampoo, several shades of hair dye, lotion, toilet paper, sanitary napkins and an array of medicines, from aspirin to antibiotics.[16] Some of it had clearly been there, unopened, for many years. Drakulić's grandmother had collected all of these things so that she and her family members would be protected in case of unexpected shortages. When she found her grandmother's hoard, Drakulić was not surprised. The economy of shortage encouraged everyone to practice similar behaviors. Whenever people saw a potentially scarce item in the store, they would purchase as much of it as they could as a guard against future shortages. For Drakulić's Bulgarian friend Blaga, the scarce item was laundry detergent. She said, "When I find it, I buy two or three big boxes. You can never be sure when it will appear again."[17]

Scarcity also encouraged theft. Stealing from one's workplace was so common that it was rarely considered immoral. A Romanian anthropologist found many examples of this practice among her informants. Workers at a pig-fattening facility carried out "sausages wrapped around one's waist" or a "salami hidden in one's sleeve." Garment workers donned their finished goods and wore them of the factory. Workers at a furniture factory designed their own pieces and smuggled them out in parts to assemble at home.[18] Anything was fair game. Slavenka Drakulić recalled that in her childhood her parents stole notepaper from their workplace to use as toilet paper, since there was none available to buy in stores (most people used newspaper for this purpose). Even after Yugoslavia started producing toilet paper in the late 1950s, she remembered, the toilet paper holders in the restrooms at school were always empty. While this was in part because they were only rarely filled, Drakulić suspected that whenever paper did appear in them, it was promptly stolen.[19]

Some of this stolen material was for personal use, some made its way onto the black market. Black market activity thrived under socialism; even the terror of the Stalinist era did not quell it. Indeed, the privations of the Stalinist period helped entrench black market behaviors in socialist society. The "black market" encompassed a wide variety of illegal or semilegal activity, from the small scale to the openly entrepreneurial. On the small scale, a person who received a gift package of a scarce or expensive item like coffee from relatives in the West might sell it for a profit or trade it for something else she needed. Others engaged in much larger operations, as in the case of János S. János was a Hungarian who created an extensive black market business during the mid-1950s. At a time when there was no wood available for sale in his village, János arranged with a young forester to steal several tons of wood from the nearby state forest to sell to local villagers. János also did a brisk business in illegally slaughtered meat. Peasants would bring him their animals—technically state property—to butcher, and he would sell the meat around the community. János did such a large trade that he eventually came under the notice of the police, forcing him to flee over the border to Austria.[20]

János's business relied on connections. He was able to start his wood-stealing venture because of his connection with the forester. The business also relied on the participation of his uncle, who had access to a truck he used to haul the wood. While János was unusual in that he used these connections to set up a black market enterprise of considerable size, many East Europeans used personal connections as a way to ameliorate living in a climate of scarcity. A sales representative for a clothing company, for example, might set aside a particularly fetching coat for a friend to purchase. A butcher might reserve a nice piece of meat for a family member, or a car mechanic might fix a friend's car after hours. Those with access to scarce goods and services could also trade them with others. The sales representative might exchange a shirt for a new pair of skates for his child's birthday. Some moved beyond favors and barter to create their own businesses on the side. The car mechanic might set up a regular business doing repairs after hours, stealing materials and tools from her employer and taking payment either in cash or in kind. Together, these kinds of activities created what scholars call the informal economy or second economy, a market-based system of private exchange that existed parallel to the official planned economy.

Dealing with the economy of shortage required constant ingenuity. Throughout the socialist period, East Europeans devoted considerable time to figuring out how to master an unpredictable system. They turned to practices like hoarding, illicit barter and black markets to be able to get what they wanted, even when it was ostensibly impossible. On the one hand, these practices undermined the centrally planned economy and exacerbated the very shortages they were meant to alleviate. Yet, they also kept the system running, despite its inefficiencies. Indeed, instead of thinking of black markets and favors as being somehow external to the socialist economy, we need to see them as being an essential part of it. There was never an ideal socialist planned economy that black markets subverted. In the actual everyday world of state socialism, the official economy and its unofficial counterpart were always inextricably intertwined.

This Is What Happiness Looks Like: Housing Construction and Modern Living

In the 1950s, there was a desperate housing shortage in Eastern Europe. One cause was the war. In East Berlin, about one-third of prewar residences had been destroyed in the fighting, while in Yugoslavia, 25 percent of the population was homeless at the end of the war.[21] Another contributing factor was postwar economic migration. In the period between 1950 and 1970, the number of people working in agriculture dropped by 40–50 percent across the region.[22] While some stayed in their home villages and commuted to work, many moved to cities. The capital cities of Budapest, Sofia, Bucharest and Belgrade all doubled (or more) in size during the socialist period.[23] Finally, much of the existing housing did not meet modern standards. Even in urban areas, many East Europeans lived crowded in cramped apartments that lacked indoor plumbing or central heating. This situation was not unique to Eastern Europe; many West Europeans lived in similar conditions in the 1950s. Under socialism, however, solutions to the housing crisis would need to emanate from the state rather than the market.

During the Stalinist period, many workers were housed in dorms and barracks because nothing else was available. The "South Side" barracks in the Hungarian industrial city of Sztálinváros were built in 1950 as temporary housing for single construction workers and meant to be in use for no more than five years. Eight years later, they had become home to hundreds of families, including 800 children, who lived in what was basically a shantytown.[24] In the Soviet Union, Nikita Khrushchev condemned the persistence of these kinds of living conditions; he launched a huge campaign in 1957 to rapidly build private family apartments for the masses. Under Soviet influence, East European leaders also began to devote substantial resources toward housing construction. In 1960, the Hungarian government promised to build 600,000 new apartments in the next 15 years, and the other countries in the region made similar plans.

As in the Soviet Union, state-sponsored housing construction in Eastern Europe concentrated on building high-density apartment blocks in urban areas or industrial centers. Beginning around 1960, these apartment blocks were generally built according to standardized models using prefabricated components, such as wall and floor panels, structural skeletons and even kitchen and bathroom units. Czechoslovak architects had been experimenting with standardization and prefabrication technologies even under Stalinism and had built their first prototype apartment buildings using these methods in 1954. The point of prefabrication was its speed; Slovak architect Peter Linton noted in a 1967 study that while it took fourteen to sixteen months to complete a five- to six-story masonry building, an eight-story building built with prefabricated panels would be finished in eight to ten months. Prefab technology made it possible to quickly build massive housing estates, such as the Jižní Město (South City) district in Prague, which was built in the 1960s and housed 100,000 people. In 2010, the Czech Republic contained 80,000 prefab apartment buildings, home to approximately one-third of the population.[25]

Prefabricated apartment buildings and large, planned housing developments were not unique to state socialist societies. Socialist architects and urban planners drew inspiration from the ideas of Western modernist architects like Le

FIGURE 3.1 An East German family celebrates the first day of school in front of a prefab apartment building, East Berlin, 1976. © Agencja Fotograficzna Caro/Alamy Stock Photo D0TCC3.

Corbusier and architects and urban planners around the world in the 1950s and 1960s experimented with prefab technologies. Yet in the West these kinds of buildings are often associated specifically with socialist Eastern Europe and the Soviet Union. Westerners often imagined them to be depressing places that exemplified a supposed grayness of everyday life under socialism. However, this was not how they were experienced by many of their residents.

The East German government took longer than its socialist allies to revise its housing policies. Throughout the 1960s, East Germans were plagued by housing shortages and substandard housing. Even at the end of the decade, a majority of East Germans did not have central heating or their own indoor toilet. A third of all residences had no running water. This was the case even in major cities. Jürgen Hinze and his family lived in the Mitte district of East Berlin in a building that had been built in 1862. He recalled that it was

> practically a ruin, dark and drafty; water ran down the walls and we had to share a toilet a half floor up in the stairwell with the neighbors ... The ceiling was busted [kaputt], the toilets no longer functioned. You couldn't touch most of the windows because otherwise they would break.[26]

It was only after East German leader Walter Ulbricht was replaced with Erich Honecker in 1971 that the East German government turned seriously to the problem of housing. In 1973, the East Germans vowed to build 800,000 apartments before 1980. The centerpiece of this initiative was the neighborhood of Marzahn on the outskirts of East Berlin, the largest prefab housing development in Europe. In only ten years, 200,000 apartments sprang up in Marzahn and surrounding neighborhoods in northeast Berlin. People who had been living in conditions like the Hinzes were thrilled to move there. Gabriele Frank, who moved to Marzahn with her husband in 1978, remembered,

> My heart was in my throat with excitement and my knees shook as I left the car and we walked up to the second floor together, the building still smelling of cement and paint. My husband opened the door to our new apartment and ... a giant empire appeared, with enough room for five family members. Central heating, warm water from the wall, and a six-meter long balcony! This is what happiness looks like. We fell into each other's arms, euphorically.[27]

A sociological study of Marzahn residents conducted in the 1980s found that 76 percent felt "a sense of well-being" in their apartment, 84 percent would "strongly urge" or "recommend" others to move to Marzahn and only 5 percent were unhappy there.[28]

Life in prefab developments was not without its travails. In Marzahn, architects carefully designed and built a community that included parks and other green spaces, shops and services, schools, and transportation to the city center. Residents of other prefab developments, however, often complained about the lack of services in their neighborhoods. In many cases, these services had been planned, but were then jettisoned to cut costs or meet housing targets. In the New Belgrade district of the Yugoslav capital of Belgrade, builders turned spaces meant as community centers, shops and services into apartments, leaving residents without needed services.[29] While the Franks in Marzahn were ecstatic about the size of their apartment, many wished for more space. Officials demanded small apartments in order to increase the total number of apartments built. In Hungary, a government decree mandated that an average apartment be no more than 570 square feet. In the massive Petržalka development outside the Czechoslovak city of Bratislava, the average three-room apartment was only 484 square feet. In Romania, a typical two-room apartment, which might house a family of four, was just over 400 square feet.[30] Many also complained that the panel construction was flimsy, creating drafts and allowing everyone to hear their neighbors.

Prefab apartments and their neighborhoods were designed to encourage their residents to live a modern, urban lifestyle. Apartments were sized for nuclear families with few children, not extended families. Kitchens, the traditional heart of the home, were small and frequently open to the main living space, without much room for storage or a traditional dining table. Instead, the center of the apartment was the living room (which frequently also doubled as a bedroom at night). The small size of the rooms required furniture scaled to their proportions. Mária Pataki, the editor of a Hungarian home décor magazine, said that the goal of her magazine was to teach Hungarians to have

FIGURE 3.2 A display showing new modern furnishings from the 1963 "Modern Living" exhibition in České Budějovice (Czechoslovakia). © CTK/ Alamy Stock Photo BX4WPB.

"modern taste," distinct from the massive and heavy bourgeois styles of the past. A 1963 article from a Hungarian newspaper extolled the new modern style, telling apartment dwellers, "the fashion is clean lines, low sizes, easy to use and clean." Prefab residents were encouraged to purchase furniture influenced by Scandinavian modern design, with a slim profile and clean, spare lines, and to cultivate a space free of knickknacks and clutter.[31]

The path to a modern lifestyle was not always smooth. Architects presumed that apartment dwellers were urbanites who lived in model conditions, yet many residents had close ties to rural life and all lived in a shortage economy. In Romania, kitchens in 1960s prefab buildings contained limited space for food storage, assuming urban residents did not need to preserve food for the winter as villagers did. Yet families continued to can fruits and vegetables, knowing that they could not count on what they might find in stores. In the Hungarian industrial town of Sztálinváros, apartment residents in the late 1950s raised pigs in their neighborhoods and slaughtered them in building laundry rooms. The town newspaper was compelled to remind readers that modern people should use their apartment pantry to "store food, not keep animals."[32]

Despite the rapid pace of housing construction, apartments were always in short supply. In Poland, 4.8 million new residences were built during the period between 1950 and 1988, but it was still not enough to keep up with demand. When Polish sociologists conducted a study in the 1980s that asked respondents about the most pressing issues in their lives, finding an apartment easily outstripped all other answers, including personal or family problems, career woes, or dealing with other shortages. Most Poles who needed housing spent at least five years on a waiting list before getting an apartment. In Poland, as in the entire region, housing was not simply doled out by the state on the basis of need. Most urban housing construction was not funded by the state directly, but by cooperatives. Prospective residents needed to contribute a portion of the costs of construction and then wait their turn for an apartment. This limited access to those who could pay the required contribution. In addition, many housing units were under the control of workplaces who could allocate them to their employees, extending the waiting period for those without such connections.[33]

The vast majority of apartment construction was in cities or suburbs. In rural areas, residents often had no choice but to build housing at their own expense. Thus, even under socialism, there was still extensive private housing construction. In Hungary, 60 percent of total housing construction was privately funded in 1975, and private construction outstripped state-funded construction for the entire socialist period.[34] Most of these privately financed dwellings were single-family houses in villages or smaller towns. These homes were often built by the residents themselves, with assistance from friends and family members. Building one's own home required not only having the money to finance the construction, but the creativity to find the necessary building materials in an economy of shortage. Almost inevitably, private home builders were forced to use theft, bribery or the black market (or all three) to finish their homes. A resident of the small Polish town of Bursztyn recalled that the town had once planned to build four apartment buildings. In the end, however, only three were completed because the materials for the fourth had all been stolen during construction to be used on private construction projects![35]

In the wake of de-Stalinization, socialist governments in Eastern Europe promised to solve the housing problem. Following Khrushchev, they declared that socialism should be able to provide its citizens with decent housing and a decent quality of life. This rhetoric sank in. By the 1970s, East Europeans considered housing to be a right. To the extent that their leaders were able to fulfill their responsibility to adequately house the population, they gained legitimacy in the eyes of their citizens. Those who were able to leave substandard dwellings with dirt floors or coal stoves and move into modern apartments could see how the socialist state was working to improve their lives. Yet even as prefab apartment buildings sprang up like mushrooms around East European cities, there were never enough resources to meet demand. Housing construction therefore strengthened socialist regimes, while simultaneously creating a source of resentment and dissatisfaction.

Creating a Classless Society

In 1959, the American National Exhibition was held in Moscow. The exhibition focused on American housing design and consumer goods. It included a supermarket, a ranch-style house fitted out with all the modern conveniences and a "Kitchen of the Future" exhibit that showed off a range of prototype electric appliances, many of which were never actually put into production, including a microwave oven, a robot maid and a dishwasher that moved on its own from kitchen to dining table. For the American organizers, the exhibition showed the superiority of the American capitalist system, embodied in the creature comforts it could offer its citizens. U.S. Vice President Richard Nixon opened the exhibition and gave Soviet premier Nikita Khrushchev a tour. In the kitchen of the ranch house, Nixon extolled the benefits of the capitalist consumer economy, offering up the kitchen's suite of sunny yellow GE appliances as evidence of Western superiority. In his response, Khrushchev did not deny the kitchen's appeal. He agreed that governments should strive to give their people a better quality of life. But he did question American excess. As the men looked at the Kitchen of the Future exhibit, Khrushchev sarcastically asked, "Don't you have a machine that puts food in the mouth and pushes it down?" He then continued, "Many things you've shown us are interesting, but they are not needed in life. They have no useful purpose."[36]

Khrushchev's comments are a reminder that even as socialist governments committed themselves to improving the standard of living, they did not abandon the cause of social justice. During the 1950s and 1960s, East European governments attempted what amounted to a social revolution. Under Stalin-ism, Communist states moved to remove former elites from power. Economic policies like nationalization, collectivization and currency reform drained the financial resources of the former bourgeoisie, while propaganda campaigns urged the population to act against capitalists and kulaks. In addition to these attacks on bourgeois privilege, governments enacted a range of policies to give new opportunities to formerly disadvantaged groups, including workers, peas-ants, the Roma and women. While overt violence against class enemies faded after 1953, these other efforts continued.

The first step in expanding equality was to end illiteracy and extend the educational system. Providing mass education was not only a matter of social justice; it was crucial to creating a modern skilled workforce. Before Commu-nists took power, educational levels in Eastern Europe were very low. While most Germans, Hungarians, Czechoslovaks and Poles achieved at least basic literacy in the interwar decades, in 1937 over one-third of the population in the Balkans did not know how to read. In Albania, that number was as high as 80 percent.[37] Before 1945, only a small minority of East Europeans went to secondary schools, let alone universities. In the Balkans, 1–3 percent of pri-mary school students went on to high school, while in East-Central Europe, it was 5–10 percent.[38] This changed rapidly after the establishment of socialism. By the end of the 1950s, adult education programs and compulsory primary education had made illiteracy a thing of the past. Within the span of a few decades, a majority of students attended secondary schools, which were reor-ganized to include schools for professional and vocational training. During the same period, the number of students going to university doubled or in some cases tripled, although the total percentage of students attending university remained low compared to contemporary standards, averaging 10–15 percent of all students.[39]

During the 1950s, affirmative action policies helped engineer a transforma-tion in the composition of the educational and professional elite. The percent-age of university students from worker or peasant backgrounds exploded, often reaching 50 percent of the total or higher. This translated into a similar increase in the representation of people from these backgrounds in the ranks of manage-rial and white-collar workers. This unprecedented social mobility did not last throughout the socialist period, however. After the 1950s, quota systems were relaxed, and by the 1970s, university students were again more likely to hail from white-collar backgrounds. Socialist policies had allowed for the creation of a new elite, but this elite then began to guard its privileges and work to pass them on to its children.[40]

Unlike under capitalism, where elites are determined primarily by their wealth, the new socialist elite was determined by its relationship to the par-ty-state. It was composed of those who ran the state, the party and the econ-omy: administrators, managers and bureaucrats. In the mid-1950s, a prominent

Yugoslav Communist, Milovan Djilas, wrote a book in which he disparagingly dubbed this socialist elite "the new class." By using this term, Djilas suggested that Yugoslavia's Communist leaders had not ended class exploitation but had merely taken the place of the bourgeoisie. Instead of being liberated, the masses just toiled under a new set of masters. Members of this new class, said Djilas, might sincerely believe they were working for the greater good of society, but their actions served primarily to maintain their monopoly on power. Djilas was imprisoned for this critique.[41]

Djilas was reacting to both the dictatorial behaviors of the new Communist elite and the economic privileges top officials granted themselves. Members of the nomenklatura were isolated from the scarcity the rest of the population faced. They had access to special stores stocked with goods not available to the general public, received preferential housing and might even have a car. While he was growing up in the 1950s and 1960s, György Péteri's father was a high-ranking state official and a member of the Hungarian Communist Party's Central Committee. Péteri remembered that his father's position allowed him

> considerably better than average housing; unlimited access to a state-owned car (from 1965 it was a black Mercedes 230 which, together with its chauffeur, Sándor Fabián, stood at my father's disposal even after working hours, with no limits as to mileage, weekdays, or time), access to the country's best resort areas at Lake Balaton and elsewhere, access to a well-equipped health care infrastructure (including the services of the National Central Hospital on Kútvölgyi Street) and access to opportunities for hunting in some of the country's absolutely finest wildlife areas.[42]

Péteri's father was one of a small number allowed to legally own a rifle and shoot big game. By taking up hunting, the Hungarian socialist elite took on behaviors associated with the country's previous aristocratic rulers, as well as providing itself with a consistent supply of high-quality meat.

However, while class did not entirely disappear under socialism and those with connections had privileges that others did not, Eastern Europe nonetheless experienced a considerable amount of social leveling during the socialist period. Income levels were much less stratified than in the West. Wage scales were weighted toward blue-collar workers, narrowing prewar pay gaps between white-collar jobs and manual work. In 1960, Polish blue-collar workers made 75 percent more than they had before World War II. In contrast, Polish white-collar workers saw their incomes decline by 25 percent from prewar levels, putting their salaries more on a level with the working class. In Hungary, educated professionals like nurses or high-school teachers typically earned 10–30 percent less than a skilled manual worker. The salaries of highly skilled technical professionals like engineers or architects were on average only 1.6–1.7 times those of blue-collar workers. Medical doctors, who had very high income levels in the West, had only slightly above average salaries in the East.[43] Even the salaries of high-level Communist officials were relatively modest compared to their elite counterparts in the West. As with György Péteri's family, their advantages were primarily in the form of access to state-owned resources, not in salary.

The case of the Roma encapsulates both the successes and failures of socialist governments as they tried to engineer a more egalitarian society. The Roma are a people who originated in northern India and migrated to Europe at some point in the Middle Ages. By the 20th century, there were Roma communities scattered across Eastern Europe, particularly in Romania, Bulgaria, Yugoslavia and Hungary, where they accounted for between 4 and 8 percent of the population in the 1990s.[44] Throughout their time in Europe, the Roma faced discrimination; in Romania, they were held in slavery until the mid-19th century. The Roma were often seen as being prone to criminality and believed to be vagabonds and nomads, although most had ceased to wander and had lived in settled communities since the 18th century. Poor, typically with darker skin than the surrounding population and often speaking their own language, the Roma tended to live in segregated communities on the fringes of society. During World War II, they were singled out by the Nazis for extermination and more than 200,000 were killed.[45]

Communist ideology officially excoriated racism, and many Communists were sincere anti-racists. Yet Communist governments saw the Roma as a problem that needed to be solved. Few respected Roma language, culture or customs; the Roma were not considered to be a nationality but a "backwards ethnic group."[46] Officials wanted to forcibly assimilate the Roma into the surrounding society, ostensibly for their own good. Behaviors commonly associated with the Roma—such as nomadism and begging—were criminalized. Roma shanty towns were bulldozed and the residents moved into apartments. Children were required to go to school and adults to get regular employment. The results of these policies were mixed. Some did integrate, but many resisted assimilation and clung to their own communities and language. Those who were relocated often resented the loss of their old homes and found ways to move back or into neighborhoods with high concentrations of other Roma. While children did attend school, few made it beyond the primary level; only a tiny percentage of Roma youth received higher education. Absenteeism was a problem and most schools were ill-equipped (or simply unwilling) to deal with a population that did not enter school already speaking the local language, as was true of a majority of the Roma population. Roma did enter the workforce en masse, although, since they often lacked adequate education, most were unskilled laborers.[47]

Despite official rhetoric, prejudice against the Roma persisted. In 1966, a resident of an apartment building in the Slovak city of Košice complained to the local authorities that a Roma family was dirty, loud and abusive, all common stereotypes, and demanded they be removed. "The directives say that gypsy [a pejorative term for the Roma] families have to be dispersed to big blocks on the edge of towns." he complained, "Now they make up almost half of the people living on our block." The local government investigated and found the complaints about the family to be baseless. The inspector noted, however, that the residents were openly hostile to the Roma, while ignoring the drunken and loud behavior of some of the white tenants.[48] These prejudices did not fade with time. In a poll taken in the late 1980s, over 70 percent of Hungarians agreed that the Roma were "parasites," "lazy," and "uneducated."[49] Yet, while socialist governments did not end the Roma's marginalization, their policies did provide many Roma with a previously unknown economic stability and gave a few avenues for further advancement. As Ivan Veselý, a Romany activist, told an interviewer in the 1990s, "Do you think I would be sitting here arguing about Marx and Weber if it were not for the communists? I would be in the ghetto in Eastern Slovakia!"[50] By giving them an education and a vocabulary of social justice, Communist regimes enabled Veselý and others like him to become advocates for their own communities, even if this had not been their intention.

Factories, Kids and Kitchen Pots: A Socialist Revolution for Women?

One day in 1951, a Czechoslovak carpenter's wife got a job. The carpenter protested: he wanted her to stay home and take care of their son. But she insisted and took a position as a secretary in a government office. As he later recounted it, from the day she started work, his life began to deteriorate. She worked long hours and had no time for him anymore. Her coworkers were Communists, and they mocked him for having bourgeois attitudes about women, insisting that his wife send their son to a nursery school and use the state laundry service, which she did. Angry and increasingly unable to even talk to his wife, the carpenter began spending all of his time at the local pub. He started acting up at work and yelling at his superiors. Eventually, in 1953, he fled over the border to Austria, leaving his family behind. He blamed the dissolution of his marriage on the Communist system, which, he suggested, destroyed families by pushing women into the workforce and telling women they were equal to men.[51]

The carpenter's story is from the Stalinist era, when Eastern Europe's Communist regimes took a radical approach to the issue of gender equality. Before the establishment of socialism, East European women lacked legal equality with men, particularly in marriage. Husbands were considered the heads of their households: wives often needed their husband's permission to get a job and had no control over their family's finances. Mária, a Hungarian, was married off in 1944 to a doctor she hardly knew who was 14 years her senior. Her new husband, she later recalled,

> treated me as if I were some sort of wilting wallflower. I was completely locked away from the outside world ... the wife at that time was supposed to be an ornament, plus she had to cook, clean and look after the children.

Mária's husband controlled all the family's purchases; she did not even get to buy her own clothes.[52]

Communists decried these traditional gender norms as bourgeois and swiftly moved to make marriage into a union of equals. Stalinist governments rewrote family and marriage laws, taking away a husband's former legal privileges. They pushed women to join the workforce and become active socialist citizens, just like men. These policies were motivated not solely by ideology but also by need; the massive Stalinist industrialization drive required women's labor to succeed. Nonetheless, many women experienced them as emancipatory. Mária herself divorced her husband when he decided to emigrate to Switzerland. She stayed in Hungary and embarked on a long and successful career, eventually obtaining a managerial position at a department store and becoming the store's trade union representative.

During the Stalinist period, Eastern Europe's socialist governments actively promoted a new model of womanhood that broke with many common perceptions about femininity. This idealized Stalinist woman was a heroine of labor who moved into occupations that had previously been dominated by men, like operating heavy machinery, driving a tractor or working as a miner. Women's magazines and other forms of popular culture constantly extolled the feats of women who had triumphed in realms previously only open to men. For example, in Romania, the country's major women's magazine published a story about Sanda Herghelegiu, a woman from a rural area who became an electrician, despite the fact that this was considered to be a man's profession. In six months, she had proved the naysayers wrong and was recognized as one of the best workers in her group.[53]

The positive stories in the press, however, hid a more complicated reality. While some women were accepted by their new coworkers, others faced resistance. Helena K., a Polish electrician, hoped to be trained for underground work in the mining industry, a job previously reserved for men. Yet even though she was accepted into a training course, the women in her group were told to sit in the bathroom and mend the miners' clothes, while the male students trained underground. Despite the official rhetoric about equality, even many Communist officials agreed with Bronisław O., a Polish male worker who complained to Polish National Radio that "these damned *babas* [hags] meddle into men's work. They should take care of kids and kitchen pots, not factories."[54]

With de-Stalinization, the woman tractor-driver gradually disappeared from the media, and policies toward women took a conservative turn. The more radical gender egalitarianism of the Stalinist period was abandoned in favor of a more traditional notion of gender relations that highlighted supposedly natural gender differences. Women were no longer encouraged to move into traditionally male occupations; instead, they were systematically pushed into fields believed to align with women's feminine nature, such as education, medicine and textiles. The workforce all over Eastern Europe became highly segregated by gender. In 1980s Bulgaria, women accounted for 75.8 percent of all those employed in education and 73.8 percent of all workers in health services and social security, but only 20.5 percent of workers in construction.[55] Jobs classified as female tended to be viewed as less skilled and were clustered at the lower end of the income scale, even when they required university degrees (by 1980, at least half of all university students in Albania, Bulgaria, Hungary, Poland and East Germany were women).[56] In the mid-1960s, women in Eastern Europe earned on average only two-thirds what men did.[57] Women in Eastern Europe were more likely than women in the West to take on positions of authority at work, but they were still underrepresented in positions of power. Even in sectors of the economy dominated by women, men still tended to have the leading positions. Women never reached parity with men in Communist party membership, and while a few women did achieve high-ranking positions in the party, Communist leaders remained overwhelmingly male.[58]

Even with this conservative turn, however, the ornamental housewife was never a socialist ideal for women. Women were expected to be workers, and their participation in the labor force increased rapidly under socialism. Across Eastern Europe, paid work became a reality for women, just as it was for men. In 1952, Bulgarian women were only 26 percent of the country's total workforce; in the late 1970s, that number had climbed to 47 percent.[59] In Romania, three-quarters of adult women worked in 1970, at a time when only just over half of French and British women did.[60] For most women, work was a necessity. Not only did governments strongly encourage all citizens to work, but supporting a family in socialist Eastern Europe usually required two incomes. Nonetheless, most women saw their work as a source of fulfillment and independence rather than drudgery. A Polish woman wrote to the popular women's magazine *Girlfriend* in 1957 and declared,

> I would never leave my job because when I was dependent on my husband for ten years I suffered. My husband gave me money as he pleased and constantly reminded me that he was working for me. When I got a job of my own, my life changed for the better.[61]

Her sentiment was echoed in a survey of 16,000 employed women conducted in Bulgaria in 1969. Of the married women surveyed, only 15.2 percent said they would stop working if their husbands earned enough on their own to support the family.[62]

Women's new roles in the workplace did not, however, precipitate a revolution in the gendered division of labor in the family. During the socialist period, over 90 percent of all men and women in Eastern Europe were married at some point in their lives.[63] As wives, most women continued to take the primary responsibility for domestic work like cooking, cleaning, laundry and childcare, in addition to their paid work. At the time most East European women entered the workforce, they were forced to accomplish these tasks without the benefit of modern conveniences. In 1960, only 6.2 percent of East German households owned a washing machine, about the same amount as owned a refrigerator. A decade later, just over half of all East German households owned these things.[64] It was only in the 1970s that washing machines and refrigerators became truly commonplace across the region. Governments and individual workplaces did try to ease women's burden by providing services like childcare facilities, cafeterias for midday meals and laundries. Yet even though the number of these services increased dramatically through the 1960s, demand often outstripped supply. Women who used laundry services in East German factories in the late 1950s might wait four weeks or more to get their cleaned laundry back.[65]

In 1969, East European women spent an average of 2.8 hours more per day on housework than men did, leaving men with substantially more leisure time than women.[66] While men did do some domestic work, the tasks men and women took on at home tended to be even more gendered than their roles in the workplace. Men's domestic labor tended to involve shopping or household repairs, while it was mostly women who cooked, cleaned and laundered. Many considered this division of labor to be natural. Mircea J., a Romanian pharmacist, recalled that when he told a male colleague that he did the dishes, the man asked, "'How can you do such feminine work?" Mircea J. saw it as an issue of fairness. As he told his colleague, "'but your wife, does she work?' He said 'yes.' And I replied, 'so she has to, without fail, work two jobs while you read the paper?'" While Mircea J.'s attitude showed that socialist egalitarian ideology had influenced how some people thought about marriage, his views were not typical for Eastern Europe in the 1960s.[67] Beliefs about the gendered nature of housework even colored state policy. In East Germany, married women and single women with young children were allowed one paid day off work each month to take care of household chores. Men were never granted this benefit, since it was assumed that this work always fell to women.[68]

Some have claimed that socialism did little to improve women's lives, emphasizing that it forced them to carry the triple burden of paid work, childcare and housework, a load that their husbands were not required to bear. While this was true, the 1950s and 1960s nonetheless witnessed a profound change in former attitudes. In 1960, an East German woman filed for divorce, claiming that her husband routinely beat her. Her husband told the court,

I have forbidden my wife to go to work, since she should stay in the kitchen. I have given her 470 Mark monthly, and for it I expect my breakfast and warm dinner prepared. This she has seldom done ... Since she hasn't done so, I have hit her on occasion, especially since she has provoked me.

This husband's views on marriage had been commonplace before the war. In 1960, however, the judge told him that his attitudes "had no place in the GDR" and were "unbefitting a reasonable person."[69] Patriarchal attitudes certainly remained in Eastern Europe, but society increasingly viewed women as independent actors and not merely as the dependents of the men in their lives.

An Iron Curtain?

In 1946, Winston Churchill declared that a Soviet-sponsored "Iron Curtain" had shut Eastern Europe off from the nonsocialist world. The image of this Iron Curtain soon took on an iconic status. In the West, many believed that East Europeans were prevented from having any contact with the outside world. The policies of East European governments helped to solidify this belief. The countries of the Soviet bloc had heavily militarized borders, fenced with barbed wire and patrolled by armed guards, and they strictly regulated the people and goods that were allowed to cross them. Nonetheless, Eastern Europe was not completely isolated from the rest of the world. News, ideas, people and things constantly crossed the supposedly impenetrable Iron Curtain, sometimes even in defiance of Communist border controls.

For most East Europeans, travel outside their home country was difficult, although the degree of difficulty changed over time and varied by country. Travel was most difficult during the Stalinist years and became somewhat easier after 1956. Those living in Soviet bloc nations who wanted to travel to the West typically needed not only a passport and a visa but a written invitation from someone in the country to which they wished to travel. Governments routinely denied passports to those who were considered politically unreliable. In 1952, only 12,000 Poles received passports for international travel, out of a total population of approximately 25 million people.[70] Despite the challenges, however, some East Europeans did manage to go to the West in the 1950s—as diplomats, on cultural exchanges, to attend academic or professional conferences, on sports teams, as journalists, or even simply as tourists—and those numbers increased in the 1960s. Yugoslavia, which was not part of the Soviet bloc, was an exception to this strict travel regime. Yugoslavia permitted its citizens to travel quite freely starting in the early 1960s. Yugoslavs began to vacation all over the European continent, and they made such frequent day trips to the Italian city of Trieste to go shopping that many shopkeepers learned basic Serbo-Croatian.[71]

Throughout the 1950s, East Berliners also enjoyed unusual access to the West. The borders between East and West Germany had been closed in 1952, but the border between East and West Berlin remained open. Throughout the 1950s, East Berliners could get to the West just by walking across town. Many did so regularly, to work, visit friends and relatives, shop or just go to the movies. In 1960, over a quarter of all moviegoers in West Berlin cinemas were residents of East Berlin. More worrisome for the East German government, however, was that the open border in Berlin gave East German citizens an easy way to emigrate to West Germany. Between 1949 and 1961, three million of East Germany's eighteen million residents fled to the West; a disproportionate number of those who left were educated professionals whose skills could not easily be replaced. To staunch the flow, East German leader Walter Ulbricht decided to close the Berlin border. Without prior warning, in the early morning hours of August 13, 1961, East German border police and factory militiamen began erecting a fence along the boundary between East and West Berlin. Over the next few months, the fence was replaced by a concrete wall surrounded by barbed wire, watchtowers and armed guards. In an instant, the everyday practice of crossing from one part of the city to another had become a criminal act.[72] On August 17, 1962, one young East German, Peter Fechter, decided to test the system. He made it almost to the final barrier only to be shot by border guards. Incidents such as this one made the Berlin Wall a symbol of the forced isolation of East Europeans.[73]

It was easier for East Europeans to travel within the socialist world. In the 1950s, most went as students, as professionals to network with colleagues or as part of cultural delegations. Underdeveloped Albania, which lacked a critical mass of technical experts, was a magnet for this kind of exchange. In the decade between 1948 and 1958, over 2,000 Albanians studied at Soviet or East European universities, while hundreds of East German, Czech, Polish, Hungarian and Bulgarian engineers, architects, urban planners, doctors and skilled workers went to Albania to help set up factories, survey land, combat disease and assist with mining.[74] In the 1960s, opportunities for leisure travel to other socialist countries increased enormously. In 1965, Bulgaria had one million foreign visitors, primarily tourists headed to its beachside resorts; 80 percent came from other socialist countries. By 1972, this number had tripled.[75] In the early 1970s, East European countries entered into open border agreements with each other, allowing their citizens to travel freely between their countries, without the need for a passport or a visa. Millions took advantage of the opportunity to travel in this way. In Poland, the number of foreign visitors from socialist countries topped eight million in 1972, the first year Poland had open border agreements with neighboring East Germany and Czechoslovakia.[76]

Regardless of their ability to physically travel, East Europeans were exposed to ideas and information from the West, primarily though the radio waves. Radio was the most common broadcast medium in Eastern Europe in the 1950s and 1960s. In 1960 most East European households had a radio, but only a small percentage had televisions, which became a truly mass phenomenon only after 1970.[77] A variety of Western radio stations, such as the BBC and Voice of America (VOA), created radio programs just for East European audiences in their own languages. In the 1960s, as many as half of all East Europeans listened to these broadcasts.[78] Unlike the BBC and VOA, which broadcast around the world, one popular station, Radio Free Europe (RFE), was created for the sole purpose of broadcasting behind the Iron Curtain. RFE was ostensibly an independent citizen initiative from the United States, funded through the charitable donations of ordinary Americans. In reality, RFE was conceived by the US government as a tool of American propaganda. It was covertly funded and advised by the CIA until the early 1970s, when the CIA connection was exposed by American journalists. From that point on, CIA involvement ceased and RFE was openly funded by the US government, just like VOA.

RFE was particularly popular because its different language services concentrated on the domestic news of the countries they served (the station broadcast to Bulgaria, Czechoslovakia, Hungary, Poland and Romania). Each desk was staffed primarily by exiles who had fled their countries because they opposed Communism. These émigrés believed that the Communist news media was full of nothing but propaganda. Their goal was to provide their countrymen with what they believed was the real truth about what was going on in their own countries, uncompromised by Communist propaganda and censorship. Particularly during its first years, RFE's programming was itself strongly shaped by its own anti-Communist ideology. Programs urged listeners to resist Communism and to distrust their governments, while portraying the West in the best possible light. After 1956, the station began to adhere more strictly to Western standards of objective journalism. Even in the early 1950s, however, RFE provided East Europeans with an alternative voice and source of information about the world, albeit one strongly colored by American national interest.[79]

Listening to Western radio stations in the privacy of one's own home was not illegal in Eastern Europe, even during the Stalinist period. Listening in large groups or discussing the broadcasts in public, however, was illegal in most countries; it was considered spreading enemy propaganda. Even though listening itself was not technically a crime, Communist governments made it clear that they considered listening to these broadcasts to be a possible indication of anti-state activity. The local press routinely excoriated these stations, especially RFE, as the source of pernicious Western disinformation and suggested that those who listened were enemies of the people. In addition to trying to discredit the broadcasts, East European governments jammed their signals. Jamming involves covering over the sound of the broadcast by transmitting competing sounds on the same frequency. The jamming was never perfect, so listeners might be able to hear the broadcast beneath the interference, particularly at certain times and locations. After the Stalinist period ended, some countries relaxed their policies towards foreign radio broadcasts, but this liberalization waxed and waned depending on local conditions. Romania stopped jamming all Western radio stations in 1963 and Hungary followed suit in 1964. Poland stopped jamming in 1956 but resumed in 1971. Czechoslovakia started to open its airwaves in 1961 but began to jam Western signals again in 1968. Bulgaria stopped jamming VOA from 1974 to 1979, but otherwise continued to do all it could to block the broadcasts.[80]

RFE and its parent organization, the Free Europe Committee (also funded by the CIA), worked to send print material to Eastern Europe as well. Like RFE's radio broadcasts, these initiatives were not disinterested. Those involved claimed to simply be serving the cause of intellectual freedom, but their actions were intended to destabilize Communist regimes. In the early 1950s, RFE printed hundreds of thousands of leaflets promoting anti-Communist resistance and used large balloons to loft them into Poland, Hungary and Czechoslovakia. The Free Europe Committee had a press arm, the Free Europe Press, that organized translations of books into all of the East European languages. They concentrated on books that had been banned in the region, such as Milovan Djilas's *New Class* and Boris Pasternak's *Doctor Zhivago*, as well as Western texts that promoted anti-Communist themes, such as George Orwell's *1984*. Free Europe Press books were distributed to interested East Europeans visiting the West, including tourists, sailors or professionals on business, to take back home with them. The Free Europe Press also organized an extensive network of private individuals and institutions in the West to mail books to private addresses in the East. In 1962, the list of recipients included over 100,000 names. They were sent a variety of texts, from literature to science, as well as reference books and textbooks. Customs officials sometimes confiscated this material; nonetheless, much of it did reach its destination.[81]

Contrary to its name, the Iron Curtain was permeable. Even at the height of Stalinism, news and information flowed across it. After Stalin's death, that flow only increased. Yet, while East Europeans did have access to alternative sources of knowledge, that access was carefully curated by those who funded it. The US government wanted to provide East Europeans with ideas that would inspire them to reject Communism. However, when unrest did strike Eastern Europe, as it would in 1956 and again in 1968, it would not be sparked by anti-Communist propaganda. Instead, the events of these years would be instigated by Communists themselves, looking for ways to reform their regimes and find a better route to socialist modernity.

Notes

1 Ivan T. Berend, *Central and Eastern Europe, 1944–1993: Detour from the Periphery to the Periphery* (Cambridge: Cambridge University Press, 1996), 184–190.
2 Mark Pittaway, *Eastern Europe 1939–2000* (London: Hodder, 2004), 59.
3 Melissa Feinberg, *Curtain of Lies: The Battle Over Truth in Stalinist Eastern Europe* (New York: Oxford University Press, 2017), 148–152.

4 Kevin McDermott, "Popular Resistance in Communist Czechoslovakia: The Plzeň Uprising, June 1953," *Contemporary European History* 19, no. 4 (2010): 287–307.

5 Jonathan Sperber, "17 June 1953: Revisiting a German Revolution," *German History* 22, no. 4 (2004): 622–623.

6 Mark Landsman, *Dictatorship and Demand: The Politics of Consumerism in East Germany* (Cambridge, MA: Harvard University Press, 2005), 101.

7 Sperber, "17 June 1953," 629–639.

8 Landsman, *Dictatorship and Demand*, 119.

9 Susan Reid, "Cold War in the Kitchen: Gender and the De-stalinization of Consumer Taste in the Soviet Union Under Khrushchev," *Slavic Review* 61, no. 2 (2002): 221.

10 Berend, *Central and Eastern Europe*, 214–219.

11 Berend, *Central and Eastern Europe*, 165–169.

12 One exception to this was Yugoslavia. For more on this, see Chapter 6.

13 Béla Tomka, *A Social History of Twentieth Century Europe* (London: Routledge, 2013), 176–178.

14 Jill Massino, "From Black Caviar to Blackouts: Gender, Consumption and Lifestyle in Ceaușescu's Romania," in *Communism Unwrapped: Consumption in Cold War Eastern Europe*, ed. Paulina Bren and Mary Neuberger (Oxford: Oxford University Press, 2012), 227.

15 Berend, *Central and Eastern Europe*, 219.

16 Slavenka Drakulić, *How We Survived Communism and Even Laughed* (New York: Harper Collins, 1991), 188.

17 Drakulić, *How We Survived Communism*, 50.

18 Narcis Tulbure, "The Socialist Clearinghouse: Alcohol, Reputation and Gender in Romania's Second Economy," in Bren and Neuburger, *Communism Unwrapped*, 262–263.

19 Drakulić, *How We Survived Communism*, 70–71.

20 Karl Brown, "The Extraordinary Career of *Feketevágó Úr*: Wood Theft, Pig Killing and Entrepreneurship in Communist Hungary, 1948–1956," in Bren and Neuburger, *Communism Unwrapped*, 277–297.

21 Eli Rubin, "Amnesiopolis: From Mietskaserne to Wohnungsbauserie 70 in East Berlin's Northeast," *Central European History* 47 (2014): 341.

22 Berend, *Central and Eastern Europe*, 185.

23 Berend, *Central and Eastern Europe*, 210–211.

24 Sándor Horváth, *Stalinism Reloaded: Everyday Life in Stalin-City, Hungary*, trans. Thomas Cooper (Bloomington: Indiana University Press, 2017), 69–74.

25 Kimberly Elman Zarecor, *Manufacturing a Socialist Modernity: Housing in Czechoslovakia, 1945–1960* (Pittsburgh, PA: University of Pittsburgh Press, 2011), 274–296.

26 Rubin, "Amnesiopolis," 349.

27 Rubin, "Amnesiopolis," 366.

28 Rubin, "Amnesiopolis," 372.

29 Brigitte Le Normand, *Designing Tito's Capital: Urban Planning, Modernism and Socialism* (Pittsburgh, PA: University of Pittsburgh Press, 2014), 132.

30 Virag Molnar, "In Search of the Ideal Socialist Home in Post-Stalinist Hungary: Prefabricated Mass Housing or Do-It-Yourself Family Home?" *Journal of Design History* 23, no. 1 (2010): 61–81; Zarecor, *Manufacturing a Socialist Modernity*, 293; Dana Vais, "Techniques of Happiness: Housing Prefabrication in Romania During the 1960s," *Centropa* 13, no. 1 (2013): 19–35.

31 Krisztina Fehérváry, *Politics in Color and Concrete: Socialist Materialities and the Middle Class in Hungary* (Bloomington: Indiana University Press, 2013), 78–110.

32 Horváth, *Stalinism Reloaded*, 87–98.

33 Michał Jarmuż and Dariusz Jarosz, "Housing Demand in the Polish Peoples' Republic," *Studiae Historiae Oeconomicae* 31 (2013): 57–68.

34 Molnar, "In Search of the Ideal Socialist Home," 70.

35 Edyta Materka, *Dystopia's Provocateurs: Peasants, State and Informality in the Polish-German Borderlands* (Bloomington: Indiana University Press, 2017), 162.
36 Greg Castillo, *Cold War on the Home Front: The Soft Power of Midcentury Design* (Minneapolis, MN: University of Minnesota Press, 2010), 166–167.
37 Ben Fowkes, *Eastern Europe 1948–1956* (London: Longman, 2000), 88; Elidor Mëhilli, *From Stalin to Mao: Albania and the Socialist World* (Ithaca, NY: Cornell University Press, 2017), 6.
38 Berend, *Central and Eastern Europe*, 204–205.
39 Tomka, *A Social History of Twentieth Century Europe*, 372.
40 Berend, *Central and Eastern Europe*, 208–210.
41 Milovan Djilas, *The New Class: An Analysis of the Communist System* (New York: Praeger, 1957).
42 György Péteri, "Nomenklatura with Smoking Guns: Hunting in Communist Hungary's Party-State Elite," in *Pleasures in Socialism: Leisure and Luxury in the Eastern Bloc*, ed. David Crowley and Susan E. Reid (Evanston, IL: Northwestern University Press, 2010), 311–312.
43 Berend, *Central and Eastern Europe, 1944–1993*, 213.
44 Zoltan Barany, *The East European Gypsies: Regime Change, Marginality and Ethnopolitics* (Cambridge: Cambridge University Press, 2002), 160.
45 Estimates of the number of Roma killed (just like the estimates of their numbers more generally) can vary quite widely. Celia Donert, *The Rights of the Roma: The Struggle for Citizenship in Postwar Czechoslovakia* (Cambridge: Cambridge University Press, 2017), 2.
46 Donert, *The Rights of the Roma*, 145.
47 Barany, *East European Gypsies*, 112–153.
48 Donert, *The Rights of the Roma*, 166.
49 Barany, *East European Gypsies*, 142.
50 Barany, *East European Gypsies*, 152.
51 Melissa Feinberg, "The Source: Radio Free Europe Information Item #687/54 (29 January 1954)—The Decline of Family Life," *Aspasia* 10 (2016): 89–101.
52 Éva Fodor, *Working Difference: Women's Working Lives in Hungary and Austria, 1945–1995* (Durham: Duke University Press, 2003), 2–3.
53 Jill Massino, "Workers Under Construction: Gender, Identity, and Women's Experiences of Work in State Socialist Romania," in *Gender Politics and Everyday Life in State Socialist Eastern and Central Europe*, ed. Shana Penn and Jill Massino (New York: Palgrave Macmillan, 2009), 18–19.
54 Malgorzata Fidelis, *Women, Communism and Industrialization in Postwar Poland* (Cambridge: Cambridge University Press, 2010), 150, 164.
55 Ulf Brunnbauer, "'The Most Natural Function of Women': Ambiguous Party Policies and Female Experiences in Socialist Bulgaria," in Penn and Massino, *Gender Politics and Everyday Life*, 82.
56 Tomka, *A Social History of Twentieth Century Europe*, 380.
57 Sharon Wolchik, "Ideology and Equality: The Status of Women in Eastern and Western Europe," *Comparative Political Studies* 13, no. 4 (1981): 454.
58 Wolchik, "Ideology and Equality," 457–462.
59 Brunnbauer, "'The Most Natural Function of Women,'" 82.
60 Jill Massino, "Something Old, Something New: Marital Roles and Relations in State Socialist Romania," *Journal of Women's History* 22, no. 1 (2010): 37.
61 Fidelis, *Women, Communism and Industrialization*, 225.
62 Brunnbauer, "'The Most Natural Function of Women,'" 83.
63 Tomka, *A Social History of Twentieth Century Europe*, 50–57.
64 Donna Harsch, *Revenge of the Domestic: Women, the Family and Communism in the German Democratic Republic* (Princeton, NJ: Princeton University Press, 2007), 183.

65 Harsch, *Revenge of the Domestic*, 174.
66 Wolchik, "Ideology and Equality," 463.
67 Massino, "Something Old and Something New," 50–51.
68 Harsch, *Revenge of the Domestic*, 110–117.
69 Paul Betts, *Within Walls: Private Life in the German Democratic Republic* (Oxford: Oxford University Press, 2010), 105.
70 Patryk Babiracki, "The Taste of Red Watermelon: Polish Peasants Visit Soviet Collective Farms, 1949–1952," in *Cold War Crossings: International Travel and Exchange Across the Soviet Bloc, 1940s–1960s*, ed. Patryk Babiracki and Kenyon Zimmer (Arlington: University of Texas at Arlington Press, 2014), 42.
71 Patrick Hyder Patterson, *Bought and Sold: Living and Losing the Good Life in Socialist Yugoslavia* (Ithaca, NY: Cornell University Press, 2011), 4–5.
72 Patrick Major, "Walled In: Ordinary East Germans' Responses to 13 August 1961," *German Politics and Society* 29, no. 2 (2011): 8–22.
73 Pertti Ahonen, "The Berlin Wall and the Battle for Legitimacy in Divided Germany," *German Politics and Society* 29, no. 2 (2011): 40–56.
74 Mëhilli, *From Stalin to Mao*, 63, 130–132.
75 Mary Neuburger, "Smoke and Beers: Touristic Escapes and Places to Party in Socialist Bulgaria, 1956–1976," in *Socialist Escapes: Breaking Away from Ideology and Routine in Eastern Europe, 1945–1989*, ed. Cathleen M. Giustino, Catherine J. Plum and Alexander Vari (New York: Berghahn, 2013), 150.
76 Mark Keck-Szabel, "Shop Around the Bloc: Trader Tourism and Its Discontents on the East-German Polish Border," in Bren and Neuburger, *Communism Unwrapped*, 374–375.
77 Tomka, *A Social History of Twentieth Century Europe*, 234–235.
78 A. Ross Johnson, "Managing Media Influence Operations: Lessons from Radio Free Europe/Radio Liberty," *International Journal of Intelligence and Counter Intelligence* 31, no. 4 (2018): 681–701.
79 Feinberg, *Curtain of Lies*, 60–87.
80 Paweł Machecewicz, *Poland's War on Radio Free Europe, 1950–1989*, trans. Maya Latynski (Washington, DC: Woodrow Wilson Center Press, 2014), 81.
81 Friederike Kind-Kovács, *Written Here, Published There: How Underground Literature Crossed the Iron Curtain* (Budapest: Central European University Press, 2014), 229–236.

4

REFORM AND RETRENCHMENT, 1956–1968

The years after the death of Stalin are often referred to as "the Thaw," after the title of a 1954 novel by the Soviet writer Ilya Ehrenburg. The term evokes feelings of change and hope, as the bleakness of winter gives way to a new spring. The Thaw has usually been portrayed as a period of liberalization. Yet while the Stalinist practice of terror did end after Stalin's death, it was not always clear what a post-Stalinist future might entail. In Eastern Europe, there was no consensus among Communist leaders about the need for change. During the years from 1956 through 1968, some countries attempted extensive reforms, while others tried to limit change as much as possible.

One issue that concerned all East European leaders was whether the Thaw would allow them greater freedom to set their own agendas independently of the Soviet Union. With the exception of Bulgaria, whose leader Todor Zhivkov remarked in 1973 that his country and the Soviet Union shared "a single body, breathing with the same lungs and nourished by the same bloodstream," Eastern Europe's Communist governments began to assert their autonomy from the USSR.[1] After 1956, East European governments began to diverge, sometimes significantly, from Soviet policies. However, this independence had its limits.

The governments of Poland, Romania and Albania successfully challenged Soviet authority because they remained committed to the Communist monopoly of power in their countries. In contrast, in 1956, Hungarian leader Imre Nagy signaled his support for multiparty elections and proposed leaving the Warsaw Pact. Soviet troops invaded to remove him from power. Cognizant of the need to stay within these limits, Czechoslovakia leaders were careful to emphasize their commitment to socialism when they launched their own reform movement in 1968. Yet their decisions unnerved Soviet leaders anyway.

DOI: 10.4324/9780813348186-5

Worried that the Czechoslovak reform effort going too far, the Soviets again authorized military intervention, signaling the new limits of East European independence.

Is It Not Preferable to Stand on Our Own Feet?

In February 1956, almost three years after Stalin's death, the Soviet Communist Party held its 20th Party Congress. Late on its last night, the delegates were called back to the Kremlin for an unscheduled extra session. To their surprise, Soviet leader Nikita Khrushchev took the floor to publicly criticize Stalin and the cult of personality that had surrounded him. While he did not denounce all aspects of Stalin's rule, Khrushchev repudiated Stalin's use of terror and admitted that many supposed enemies of the people had been falsely accused.[2] Khrushchev's speech had enormous repercussions throughout the socialist world. In its aftermath, those who had celebrated Stalin and believed in his policies suffered a crisis of conscience. If some of Stalin's acts were now revealed to be crimes, how could Communists continue to have faith in their party and its leaders? This was a question that all Communists would wrestle with in the coming years.

Because it was given in a closed session and not included in the official publication of the proceedings of the congress, Khrushchev's address has become known as the Secret Speech. However, it was never intended to be kept secret. Shortly after its initial reading, copies of the speech were sent to party organizations throughout the Soviet Union specifically so that they could be read out at party meetings all across the country.[3] Copies were also given to Eastern Europe's Communist leaders. In most of the region, the full text of Khrushchev's speech was kept in the hands of the party elite. The exception was Poland, where tens of thousands of copies were printed. These were ostensibly for internal party use—they were labeled "For the Exclusive Use of Party Organizations"—but soon were openly available for purchase at Warsaw's Różycki Flea Market. It was via Poland that the text made its way into the hands of Western intelligence and into the Western media.[4]

The Stalinist system in Poland had begun to change even before the revelations of the 20th Congress. The Polish security service found itself under scrutiny after one of its leading officials, Józef Światło, defected to the West in late 1953. In 1954, Radio Free Europe's Polish service broadcast a series of interviews with Światło in which he detailed his department's use of terror, allowing listeners to hear how innocent people had been arrested and tortured. Światło's revelations sparked criticism of Stalinist methods within the Polish Communist Party. The security service was reorganized and its staff was reduced. Some political prisoners, including Władysław Gomułka, a former Communist party leader who had argued with Stalin, were released. The media warily began to include a wider range of voices.[5]

Uniquely in Eastern Europe, Polish leaders initiated a widespread discussion of the Secret Speech throughout the ranks of the Communist party. The text was read at thousands of party meetings throughout the country in late March and early April 1956. The revelations, which occurred in tandem with the unexpected death of Polish Communist Party chief Bolesław Bierut, sent shockwaves throughout Polish society. Attendees responded with shock, horror and anger. "Can we trust role models, when the supreme one lied to us?" asked participants at a party meeting at the State Higher Drama School in Łódź. Some questioned Stalinist policies, such as collectivization. "When are we going to dissolve production cooperatives, since it's an idea of Stalin's?" wondered someone at a meeting in Kraków Province. Others cast doubt on the competence of Polish leaders and challenged Soviet influence in Polish affairs. If Stalin had acted so criminally, they wondered, why had Poland followed the Soviet model so blindly? "Is it not preferable to leave our eastern friends and stand on our own feet?" demanded people at a meeting at Łódź Polytechnic?[6]

Polish Communist leaders disseminated the Secret Speech because they wanted to create support for change, but they also believed they could control the pace and extent of that change. Instead, people became emboldened and began to make their own demands, calling for new leaders, an improved standard of living and an end to Soviet influence over domestic policy. As one Polish Communist activist from Lower Silesia wrote,

> The Twentieth Congress of the CPSU [Communist Party of the Soviet Union] motivated people, loosened their tongues, and the people we once considered to be devoted to our regime, our government, today are coming out against us. When we ask why they are doing this, they usually answer: 'I didn't speak up then, now after the Twentieth Congress I can.'[7]

This new climate of expectation erupted into violence in the city of Poznań on June 28, 1956. On that day, workers around the city went on strike to demand better pay and lower prices on basic consumer goods. They marched toward the city center chanting slogans like "We want bread!" and "We want to live like human beings!" As the march went on, the crowd began to shout political demands in addition to their economic concerns, including "Freedom!" and "down with the Russkis!" They sang Polish patriotic songs and started to destroy Soviet and red flags. The crowd, estimated to be about 100,000 strong, marched peacefully to the town hall, intending to present its demands to local authorities. Unhindered by the police, they occupied the local Communist party headquarters.[8]

At some point, the crowd became more revolutionary. Socioeconomic demands for better pay gave way to overt political revolt. Some of the demonstrators marched to the local office of the security service and attacked it, shouting, "death to the political police!" "murderers!" and "Godless reds!"

Shooting broke out and the march became a battle that engulfed much of the city. Army units were sent out onto the streets. When the dust had settled, 73 had been killed, 239 wounded and 247 arrested; most were workers. Across Poland, the events in Poznań were widely seen as a national uprising against Soviet domination.[9]

While peace was quickly restored, public dissatisfaction grew. Many placed their hopes on Władysław Gomułka. A victim of the Stalinist purges, Gomułka was viewed by many Poles as a nationalist who would defend the country against the Soviets and right the wrongs of the past. The situation came to a head in late October 1956, around the Eighth Plenum of the Central Committee of the Polish Communist Party. In the days before and after the plenum, particularly from 19 to 24 October, there were thousands of mass meetings, rallies and demonstrations all over the country. In response to the unrest, Soviet troops within Poland mobilized, and Soviet leaders appeared in Warsaw to discuss the situation with their Polish counterparts. In talks with the Soviets, Gomułka emphasized his commitment to socialism and to Poland's alliance with the Soviet Union. The Soviets were convinced and the Polish Central Committee elected Gomułka as its chief on October 21, bringing the crisis to a gradual end. Although he never claimed to be anything but a sincere Communist, Gomułka's election was widely celebrated as a national victory against Soviet domination. According to an anonymous letter sent to the Central Committee, the events of October 21 "opened a new period on our social and political life. The nation was profoundly shaken by the joy of liberation, the happiness of awakening and the dawn of the new free life…"[10]

During the Polish October, the masses played a decisive role in determining the future of the socialist system in Poland. Gomułka's ascension to power did not end Communist dictatorship, but it showed that the system was capable of transformation. As a result of 1956, Poland gained considerably more autonomy in its internal affairs, albeit within strictly defined limits. Soviet troops remained in Poland, but Polish leaders no longer felt compelled to follow Soviet models in many areas of domestic policy. Bowing to popular pressure among the peasantry, Gomułka ended the push to collectivize agriculture and lowered compulsory deliveries for private farmers. Within a few months, over 80 percent of existing agricultural cooperatives had been disbanded. Private farming would become the norm in Poland for the remainder of the socialist period. The year 1956 also marked a significant turning point in the use of political repression. While it was still possible for Poles to be prosecuted for political offenses, the number of arrests for such crimes declined substantially. The security service was reduced to about half its former size. The persecution of the Catholic clergy also abated and the Church gained a considerable amount of autonomy over its own affairs. By ameliorating or removing the most widely disliked elements of the Stalinist era, the Polish government was able to bolster its legitimacy and achieve a new stability that would last for more than two decades.[11]

An Unlikely Revolutionary

Inspired by what was happening in Poland, Hungarian university students organized a demonstration in Budapest on the 23rd of October 1956. The Hungarian students hoped to spark similar changes in their country. However, events in Hungary would follow a very different trajectory.

The years leading up to 1956 had been tumultuous ones in Hungary. The country's Stalinist leaders, led by Mátyás Rákosi, were noted for their brutality, which made them very unpopular with the country's non-Communist majority. Their excessive use of terror alarmed the Soviets, who worried that it might provoke an uprising. In June 1953, only months after Stalin's death, Soviet leaders summoned the Hungarian leadership to Moscow to express their concerns. They ordered Rákosi to give up his post as prime minister, although he was allowed to remain as the head of the Hungarian Communist Party. The Soviets installed Imre Nagy, a Hungarian Communist who had lived in Moscow for many years, as prime minister and charged him with developing a "New Course" that would moderate his predecessor's policies. This left Hungary in the unique position of having power split between two men—Nagy and Rákosi—who disagreed on many issues of policy. Rákosi was the embodiment of the Stalinist policies that Nagy had been asked to reform.

A committed Communist, Imre Nagy believed that socialism could only succeed in Hungary if it was implemented gradually. The goal of his New Course was to gain more widespread support for socialism by moving away from the Stalinist model that Mátyás Rákosi had so faithfully followed. Nagy was the first East European leader to attempt to "de-Stalinize" or to reject some of the tenets of Stalinism, such as the use of terror as a political strategy. As part of the New Course, Nagy slowed the pace of collectivization and devoted more resources to improving the standard of living. He also worked to curb the activities of the secret police and to release and rehabilitate those who had been wrongly imprisoned during the Stalinist terror. When some of these former "traitors" began to appear on the streets of Budapest, it caused a sensation. Why, some began to ask, had they been arrested in the first place?[12]

Nagy's policies were popular with many ordinary Hungarians, but he had trouble building support within the ranks of the Hungarian Communist leadership. Nagy's primary allies were among the Communist intelligentsia: writers, journalists and students. Many of these intellectuals felt betrayed after they learned the truth about the show trials and looked to the New Course as a positive step forward. As the writer István Örkény lamented in late 1953,

> It was not our intention to write books that offer a distorted picture of the world, books as hollow as an empty nut... Yet we have written such books. And what should the mission of the writer mean now?... that the

writer and no one else has the responsibility for what he writes. That he may experiment and stop being a mere illustrator.[13]

From the moment Nagy became prime minister, Rákosi worked to undermine him. While consolidating his own support at home, Rákosi played the rivalries among the Soviet leadership to his own advantage. When Nagy's primary Soviet supporter, Georgy Malenkov, was sidelined when Khrushchev moved to consolidate his own power, Nagy became expendable. In 1955, Rákosi used this situation to facilitate Nagy's removal from office and his expulsion from the party. Then Rákosi reversed the New Course. The newly emboldened intellectuals, however, refused to accept a return to Stalinism. They continued to publicly criticize Rákosi's rule and rallied around Imre Nagy, making him into the symbol of reform. Concerned that the situation in Hungary had failed to stabilize, the Soviets again intervened. This time, they asked Rákosi to step down, replacing him with his close comrade Ernő Gerő. Unfortunately, in the eyes of those who sympathized with Nagy and his anti-Stalinist reforms, Gerő was no better than Rákosi.

When the Hungarian students took to the streets on the morning of October 23, 1956, they did not intend to start a revolution. They marched in solidarity with what had happened in Poland and to demand that Hungarians also be allowed to choose their own reformist leader: Imre Nagy. Yet after the demonstration had concluded, the crowds on the streets continued to grow, with workers and other passersby joining the students. As the hours passed, the protests grew bolder. The journalist Paul Lendvai recalled hearing increasingly radical slogans from the crowd, such as "Russians go home!" "Rákosi into the Danube, Imre Nagy into power!" and "Don't stop halfway, sweep Stalinism away!"[14] People congregated at different locations around the city; 150,000–200,000 gathered on Parliament Square, where they demanded to hear from Imre Nagy.[15]

In the evening, Nagy finally addressed the restive crowd. But Nagy was a poor speaker and his words did little to satisfy the masses gathered on the square. Most considered what he said to be mere Communist jargon which did not acknowledge their desire for substantive change. Meanwhile, elsewhere in the city, a group of young people attacked a giant statue of Stalin and managed to hurl it to the ground. At around the same time, another group attacked the main building of the Hungarian radio, hoping to get their demands read on the air. Shots were fired and fighting ensued. By the morning of October 24, the city was in chaos. Martial law was declared and Soviet tanks appeared on the streets. Over the next several days, fighting continued as approximately 15,000 Hungarians took up arms, not only in Budapest but all over the country. Many more took part in demonstrations. Initially, those on the streets were fighting not to destroy the socialist system but to return Nagy to power. When

FIGURE 4.1   Hungarians surround the demolished statue of Stalin in Budapest, 1956. © Photo by Hulton Archive/Getty Images.

several hundred people were killed over the next few days, however, the situation radicalized. As there was no one center of resistance, demands were shifting and fluid, changing from day to day and even hour to hour.[16]

After addressing the crown on October 23, Imre Nagy retreated to the Central Committee building. Ever a loyal Communist, Nagy believed that solutions should be made among party leaders, not on the street. In the early hours of the morning on October 24, Nagy was appointed prime minister. For the next few days, as violence raged throughout the country, Nagy talked and bargained with his old comrades over the composition of a new government in a state of disconnect from the rapidly evolving situation on the street. According to observers, Nagy was simply not capable of taking charge of such a moment. One of the insurgents, István Eörsi, wrote later of Nagy:

> He was an unhurried man, shaped by doubts and also by deep-rooted party discipline, who simply needed more time to make decisions than one should or could afford in a revolution. He was always two, three days behind in his decisions.[17]

On October 28, friends and allies convinced Nagy that he needed to act. Spurred out of his passivity, Nagy decided to make common cause with the people on the street. With Soviet knowledge, he recognized the legitimacy of the insurgents, calling their actions a national democratic movement. He declared a cease fire and amnesty for all insurgents, pledged to dissolve the secret police and promised that Soviet troops would withdraw from Budapest. These concessions, however, did little to calm the situation and the unrest continued. A few days later, on October 30, Nagy went further. He proclaimed that Hungary would return to the multiparty system from 1945 and announced the creation of a new government that included representatives from opposition parties, several of whom had until recently been in jail.[18]

While Soviet leaders had initially seemed inclined to accept Nagy as they had done with Gomułka in Poland, the decision to reinstate the multiparty system convinced Khrushchev that Nagy had lost control of the situation. He remembered later that on the night of October 30, "I could not sleep. Budapest was like a nail in my head." The next morning, he asked the Soviet Politburo to authorize military intervention in Hungary. The Soviets reached out to János Kádár, a moderate Hungarian Communist who had been in jail until he was released by Nagy during the New Course, and asked him to support the invasion in exchange for the leadership. Kádár agreed.[19]

Realizing that Soviet troops were moving to invade Hungary, Imre Nagy made one last, desperate move. He declared Hungary was leaving the Warsaw Pact in favor of neutrality and asked for the support of the United Nations. His appeal, however, fell on deaf ears. While the United States had publicly been committed to the rollback of Communist regimes in Eastern Europe, and although Radio Free Europe had urged Hungarians to ever more radical steps during the revolution with the implied promise of American support, the US government was not willing to risk a war with the Soviet Union for the sake of Hungary. On November 4, 1956, Soviet troops entered Budapest. Hungarians again took up arms. By the time the fighting was over, thousands of Hungarians and hundreds of Soviet soldiers had lost their lives. Imre Nagy was taken prisoner by the Soviets and was executed after a show trial in 1958. János Kádár became the leader of the Hungarian Communist Party. He would hold that position for the next 32 years.[20]

The events of October 1956 in Poland and Hungary dramatically illustrated the limits of national autonomy in post-Stalinist Eastern Europe. In Poland, public discontent was able to help shape the course of events, sweeping Władysław Gomułka into power. This was only possible, however, because the Communist monopoly on power was never threatened, nor was Poland's alliance with the Soviet Union ever in jeopardy. Poland gained control over its own domestic agenda but remained firmly in the Soviet camp. Demonstrators in Hungary did not respect these boundaries. When Nagy's proposed reforms began to challenge the Hungarian Communist Party's hold on power, the Soviets felt they had no choice but to intervene. The countries of Eastern Europe might be able to deviate from the Soviet model, but they could not reject socialism.

A Fruit Growing Colony?

In Poland and Hungary, reformist factions within each country's Communist party welcomed Khrushchev's repudiation of Stalin and his tactics. Elsewhere in Eastern Europe, there was less enthusiasm for change. Stalinist leaders in Albania, Czechoslovakia, East Germany and Romania maintained their hold on power and resisted expansive reforms. Nonetheless, leaders in these countries also began to assert their independence from the Soviet Union. This was particularly true in Albania and Romania, where Communist leaders gained new legitimacy not via liberal reforms but by challenging Soviet dominance.

As the poorest country in the Soviet bloc, Albania depended on its allies for economic and technical aid. Yet the Albanians were wary of being exploited by their more powerful allies. In 1948, Albanian leader Enver Hoxha joined the Soviet Union in denouncing Yugoslavia, Albania's neighbor and patron, in order to curtail Yugoslav influence in his country. Hoxha wanted the Soviets to help turn Albania into a modern industrial nation. During the 1950s, the Soviets sent Albania legions of technical experts and millions of dollars in aid.[21] Yet while they financed a textile complex, a cement factory and other industrial enterprises in Albania, Soviet leaders advised Hoxha to concentrate on developing agriculture rather than industry. The Albanians ignored them and kept their focus on industry, much to the annoyance of the Soviets.

On a visit to the country in 1959, a frustrated Khrushchev responded to Albanian requests for yet more aid by saying, "You fed us lunch and then promptly demand all these things from us. If we had known about this, we would have brought lunch with us." He urged the Albanians to concentrate on growing fruits and vegetables, not oil extraction.[22] As Enver Hoxha saw it, however, Khrushchev "wanted Albania to be turned into a fruit growing colony which would serve the revisionist Soviet Union, just as the banana republics in Latin America serve the United States of America."[23]

Like some of Eastern Europe's other Stalinist leaders, Hoxha felt blindsided by Khrushchev's rejection of Stalin and his legacy. As the instigator of terror in Albania, Hoxha had little desire to rehabilitate rivals he had eliminated as traitors. Hoxha was even more uneasy about changing Soviet policy toward Yugoslavia. In 1956, Khrushchev restored relations with Yugoslavia and pressed Albania to do the same. Ignoring Hoxha's misgivings, Khrushchev invited the Yugoslav ambassador to toast with the recalcitrant Albanians at a dinner in Moscow in 1957. As Hoxha wrote later, "We all toasted and shook hands. Truth be told, the atmosphere at dinner was warm, but we felt hurt inside."[24]

The mutual frustrations and misunderstandings between the Soviets and the Albanians came to a head in 1960, as tensions mounted between the Soviet Union and China. Pressed by Khrushchev to join the Soviet critique of the Chinese, Hoxha refused, publicly claiming the Khrushchev had betrayed Marxism-Leninism. In response, the Soviet Union moved to exclude Albania from its orbit, as it had with Yugoslavia in 1948. The Soviets cut off economic aid to Albania and severed diplomatic relations, urging their East European allies to do the same.[25] At first, the Albanians cultivated their ties with the Chinese, but Enver Hoxha gradually grew more and more isolationist, preferring his own brand of ideological purity to any form of compromise.

Like Hoxha, Romanian leader Gheorghe Gheorghiu-Dej was skeptical of Khrushchev's turn against Stalin. Despite Gheorghiu-Dej's growing distrust, Romania remained overtly loyal to the Soviet Union throughout the 1950s. This changed in the early 1960s, when Romania rebelled against Soviet plans to coordinate economic planning across the Council for Mutual Economic Assistance (CMEA). In this scheme, Romania would become a supplier of raw materials for the more industrialized regions of northern Eastern Europe and the Soviet Union. This was anathema to Romanian leaders, who clung to the Stalinist model of intensive industrialization. Like the Albanians, the Romanians resented being characterized as an agricultural resource for their more advanced allies. The situation reached a boiling point in April 1964, when the Romanian government published a formal statement asserting its independence from Soviet foreign policy.[26]

Unlike Albania, Romania did not completely break with the Soviet Union and remained one of its allies. Romanian leaders, however, often refused to follow the Soviet lead in foreign affairs, most famously when the country refused to support the Warsaw Pact invasion of Czechoslovakia in 1968. This willingness to cross the Soviet Union caused Western governments to look favorably on Romania. US President Richard Nixon visited the country in 1969 as a show of Western support for Romania's defiant rejection of Soviet priorities.

Defying the Soviet Union was one element in the Romanian Communist Party's turn toward nationalism. Beginning under Gheorghiu-Dej and continuing under his successor, Nicolae Ceaușescu, the Romanian Communist Party revived Romanian nationalism as a political language. Formally, Communism de-emphasized the nation, promoting class solidarity across national lines. Nonetheless, different Communist regimes often used nationalism to promote their policies and gain the support of the population. In post-1964 Romania, the socialist nation, rather than the working class, took on a central role. Ceaușescu's regime portrayed itself as using socialism to bring the Romanian nation to its fullest potential.[27] Ceaușescu's turn to nationalism resonated with many Romanians, especially the country's intellectual elites. His fusion of Communist rule with nationalist ideals would remain characteristic of Romanian politics until the end of Communism in 1989.

Well into the 1970s, Ceaușescu was praised in the West as a maverick for standing up to the Soviet Union. Yet Romanian leaders pursued national autonomy to enable the continuation of Stalinist practices rather than the reverse. After a brief period of liberalization, Ceaușescu established a brutal dictatorship in which he glorified himself as the "Genius of the Carpathians" and the "Danube of Thought."[28] The slogan "Party, Ceauşescu, Romania," which equated the nation, the Communist Party and their leader, was a hallmark of his rule. For Ceauşescu, challenging the Soviet Union was the path to personal power.

Socialism with a Human Face

They year 1968 was marked by protest around the world. In the West, the protests of 1968 were typically organized by students inspired by the radical left. They protested against capitalism, imperialism and the Vietnam War; advocated countercultural lifestyles, and agitated for a less hierarchical world. Eastern Europe was part of the global protest wave of 1968, but events there had their own dynamic. Young people did take to the streets to demand change in Eastern Europe in 1968, particularly in Poland and Yugoslavia. However, the largest movement for change in Eastern Europe in 1968 was not led by radical students. Instead, it came out of the Czechoslovak Communist Party. In 1968, Communist reformers in Czechoslovakia launched an ambitious project to create a more democratic and humane form of socialism. Their failure would resonate throughout the entire socialist world.

Czechoslovak leader Antonín Novotný, who took over the party after the death of Klement Gottwald in 1953, was a neo-Stalinist who resisted reforms. For a while, the country's relatively robust economy insulated him from popular pressure to initiate change. An abrupt economic downturn in 1963 made this stance less tenable. Reform elements within the Czechoslovak Communist Party (KSČ) began to call for the decentralization of the planned economy and greater freedoms for writers, artists and academics. Novotný and his allies did their best to resist these reformist tendencies, but censorship had loosened enough by the mid-1960s to allow the production of books, films and plays critical of the existing system. For example, Milan Kundera's 1965 novel, *The Joke*, told the story of an early supporter of Communism who became bitter and disillusioned after he was expelled from the university for sending an ironic postcard. The book suggests that the idealistic dreams of Czechoslovakia's young Stalinist revolutionaries were chimeras, quickly replaced by cynicism and shameless careerism.[29]

These tensions burst into the open at the fourth congress of the Czechoslovak Writers' Union in June 1967, where several prominent writers, including Milan Kundera, Pavel Kohout, Václav Havel, Ivan Klíma and Ludvík Vaculík, publicly advocated freedom of speech and sharply condemned the Novotný regime for stifling thought and innovation. In a particularly incendiary speech, Vaculík declared that in the years since the Communists came to power, "I am afraid that we have not advanced on the world scene and that our republic has lost its good name. We have not contributed any original thoughts or good ideas to humanity."[30] The Novotný regime did not appreciate the writers' message. The Ministry of Culture moved to exert more control over the Writers' Union, and three of those who made provocative comments (including Vaculík) were expelled from the KSČ.

Despite the Novotný government's attempts to quell dissent, pressure for change built inside the ranks of the party. In January 1968, Novotný was ousted from power. He was replaced by Alexander Dubček, a compromise candidate who was little known before he assumed leadership. Although he was actually quite moderate in his views, Dubček would become the face of the Czechoslovak reform movement. During the first few months of Dubček's tenure, reformist officials began to draft a plan for creating a new, democratic model of socialism, sometimes referred to as "socialism with a human face."

The need to reinvigorate the economy was at the heart of the Czechoslovak reforms. Economists at the Czechoslovak Institute of Economics, led by Ota Šik, insisted that the highly centralized system of economic planning that had developed under Stalinism needed to be fundamentally overhauled. They proposed moving from the former command system to a kind of market socialism, where a great deal of decision-making power would devolve to the level of individual enterprises and wages and prices would be partially determined by the market.[31] Czechoslovakia was not the only socialist state to consider implementing some kind of market-based reform during this period. Yugoslavia had moved away from a strict model of central planning already in the early 1950s and became even more market-oriented after a further series of reforms in 1965. In January 1968, Hungary adopted a package of reforms called the New Economic Mechanism (NEM) that was similar to many of the Czechoslovak proposals.

In Czechoslovakia, however, reformers insisted that changes in the economic system had to be accompanied by a larger program of democratization. In support of this, Czechoslovakia abolished censorship in March 1968. The result was an extraordinary flowering of public debate that gave the reform era its name: the Prague Spring. Almost overnight, Czechoslovak newspapers and magazines began to publish articles on controversial topics, while radio and television stations broadcast uncensored critical interviews with government officials and took live calls from the public on the air. People began to actively take part in public life, going to political meetings and forming new civil associations and clubs. Once people began to speak freely, their demands quickly became more and more radical. Many called for increased democratization, more openness and more reform; some even discussed the possibility of allowing truly opposition political parties to contest elections.[32] The atmosphere in the media was raw and exciting, even joyous. A young bureaucrat caught by a television crew on the street summed up the moment to a reporter by saying, "Yesterday I didn't think I could say what I think. Today I think maybe I can."[33]

The incredible outspokenness in the Czechoslovak press attracted the notice of Soviet and other East European leaders, who were concerned that the KSČ had unleashed a force it could not control. At a meeting in Dresden on March 23, Leonid Brezhnev, who had succeeded Khrushchev as the head of the Soviet Union in 1964, warned Alexander Dubček that members of the intelligentsia were engaged in what amounted to a counterrevolutionary conspiracy. Invoking the case of Hungary in 1956, Brezhnev cautioned Dubček about the need to impose some kind of limit on this increasingly raucous new public sphere.[34] According to the Czechoslovak foreign minister, Jiří Hájek, the Soviet perspective was fundamentally different from that of the Czechoslovak reformers, making it difficult to persuade them the situation was not as dire as they believed. As Hájek remarked,

> the Soviet comrades do not understand the situation in our country. They are not familiar with Czechoslovak history, the composition of Czechoslovak society, the mentality of our people or our democratic traditions. That is why the openness in the Czechoslovak press and radio has evoked such bewilderment, and why opinions have been expressed that this development is abetting the enemies of socialism.[35]

The KSČ released an outline of its reform plan, known as the Action Program, on April 10, 1968. While insisting that the Communist party would maintain its hold on power, the Action Program emphasized the need for the freedom of expression, including political debate and dissent. It affirmed the right to freedom of association, assembly and travel; called for the decentralization of the economy and promised the rehabilitation of those unjustly imprisoned during the 1950s. The authors of the Action Program insisted that democratization was not a threat to socialism, but the only way it could evolve and grow.[36] Brezhnev, however, was not convinced. At the May 6 meeting of the Soviet Politburo, he called it "a bad program, opening up possibilities for the restoration of capitalism in Czechoslovakia."[37]

The worries of Warsaw Pact leaders were exacerbated by events in Poland. In March, Polish students erupted in protest. The impetus was the Polish government's decision to cancel a Warsaw production of a 19th-century play, *Dziady* (Forefather's Eve), by Adam Mickiewicz. Some audience members had taken to wildly applauding the play's anti-Russian lines, causing a sensation.[38] In the fallout from the protests against the play's cancellation, two students, Adam Michnik and Henryk Szlajfer, were expelled from Warsaw University. In the wake of their expulsion, their fellow students organized a public demonstration on March 8 that was attended by thousands. The event dissolved into chaos when busloads of club-wielding party activists and police appeared. Hundreds of students were beaten, and some of the student leaders were arrested.

The Polish students were not simply following events in Prague. Some of them, like Michnik and Szlajfer, had been engaged in oppositional activities for years. Many of these student radicals were Marxists who had a different vision of socialism than the one promulgated by the Gomułka regime. They were part of a global countercultural young left that was inspired by a variety of Marxist thinkers, from Trotsky to Mao. The Polish students had also been strongly influenced by the work of two young activists, Jacek Kuroń and Karol Modzelewski. In 1965, Kuroń and Modzelewski released their *Open Letter to the Party*. In this text, they charged that the Polish Communist regime had devolved into an oligarchic bureaucracy that cared more about keeping itself in power than the needs of the working class. The solution, they said, was a further proletarian revolution. The *Open Letter* landed Kuroń and Modzelewski in jail. It also circulated among radical Polish students, providing some of the intellectual framework for their later protests. The *Open Letter* was smuggled out of Poland and published in the West, where it would be translated into many languages and read by left-leaning students around the world, including in other East European countries.[39]

After the events of March 8, protests quickly spread around Poland. While most demonstrations and rallies were located around universities, some young workers also protested. Like many of those in Czechoslovakia, the Polish students emphasized their support for socialism but demanded reforms, including freedom of speech, and adherence to the rule of law.[40] One of the student activists, Jan Walc, later recalled how he and his fellow activists felt inspired by a sense of higher purpose. He said,

> It was a moment when we felt that we were going down in the history of our country. Indeed, our time had come and we didn't have to be jealous of our parents' generation any longer, in that they, during the war, had a chance to prove themselves, a chance we'd been denied.[41]

As Walc implies, many of the Polish student protesters were the children of socialists who had fought to establish Communism in Poland. They saw themselves less as fighting against their parents than working to finally realize what their parents had wanted to achieve.[42]

The Polish government did not see their actions in this benign light. It swiftly cracked down on the protesters. By March 27, over 2,500 people had been arrested, including almost 600 students. Hundreds of students were expelled from universities, conscripted into the military or interrogated and beaten by the police. Professors and other people alleged to be connected with the demonstrators (such as their parents) were fired from their jobs. This repression continued for months.[43]

One prominent element of the Polish government's attack on the protestors was its brutal anti-Zionist campaign. Within a few days after the March 8 demonstrations, newspaper articles alleged that the protests were orchestrated by "Zionists" (understood to be Jews) who cared more for Israel than for Poland.

This message was quickly repeated throughout the media. Across the country there were tens of thousands of meetings by local Communist party organizations that urged Poles to resist this Zionist scourge. While they claimed to be against antisemitism, Communist leaders consistently used antisemitic tropes to describe Zionists, referring to them as foreign elements working together in a conspiratorial fashion to undermine the Polish state.[44] The nastiness of this campaign convinced over 15,000 people of Jewish ancestry to emigrate, comprising over half of the total number of Jews resident in Poland.[45]

By caricaturing the demonstrators as elite and Jewish, the Polish government was able to successfully marginalize them. While the students had hoped their demands would resonate with workers, most seemed to accept the regime's characterization of the protests. A Polish graduate student, Ewa B., told a British embassy employee,

> There is not much hope now. The workers don't understand what the trouble is about, and they would much rather keep their jobs, their flats, their television sets and their vodka than go out on to the streets in support of intellectual notions. You can't blame them; they simply aren't dissatisfied enough to come out in support.[46]

Unable to garner wider support, the Polish demonstrations fizzled out.

A few months later, at the beginning of June, students at the University of Belgrade in Yugoslavia erupted in protest. Along with some sympathetic faculty, they occupied university buildings, organized happenings and teach-ins and called for a week-long university-wide strike. An estimated 40,000 Belgrade students took part in the demonstrations, which quickly spread to the cities of Zagreb and Sarajevo. During the June protests, the Yugoslav students agitated against police brutality (the protests were sparked by police beating students trying to get into a rock concert) and a stultifying university bureaucracy. Like the Polish students, the Yugoslav protesters were inspired by the work of revisionist Yugoslav Marxist intellectuals, who charged that Yugoslavia's socialist government had merely created its own elite and not liberated the working class. The protesters criticized the Yugoslav system for becoming too bureaucratic and for creating new forms of economic inequality that effectively replicated the capitalist class system. Some called for an end to this new "red bourgeoisie." After a week of demonstrations, Yugoslav leader Josip Broz Tito gave a televised speech in which he claimed to agree with the students and promised reforms. Tito's speech effectively neutralized the demonstrations, but other than some improvements to student living standards no lasting reforms were implemented. Instead, state harassment of critical intellectuals and other nonconformists increased.[47]

While protests in Poland and Yugoslavia were quickly contained, the radical voices in the Czechoslovak media continued unabated. Writers, journalists and other members of the intelligentsia were intent on pressuring the KSČ to stay on its reform course. The writer Ludvík Vaculík published a particularly provocative manifesto on June 27 entitled "2,000 Words to Workers, Farmers, Scientists, Artists and Everyone." In this piece, which was signed by dozens of prominent intellectuals, Vaculík claimed the success of the reforms depended on sustained grassroots political engagement. Citizens should insist that corrupt or incompetent officials resign. If they refused to go, people should encourage them to leave, via actions like "public criticism, resolutions, demonstrations, demonstrative work brigades, collections to buy presents for them on their retirement, strikes and picketing at front doors."[48] What Vaculík proposed was a new culture of public accountability, where state and party officials answered to their constituents, not simply to their superiors.

Vaculík's essay provoked concern among Warsaw Pact leaders and more conservative Czechoslovak Communists alike. Both groups worried that the reforms had gone too far, weakening the KSČ's monopoly on power. For months, Soviet leaders had demanded that the Czechoslovak government reinstitute censorship precisely to prevent manifestos like the "2,000 Words" from getting into print. Yet nothing had changed. In a sign of their displeasure, the leaders of all the other Warsaw Pact nations sent a strongly worded letter to the Central Committee of the KSČ on July 26, 1968, expressing their "profound anxiety." The KSČ, they declared, was losing control of events. Under the banner of democratization, anti-socialist reactionaries, such as Vaculík, were undermining Communist power in Czechoslovakia. This, they said, was unacceptable. "We cannot assent to hostile forces pushing your country off the path of socialism," they warned, adding "this is no longer your affair alone."[49]

At subsequent meetings with the Soviets in the Slovak village of Čierná nad Tisou on July 29 and with Warsaw Pact members in Bratislava on August 3, Alexander Dubček promised to take steps to alleviate his allies' concerns. Unbeknownst to him, however, a few conservative KSČ Central Committee members wrote to Brezhnev to say they did not believe the KSČ was capable of mastering the situation and requesting Soviet assistance. On August 17, the Soviet Politburo voted to invade Czechoslovakia to halt the reforms. A few days later, on the night of August 20, Warsaw Pact forces moved to occupy the country.[50] The Soviet-led invasion of Czechoslovakia was justified by what became known as the Brezhnev doctrine, named for Soviet leader Leonid Brezhnev. First formally articulated in *Pravda* in September 1968, this policy affirmed the right of the Soviet Union to intervene to preserve socialism anywhere it was threatened, even inside a sovereign nation.[51]

On the morning of August 21, Czechoslovaks gathered on the streets to watch Soviet tanks take over their cities. Unlike in Hungary in 1956, there was little armed resistance to the invasion. The largest skirmish was, perhaps fittingly, at the headquarters of the Czechoslovak radio, where journalists continued to broadcast as shots were fired outside the building and troops stormed

FIGURE 4.2 A Czechoslovak woman tries to speak to Soviet soldiers on the streets of Prague, 1968. © Photo by Bettman via Getty Images.

the premises. Instead, Czechoslovaks engaged in nonviolent acts of protest, such as the removal of highway and street signs to confuse the troops and plastering walls with signs and graffiti condemning the invaders, to the extent that the entire city of Prague became "one great poster."[52] As the invaders occupied the country, Alexander Dubček and other leading Czechoslovak officials were taken to Moscow, where they were forced to sign a secret agreement saying that they would reestablish state control over the media, ban unruly civic organizations and remove the most radical reformers from positions of power. Czechoslovakia, the Soviets insisted, must be "normalized" as quickly as possible.[53]

Initially, it was not clear what returning to "normality" would entail. Alexander Dubček remained in his post for more than half a year after his return from Moscow, and he and his allies hoped that by cooperating with the Soviets some part of the reform program could be salvaged. Gradually, it became clear that this would not happen. Seeing this, on January 16, 1969, a young university student named Jan Palach lit himself on fire in the center of Prague, hoping to "wake up the people of this land" and demanding the return of a free media. His death evoked tremendous grief but failed to spark further protest, but instead serving as a symbolic end to the reform movement of the Prague Spring.[54]

The New Normal

In April 1969, Gustav Husák replaced Alexander Dubček as the head of the Czechoslovak Communist Party; he would remain in power until 1987. Although known as a moderate, Husák would be responsible for reversing most of the 1968 reforms, a process called normalization. Under Husák, reformers would be expelled from the KSČ, and anyone who refused to acknowledge the necessity of the Soviet invasion would face consequences. Just over 20 percent of Communist party members in Czechoslovakia were removed from party membership rolls after going through a formal screening process. Tens of thousands lost their jobs, particularly among the ranks of the intelligentsia. Almost 2,000 reporters were removed from the Journalists' Union, and over half of the editors of the Communist party's own daily newspaper *Rudé právo* (Red Right) were fired. Writers, professors and journalists were forced to find work as boiler stokers or construction workers. Some, like the writer Milan Kundera, chose to emigrate; the borders were unofficially open for months after the August invasion, allowing those who wished to leave to do so.[55]

Husák emphasized the need for calm and order in the aftermath of the failed reform movement, noting that "[A] normal person wants to live quietly and this party wants to safeguard the quiet life."[56] Under his rule, the Czechoslovak state encouraged its citizens to prioritize their private lives over politics. Those who renounced public engagement and protest could take refuge in a quiet life. After a few years, many who had been removed from their jobs in the name of normalization were allowed to return if they agreed to repudiate their former beliefs and censor their political opinions. Most found this an acceptable bargain.

Hungary's János Kádár also encouraged his people to focus on their domestic lives. In the immediate aftermath of the failed revolution of 1956, tens of thousands were imprisoned for their participation and 200,000 fled the country. By the early 1960s, however, Kádár's government turned to carrots over sticks. Like Husák, Kádár emphasized quiet political conformity over ideological enthusiasm, famously declaring in 1961, "Those who are not against us are with us." In the same speech, he stressed that the point of socialism was not ideology but to give people a better quality of life.[57]

Historians have often asserted that after 1968 most East Europeans lost faith in socialism as an ideology. The invasion of Czechoslovakia suggested to many that the region's socialist governments would never be able to embrace meaningful reform. According to this interpretation, leaders like Husák and Kádár realized that their citizens would never enthusiastically embrace socialism again, if they ever had. In order to maintain the Communist monopoly on power in the absence of popular support, they encouraged political apathy. In exchange for quiet obedience, they would promise their citizens a better quality of life, providing them with perks like a lot of free time, the chance to acquire a weekend cottage or a good supply of cheap beer. As the historian Timothy Garton Ash put it,

> In effect, the regime said to the people: Forget 1968. Forget your democratic traditions. Forget that you were once citizens with rights and duties. Forget politics. In return, we will give you a comfortable, safe

> life … We won't ask you to believe in us or our fatuous ideology… All
> we ask is that you will outwardly and publicly conform.[58]

Cowed by their failure to achieve significant reform and win more personal
freedoms, most people would take the deal. Life in Eastern Europe after 1968
would be characterized by this materialist social contract, where socialist dictatorships offered a better quality of life in exchange for political disengagement.

The idea of a consumerist bargain between the rulers and the ruled in
Eastern Europe after 1968 has been useful in thinking about the ways everyday life changed in the region during the 1970s and 1980s (a topic that will
be explored in Chapter 5). However, some historians have argued that this
concept does not encompass the full range of ways East Europeans related to
socialism after 1968. While some East Europeans may have seen socialism as
no more than a set of empty slogans to be mouthed in exchange for being left
alone, for others it continued to have meaning. Historians still actively debate
the extent to which socialism had resonance with ordinary East Europeans.
Recent research suggests that young people in different countries continued to
be influenced by socialist values, although not always in the ways their leaders
might have wished.

In Hungary, young socialist activists drew inspiration from feeling like a
part of a global socialist movement well into the 1970s. Hungarian officials promoted socialist internationalism among young people, hoping that they would
find their own revolutionary consciousness by becoming familiar with the an-
ti-imperialist struggles of Cuba and Vietnam. To their chagrin, some young
Hungarians were inspired by revolutionary struggles in the decolonizing world
to criticize their own leaders. During the Vietnam War, for example, some
Hungarians reproached Soviet and Hungarian leaders for not doing more to
help the North Vietnamese win the war. As with the radical Polish students of
1968, some Hungarian young people were influenced by Maoism, which was
not acceptable to Hungarian party leadership after the disintegration of Si-
no-Soviet relations in the early 1960s. In 1968, a group of Hungarian students
were arrested, charged and jailed for supposedly creating a Maoist conspiracy
to overthrow the Hungarian government.[59]

After 1970, many Hungarians were fascinated with Salvador Allende's Chile.
Hungary was experimenting with its own turn toward a more market-based
socialist economy after 1968 (the NEM) and Hungarians eagerly watched
Allende's socialist experiment. The idea that a socialist government could be
democratically elected within a multiparty system particularly drew the attention of some young people. Historians James Mark and Péter Apor argue that
the example of Chile allowed Hungarians to hope for a more democratic form
of socialism in their own country well after the crushing of the Prague Spring.
As Ferenc Redő, a Communist youth activist at Eötvös Lóránd University in
Budapest remembered,

That a majority of the Chilean people had voted for change … and had been able to create their socialist change of direction in this way—that was very inspiring, and it brought out the fight in me, that perhaps you could do something successfully 'by the rules.'

After Allende was overthrown in a coup in 1973, this optimism among Hungarians about democratic socialist reform also gradually faded.[60]

There were many ways of relating to socialist values, some of which were not overtly political. In Romania after 1969, young people from the Communist Pioneer organization (which enrolled approximately 70 percent of all schoolchildren) gladly signed up for summer excursions to carry out research projects in the countryside called the "Expeditions of the Daring" (*Expedițiile Cutezătorii*). Rather than being vehicles to expose students to propaganda, these expeditions created spaces for their participants to learn how to be good socialist citizens through their involvement in group activities. Those chosen spent three weeks traveling on foot, living in tents and carrying out ethnographical, geological or historical research, such as documenting folk costumes in remote villages, recording peasant songs or digging for archeological finds. Students learned to work as a group, to think in terms of the scientific method, to respect their national heritage and to be self-reliant. One man, Cristi, who went on an expedition as at the age of 13 in 1973, later recalled, "It is great that you can simultaneously play and accomplish relatively serious tasks. For us, this felt very much like child's play."[61]

According to historian Diana Georgescu, activities like the Expeditions of the Daring show people, both students and their adult teachers, interacting with the socialist state in ways that were anything but apathetic. In these expeditions, learning to become a socialist citizen was not a process of simply learning to obey. Rather, it involved becoming self-reliant and resourceful, using one's education in the service of a greater good. This seemingly nonpolitical example shows the ways in which even after 1968 East Europeans lived within a culture that was imbued with socialist values and ideals. This culture was not simply promulgated from above but formed through the actions of ordinary people living their everyday lives.[62]

To Know Everything

During the Secret Speech, Nikita Khrushchev excoriated Stalin for creating a reign of terror and revealed that the Soviet security service had abused its power to create false confessions for supposed spies and traitors. As they moved away from Stalinism in the 1950s, the governments of Eastern Europe were also pushed to admit the crimes committed by their own security forces. They did this to varying extents. In Hungary, show trial victim László Rajk was formally rehabilitated in 1955 and allowed a public reburial in October 1956, on what would become the eve of the Hungarian Revolution. In Czechoslovakia, the Novotný regime began to quietly release some of the survivors of show trials from jail in the mid-1950s. It admitted that those executed in the Slánský trial were innocent only in 1963, but still kept the details of the trial from the public. The larger story did not emerge until the Prague Spring.

While show trials and mass arrests of political foes ended with Stalinism, se-cret police forces continued to exist everywhere in Eastern Europe. Their role remained the same: to investigate anti-state activity, both at home and abroad. Most countries have police forces dedicated to state security. What made the security services in Eastern Europe different from their Western counterparts was their large size and their broad powers to conduct surveillance. In their quest to eliminate opposition to Communist rule, East European security forces routinely spied on their own citizens, usually without their knowledge. According to the Romanian scholar Florian Banu, the goal of the Romanian security service, the Securitate, was "to know EVERYTHING, to control EVERYTHING and to repress EVERY anticommunist gesture, idea, or atti-tude."[63] While no security service could ever reach such a goal, agents did their best to gather as much information as they could on any potential opposition. Given their mission, security agents tended to prioritize certain groups for ob-servation, including government and party elites, the military, those in regular contact with Westerners and those who worked in sensitive industries.

The secret police forces of Warsaw Pact countries used similar methods to monitor their populations. Agents observed and recorded the movements of those suspected of oppositional activity; they tapped their phones and read their mail. As the technology became more available in the 1970s, they installed listening devices in suspect's homes. Perhaps most crucially, they supervised networks of civilian informers tasked with providing information on specific individuals, groups or workplaces. While they operated in similar ways, sur-veillance was more pronounced in some countries than in others. Romania and East Germany had much larger operations than their allies. The East German Ministry of State Security, colloquially known as the Stasi, employed one per-son for every 180 East German citizens in 1989, in addition to having a net-work of over 173,000 civilian informers.[64] The Romanian Securitate had less than half as many employees than the Stasi but claimed more than two and a half times as many informers, albeit for a larger population.[65] In contrast, Czechoslovak state security employed one person per every 867 inhabitants, while the ratio in Poland was one employee for every 1,574 people.

While ordinary East Europeans certainly knew about the possibility of sur-veillance, most of them did not live in constant fear of being watched. Even in heavily surveilled East Germany, many of those who were monitored were not aware of it at the time. As one East German remembered, "Of course, we all knew it [about the existence of informers], we all knew it. But each one of us thought that he wasn't personally affected."[66] Those who were openly involved in oppositional activity tended to be more aware that that they were being observed. Dr. Ulrich Woronowicz, an East German Lutheran pastor, visited political prisoners, counseled people who wanted to leave East Germany and sometimes gave sermons critical of the regime. Woronowicz noticed that Stasi agents sometimes followed him, knew from the clicking sounds that his phone was tapped and assumed that informers reported on his activities, although he did not know that there were actually 27 of them.[67]

Rather than a constant state of being, fear of regime surveillance tended to be situational. Most East Europeans rarely, if ever, came into contact with a secret police agent, but doing so was frightening. Agents generally approached people because they wanted information. For example, an East German doctor interviewed in 2006 recalled being asked by a Stasi agent for information about a colleague who had applied to emigrate (the East German state routinely tried to prevent highly educated professionals like doctors from leaving the country). She complied, afraid that if she did not it might cost her husband his job or prevent her child from receiving an advanced education.[68] Knowing that she had been approached by the Stasi for information, this woman might then be more circumspect in dealing with her coworkers, wondering if they might ever be asked to give information on her.

People agreed to become regular informers for a variety of reasons, including patriotism, financial gain or even a desire for adventure. Some were coerced with compromising material about marital affairs or illegal activities. Others, like doctor, feared the consequences of noncompliance. Some agreed to inform but then tried to only reveal banalities in their reports. All wound up becoming part of a repressive state that could not have existed without their cooperation. This often created an emotional toll on the informers, whatever their initial attitude toward their task.[69]

One Romanian informer, who went under the code name Beniamin, remembered that his handler had initially approached him by praising his abilities, emphasizing how Beniamin would be helping his country, as well as himself, with his cooperation. In their relationship, the handler was generally friendly and helpful, although Beniamin also said that he seemed to be incredibly knowledgeable about Beniamin's life, which was a way of showing the Securitate's power. When he spoke about the experience decades later, Beniamin recalled being wracked with guilt and anxiety over his work with the secret police, despite his positive relationship with his handler. "I was doing something horrible and I knew it," he said. "This was not something I could be proud of." While these feelings could have been something Beniamin applied to his experience retroactively after the fall of Communism, they reflect the emotional strain of being forced to keep his cooperation a secret, deceiving even his closest friends and family about his activities.[70]

In the wake of de-Stalinization, the Communist regimes of Eastern Europe renounced their former practices of terror. Yet, the secret police continued to exist and even grew significantly in size in some countries during the years after 1968. The tactics the security forces used, however, changed. In the place of mass arrests, the security forces turned their energy to monitoring the population, creating more extensive and capable systems of surveillance than had existed in the first decades of socialism. These systems of surveillance, which were a distinctive characteristic of life in Communist Eastern Europe, were embedded within the contours of everyday life. Some, perhaps even a majority of people, were able to spend most of their lives without coming into open contact with this system, while, unbeknownst to them, some of their neighbors were compelled to participate in it. After the fall of Communism in 1989, many were shocked when the true scale of the surveillance that surrounded them was revealed. Yet this was the price, as Czechoslovak leader Gustav Husák said, for safeguarding the quiet life that so many longed to lead.

Notes

1 Marie-Janine Calic, *The Great Cauldron: A History of Southeastern Europe*, trans. Elizabeth Janik (Cambridge, MA: Harvard University Press, 2019), 482.
2 Kathleen E. Smith, *Moscow 1956: The Silenced Spring* (Cambridge, MA: Harvard University Press, 2017), 43–54.
3 Susanne Schattenberg, "'Democracy or Despotism'? How the Secret Speech Was Translated Into Everyday Life," in *The Dilemmas of De-Stalinization: Negotiating Cultural and Social Change in the Khrushchev Era*, ed. Polly Jones (London: Routledge, 2007), 65.
4 Paweł Machcewicz, *Rebellious Satellite: Poland 1956*, trans. Maya Latynski (Washington, DC: Woodrow Wilson Center Press, 2009), 36.
5 Anthony Kemp-Welch, *Poland Under Communism: A Cold War History* (Cambridge: Cambridge University Press, 2008), 62–68.
6 Machcewicz, *Rebellious Satellite*, 18–33.
7 Machcewicz, *Rebellious Satellite*, 67.
8 Machcewicz, *Rebellious Satellite*, 91–109.
9 Machcewicz, *Rebellious Satellite*, 110–121
10 Machcewicz, *Rebellious Satellite*, 203.
11 Machcewicz, *Rebellious Satellite*, 234–251.
12 Charles Gati, *Failed Illusions: Moscow, Washington, Budapest and the 1956 Hungarian Revolt* (Washington, DC: Woodrow Wilson Center Press, 2006), 51–67.
13 Gati, *Failed Illusions*, 61.
14 Paul Lendvai, *One Day that Shook the Communist World: The 1956 Hungarian Uprising and its Legacy*, trans. Ann Major (Princeton, NJ: Princeton University Press, 2008), 9.
15 Gati, *Failed Illusions*, 145.
16 Gati, *Failed Illusions*, 155–160.
17 Lendvai, *One Day that Shook the Communist World*, 67
18 Csaba Békés, Malcolm Byrne and János Rainer, "From Demonstrations to Revolution: Introduction," in *The 1956 Hungarian Revolution: A History in Documents*, ed. Csaba Békés, Malcolm Byrne and János Rainer (Budapest: Central European University Press, 2002), 203–208; Gati, *Failed Illusions*, 171–176.
19 Gati, *Failed Illusions*, 186–194 (quote on p.141).
20 Lendvai, *One Day that Shook the Communist World*, 151; Gati, *Failed Illusions*, 194–203.
21 Calic, *The Great Cauldron*, 479.

22 Elidor Mëhilli, *From Stalin to Mao: Albania and the Socialist World* (Ithaca, NY: Cornell University Press, 2017), 191–197.

23 Miranda Vickers, *The Albanians: A Modern History* (London: I.B. Taurus, 1999), 184.

24 Mëhilli, *From Stalin to Mao*, 194.

25 Calic, *The Great Cauldron*, 483.

26 Vladimir Tismaneanu, *Stalinism for All Seasons: A Political History of Romanian Communism* (Berkeley: University of California Press, 2003), 143–148; Calic, *The Great Cauldron*, 482.

27 Katherine Verdery, *National Ideology Under Socialism: Identity and Cultural Politics in Ceaușescu's Romania* (Berkeley: University of California Press, 1991), 118.

28 Calic, *The Great Cauldron*, 475.

29 Milan Kundera, *The Joke* (New York: Harper, 1993)

30 Kevin McDermott, *Communist Czechoslovakia, 1945–1989: A Political and Social History* (New York: Palgrave Macmillan, 2015), 117.

31 H. Gordon Skilling, *Czechoslovakia's Interrupted Revolution* (Princeton, NJ: Princeton University Press, 1976), 57–62, 412–450.

32 Skilling, *Czechoslovakia's Interrupted Revolution*, 183–224.

33 Paulina Bren, *The Greengrocer and His TV: The Culture of Communism after the 1968 Prague Spring* (Ithaca, NY: Cornell University Press, 2010), 25.

34 Kieran Williams, *The Prague Spring and Its Aftermath: Czechoslovak Politics, 1968–1970* (Cambridge: Cambridge University Press, 1997), 71–72.

35 Bren, *The Greengrocer and His TV*, 25.

36 The text of the Action Program is available online in English at https://archive.org/details/actionprogrammeo08komu. See also Skilling, *Czechoslovakia's Interrupted Revolution*, 217–221.

37 Williams, *The Prague Spring and Its Aftermath*, 73.

38 "Student Demonstrations in Poland and Their Consequences," Report by New Zealand Embassy Bonn, 8 April 1968, FCO 028/000294, National Archives, UK, cited in Melissa Feinberg, "1968 and its Aftermath in Eastern Europe," from Cold War Eastern Europe online document collection, http://www.coldwareasterneurope.com/Overview/Subject-Essays/Melissa-Feinberg (accessed March 7, 2021).

39 Malgorzata Fidelis, "Tensions of Transnationalism: Youth Rebellion, State Backlash and 1968 in Poland," *American Historical Review* 125, no. 4 (2020): 1237–1245.

40 Marcin Zaremba, "1968 in Poland: The Rebellion on the Other Side of the Looking Glass," *American Historical Review* 123, no. 3 (2018): 771.

41 Robert Gildea, James Mark and Annette Warring eds., *Europe's 1968: Voices of Revolt* (Oxford: Oxford University Press, 2013), 53.

42 Gildea, Mark and Warring, *Europe's 1968*, 52–58.

43 Dariusz Stola, "The Hate Campaign of March 1968: How Did It Become Anti-Jewish?" *Polin* 21 (2009): 17.

44 Stola, "The Hate Campaign of March 1968," 20–32.

45 Jerzy Eisner, "1968: Jews, Antisemitism, Emigration," *Polin* 21 (2009): 56.

46 "Political and Civil Unrest: Three Student Views," (Derek Tonkin to R.O. Miles). 28 March 1968, FCO 28/294, National Archives, UK, cited in Feinberg, "1968 and its Aftermath."

47 These were the revisionists Marxists around the journal *Praxis*. Madigan Fichter, "Yugoslav Protest: Student Rebellion in Belgrade, Zagreb, and Sarajevo in 1968," *Slavic Review* 75, no. 1 (2016): 99–121.

48 The text is available in Jaromír Navrátil, et al. eds., *The Prague Spring 1968: A National Security Archives Document Reader* (Budapest: Central European University Press, 1998), 177–181 (quote on p. 180).

49 "Letter from Warsaw Meeting of Communist Parties Criticizing Czechoslovak Reforms," *International Legal Materials* 7, no. 6 (November 1968): 1265–1267.

50 Williams, *The Prague Spring and Its Aftermath*, 121–125; Kevin McDermott, *Communist Czechoslovakia, 1945–1989* (London: Palgrave Macmillan, 2015), 143–145.
51 The text is available online through the Internet Modern History Sourcebook at https://sourcebooks.fordham.edu/mod/1968brezhnev.asp
52 Skilling, *Czechoslovakia's Interrupted Revolution*, 776–777.
53 Skilling, *Czechoslovakia's Interrupted Revolution*, 800; Williams, *The Prague Spring and Its Aftermath*, 137–143.
54 Bren, *The Greengrocer and His TV*, 33.
55 McDermott, *Communist Czechoslovakia*, 156–159; Bren, *The Greengrocer and His TV*, 180.
56 Bren, *The Greengrocer and His TV*, 89.
57 Roger Gough, *A Good Comrade: János Kádár, Communism and Hungary* (New York: I.B. Taurus, 2006), 135.
58 Timothy Garton Ash, *The Uses of Adversity: Essays on the Fate of Central Europe* (New York: Random House, 1989), 62.
59 James Mark and Péter Apor, "Socialism Goes Global: De-colonization and the Making of a New Culture of Internationalism in Socialist Hungary, 1956–1989," *Journal of Modern History* 87, no. 4 (2015): 852–891.
60 Mark and Apor, "Socialism Goes Global," 878–885 (quote on p. 884).
61 Diana Georgescu, "Small Comrades as Historians and Ethnographers: Performativity, Agency and the Socialist Pedagogy of Citizenship in Ceauşescu's Romania," *Slavic Review* 78, no. 1 (2019): 74–102, quote on 85.
62 Georgescu, "Small Comrades," 100–102.
63 Katherine Verdery, *Secrets and Truths: Ethnography in the Archive of Romania's Secret Police* (Budapest: Central European University Press, 2014), 21.
64 Jens Gieseke, *The History of the Stasi: East Germany's Secret Police, 1945–1990*, trans. David Burnett (New York: Berghahn Books, 2014), 49; 81.
65 Verdery, *Secrets and Truths*, 207–208.
66 Gary Bruce, *The Firm: The Inside Story of the Stasi* (Oxford: Oxford University Press, 2010), 147–150.
67 Bruce, *The Firm*, 132, 150.
68 Bruce, *The Firm*, 148.
69 Gieseke, *History of the Stasi*, 89–92.
70 Verdery, *Secrets and Truths*, 174–179.

5

CONSUMERISM AND ITS CONSEQUENCES DURING LATE SOCIALISM

In the years after 1968, the governments of Eastern Europe achieved a new stability. With the exception of Poland, there was little overt unrest during the 1970s and 1980s. In these decades, known as the period of late socialism, most people preferred to work within the system rather than against it. Instead of advocating political change, they concentrated on achieving a better quality of life and a higher standard of living. This domestic stability was mirrored in the international arena. The 1970s was a period of détente, or improved relations between East and West, that lowered Cold War tensions throughout the region.

If the 1950s were a time of scarcity in Eastern Europe, the 1970s were a moment of relative abundance. While periodic shortages remained a fact of life, in the 1970s Eastern Europe began to develop a consumer society. More and more East Europeans were able to purchase things for pleasure rather than necessity. Consumer durables like televisions, refrigerators and washing machines became widely available. New prosperity also brought more time for leisure: tourism became a mass phenomenon and weekend houses sprouted up in the countryside. Most East Europeans enthusiastically embraced these new possibilities. Their rising expectations put pressure on their governments, which were now forced to see their citizens as consumers, not merely as producers.

This new good life of late socialism was not available to everyone. Privileges like travel visas, access to new apartments or good jobs were typically withheld from those who openly criticized their governments. Public critics of Eastern Europe's socialist governments, known as dissidents, faced repression and even jail for their outspokenness. For these critics, the era's new consumerism was no more than a bribe to their countrymen, offering them a better standard of living in return for supporting governments they did not believe in. Ironically, some Communists also criticized the consumer society of late

DOI: 10.4324/9780813348186-6

socialism, charging that it encouraged selfish materialism at the expense of the greater good. Most East Europeans, however, did not share these qualms. They celebrated their entry into consumer society as the just reward for their work building socialism.

Fridge Socialism

On December 12, 1970, Polish leader Władisław Gomułka announced that the price of bread, meat and dairy products would go up by 25 percent. These measures were intended to alleviate some of the strain on an ailing Polish economy. Poles were incensed at the prospect of such a large increase in the price of food, particularly as it was just two weeks before Christmas, a time devoted to feasting. Workers in several cities along the Baltic coast went on strike in protest. When the police tried to disperse the strikers, the situation quickly escalated into violence. After the Communist party headquarters in Gdánsk was burned by rioters, Gomułka sent over 20,000 troops and 500 tanks to pacify the city. Forty-one people were killed and over one thousand were wounded before order was restored. The use of Polish soldiers against striking workers shocked even members of the Polish Central Committee. Gomułka, who was in ill health, was forced to step down. He was replaced with Edward Gierek, who eventually agreed to freeze food prices for the next two years.[1]

By 1970, Polish workers had come to see cheap food and housing, along with free education and free health care, as basic rights. When their government tried to raise the price of food, they saw this as an infringement on their rights as socialist citizens. Realizing that providing a basic standard of living was the basis of its legitimacy, the Polish government was forced to acquiesce to their expectations. Unless he wanted to face more angry masses on the streets, Edward Gierek had to find some way to maintain food prices, even though this was not economically feasible. For the short term, Poland would have no choice but to bridge the gap with loans from Western banks. The availability of such loans to East European governments was a side effect of détente, which opened a variety of contacts between Eastern Europe and the West in the 1970s.

The idea that life's material necessities had the status of rights was entrenched throughout Eastern Europe by the 1970s. Socialist governments heavily subsidized the cost of basic necessities, including food, housing, utilities and healthcare. As the percentage of their income needed for these things decreased, East Europeans found themselves with more money to spend on their own desires. During the period of late socialism, shopping and spending took on a larger role in people's lives, giving rise to a more consumer-oriented society. While it shared some characteristics with the West, this socialist consumer society had its own distinct features. While the amount of goods in stores had increased immensely since the lean 1950s, socialist consumer society still operated within an economy of shortage. Perhaps even more crucially, it existed within a culture shaped by socialist values, where the pursuit of personal gain was sometimes viewed with suspicion.

After 1968, many East Europeans chose to concentrate their spending on the purchase of consumer durables like televisions, refrigerators and washing machines, as was also typical in the West. These kinds of goods were much more expensive in Eastern Europe, however. Governments kept prices high in order to recoup some of what they spent subsidizing necessities and as a means of managing inflation. In 1966, a typical Yugoslav worker only needed to work 16 hours to pay the monthly rent on an average apartment, but a television, still rare in 1966, cost the equivalent of 629 hours of work.[2] As most purchases were for cash only (credit cards did not exist in the socialist world), potential buyers might spend years saving for one significant item.

East Europeans were willing to sacrifice for the pleasure of watching television or the convenience of being able to wash clothes at home. In 1960, only a small minority of East Europeans owned major appliances. By the mid-1980s, most households across the region had refrigerators and washing machines. While the standard of living improved everywhere in the 1970s, the Balkans lagged behind the northern tier of countries in the distribution of consumer durables across the population. In Poland, Czechoslovakia and Hungary, practically every family had a television by the mid-1980s; in the Balkans, there were 80–90 televisions per every 100 households, with the exception of Albania, which had only about half as many televisions as its neighbors.[3]

As society became more focused on acquiring the material accoutrements of modern life, owning the latest appliance increasingly became a sign of social status. For many, the ultimate dream was to buy a car. In the 1950s, East

FIGURE 5.1   A worker inspecting refrigerators at a factory in Bucharest (Romania), 1957. © Photo by Keystone/Getty Images.

European governments tended to discourage private car ownership in favor of public transportation or car sharing. By 1970, they had changed their attitude. Increasing the supply of private cars enhanced social stability. The goal of purchasing a car encouraged people to hold on to their jobs, work hard and save their money, which increased productivity and removed excess cash from circulation, leaving less money to chase scarce goods. Like other nonessential items, even the cheapest cars were very expensive in Eastern Europe. In 1972, the Polish Fiat 126p, manufactured in Poland under a license purchased from the Italian Fiat company, was created to be an affordable car. Yet it cost more than twice the annual salary of an average Polish worker. Despite the high prices, private car ownership in Eastern Europe grew dramatically in the decades after 1968. In Hungary in 1957, there were only 3,980 privately owned cars. In 1980, there were approximately one million.[4] In Poland, the number of private cars doubled during the years between 1975 and 1979.[5]

Demand for cars always exceeded their supply. East Europeans who wanted to buy a car often found that there were no cars ready for them to buy. To obtain one, they needed to put their names on a waiting list; it might take years before their names were called. The German Democratic Republic (GDR or East Germany) had the highest rate of private car ownership in the Soviet bloc at 200 cars per every 1,000 people in 1985. Paradoxically, East Germans also had the longest waiting times for new car purchases. Most East Germans who ordered Trabants—the cheapest East German-made car, with a two-stroke engine and a plastic body—in 1976 only received their cars in 1989. The Wartburg, East Germany's version of a luxury car, was even harder to acquire. The wait to receive a car in East Germany was so long that it encouraged everyone to get in the queue to buy a car, whether they needed one or not. Given the extended waits, a black market in places on the waiting list developed, with the price increasing as the delivery date for the car neared. A spot at the top of the waiting list could command a price higher than that of the car itself.[6]

Because cars were expensive and hard to get, they became a prominent indicator of social status. In Poland in 1977, only 2 percent of the families of unskilled workers owned a car, while 20 percent of the families of white-collar workers did. The kind of car one owned was also a sign of wealth and educational level. East Europeans were generally only able to purchase cars made within the Soviet bloc, but there were distinctions even among locally produced cars. In Poland, educated professionals were more likely to drive the more expensive Polski Fiat 125p, while manual workers or farmers bought the smaller, more cheaply made 126p.[7] When an East German doctor wrote to the Ministry of Trade and Procurement in 1977 to ask to be allowed to purchase a new car without a wait (he argued that he needed the car to make house calls to underserved patients in the countryside), he didn't ask for just any car but specifically requested a Wartburg, which was three times more expensive than the more plebian Trabant. He claimed he needed the Wartburg because it was more dependable, but he also emphasized that he had previously owned one, marking him as a person of means and respectability.[8]

Another way to obtain a car without a wait was to purchase it through a hard currency store. All the countries in the Soviet bloc had their own version of these stores, which were initially established to serve the needs of Western tourists. They were eventually opened to local residents who had earned foreign currency while working abroad or had received cash gifts from friends or relatives in the West. Because Soviet bloc countries used nonconvertible currencies that were worthless in Western markets, socialist governments needed to have access to hard currency if they wanted to import goods from the West. The most effective way of gaining hard currency was by producing goods for export, but hard currency stores were a useful means of adding to a state's hard currency reserves. In 1987, the Czechoslovak chain of hard currency stores, called Tuzex, brought in a profit of $230 million, more than the state's leading Western export: glass.[9]

Hard currency stores like Tuzex created a two-tiered system of consumption where those who had access to hard currency were heavily favored. Some found this institutionalized inequality ideologically problematic, particularly because it rewarded people for having contacts with the capitalist West rather than for being good socialist citizens. A taxi driver who picked up tourists from the airport and accepted tips in hard currency was more advantaged than an upper-level state official who had no opportunity to travel. One Czechoslovak commented on the irony of this situation in a letter to the humor magazine *Dikobraz*, saying,

> As long as you're filling out information in your personnel file, you'd better not show off about your relatives in a capitalist country because you're probably a scoundrel as well. But if, however, they send you hard currency once in a while, then you're a beloved citizen of our state and we have special stores for you.[10]

In the end, the need for hard currency overrode ideological concerns, making these kinds of stores a permanent part of the consumer landscape of late socialism.

With enough Western currency, the privileged customers to these stores could purchase scarce goods like cars and receive them immediately, although in Bulgaria even those who bought cars in hard currency might still have to wait months or years for them. Even apartments or land for vacation houses could be bought in this way. In addition to scarce domestically produced goods, Eastern Europe's hard currency stores sold Western-made goods that were not legally available anywhere else in the country. Buyers at Czechoslovak Tuzex stores could purchase a wide range of Western products, from Sony videotape recorders to Levi's jeans, Johnnie Walker whiskey, German chocolates and French perfume. Other countries offered a similar array of products. Even Western cars, from Chrysler to Volkswagen and Mercedes, could be bought in some of Eastern Europe's hard currency stores.[11]

Hard currency stores served a pragmatic need: they helped governments get the dollars or West German marks they needed for foreign trade. They were not meant to advocate Western-style consumption. Bulgarian officials even refused to stock items they deemed particularly representative of Western decadence, interestingly mostly goods directed at women, including nail polish, lipstick, birth control pills, condoms and playing cards.[12] Yet the existence and exclusivity of these stores served to solidify popular perceptions of the West as a consumer utopia and helped make Western goods into objects of consumer fantasy. Because they were hard to get, objects from the West took on a cult status for some East Europeans. A Czech man who was a child in the 1970s recalled decades later that

> the West was an exotic place to me. Yeah, literally. We collected Donald Duck chewing wrappers, candy wrappers, stuff like that, when we could get them. They were just nice to look at and collecting was a cool hobby—having something from outside the Iron Curtain.[13]

Bulgarian women interviewed by American anthropologist Kristen Ghodsee between 1999 and 2006 illustrated the allure of Western goods by talking about their experiences with cosmetics and perfumes. In late socialist Bulgaria, there were only two main cosmetics companies, Alen Mak and Aroma. Although a few beauty products were imported from elsewhere in the Soviet bloc, most of the skin creams and makeup available to Bulgarian women were made by one of these companies, making the scope of consumer choice very limited. Most annoyingly for Bulgarian women, the Bulgarian products were all scented with rose oil. Bulgarian rose oil was a prominent Bulgarian export product, used in perfumes throughout the world. What might have been a selling point elsewhere, however, was precisely what young Bulgarian women wanted to avoid. They longed for something different, without the telltale aroma of rose. Those who could hunted down the small amount of French perfume that was imported into Bulgaria via barter agreements and for sale in only a few locations in central Sofia, the capital. For these women, the smell of Christian Dior represented the material distillation of prestige.[14]

Residents of nonaligned Yugoslavia had a somewhat different consumer experience than citizens of other East European countries. Their freedom to travel allowed them to purchase Western goods easily, limited only by the purchasing power of the Yugoslav dinars. At the same time, the decentralization of the Yugoslav economy meant that Yugoslav firms, unlike most of their socialist counterparts, had a much greater incentive to make a profit. To do so, Yugoslav firms needed to create markets for their products and be more responsive to the needs of consumers. The result was that Yugoslavs were able to satisfy most of their consumer desires at home. A 1968 article in the Croatian women's magazine *Svijet* informed shoppers considering a trip to the Italian city of Trieste that they would find little there they could not get in Ljubljana (the major Yugoslav city closest to Trieste). Ljubljana's retailers, the author claimed, had made "much more serious efforts in the battle for the market and for consumers" and could reasonably compete with the Italians.[15]

As people throughout Eastern Europe became increasingly focused on shopping and spending, some worried that this emphasis on consumption was taking them away from proper socialist values. One Yugoslav writer, Pero Zlatar, compared Yugoslavia in 1970 to a decadent Babylon, which left people "surrounded by paradoxes." What is an average Yugoslav woman's main preoccupation today, he asked? "The living standard, above all."[16] In neighboring Hungary, where the New Economic Mechanism (NEM) had also created a significant rise in overall consumption, critics of the new consumerism disparaged what they called "fridge socialism," referring to lifestyles enabled by the growing availability of consumer durables. As one asked,

> Does the car, the little weekend house, and the attainment of individual goods in general slide us into imitating the bourgeois way of life? Does it escalate the spread of individualism? According to my personal experiences so far, it does![17]

Critics like these worried that their fellow citizens were becoming lazy, entitled and too focused on personal pleasure rather than the good of the larger community. Too much materialism, they felt, was antithetical to socialism. Yet they also believed that socialism should improve people's lives. Where did rational improvement end and bourgeois decadence begin? Such qualms were common among socialist elites, but rarely expressed by others. Most East Europeans took pleasure in their better standard of living and looked forward to their next purchase.

Grilling Bacon over a Bonfire

In 1971, a Czechoslovak woman who had emigrated to the United States after the Soviet invasion of 1968 decided to return to her home country. As she got off the plane at Prague's Ruzyně airport, a reporter asked her what had motivated her to come back. Her response was surprising. Life, she claimed, was more fun in socialist Czechoslovakia. In the West, everything was expensive.

> If you were to wish to live the same way as you lived in Czechoslovakia, she said. "going to the theater, the cinema, out to dinner once in a while, or to some club—clubs, by the way, are a very expensive affair—then you'll practically have to hand over your whole salary.

In Prague, she could swim at a public pool for practically nothing, whereas in the United States, she hadn't encountered any public pools at all.[18] The Czechoslovak media published this woman's story precisely because it contradicted common stereotypes. In the West, life in socialist Eastern Europe was usually portrayed as dull, gray and boring. Yet by the 1970s, most East Europeans had access to an array of new leisure opportunities.

During the late socialist period, a majority of East Europeans had a five-day work week, giving them more free time than previous generations. Václav Janoščík, a Czech lawyer, recalled having plenty of leisure time as a young man in the 1970s. He said,

> I'd go to work in the morning and after work I'd spend the afternoons on my hobbies, whether it was volleyball or climbing. But quite often we'd just go to a pub because this was where we met. And then we'd stretch the evening out by meeting friends or listening to music.[19]

Janoščík's carefree experience was most typical of the young and unmarried. Married people with children spent much of their "free" time on housework and childcare. This was particularly true of women, who typically had greater domestic burdens than their husbands. Others devoted their off hours to a second job, in order to save for a car or apartment, or just to make ends meet.

The pub figured prominently in Janoščík's recollection of how he spent his free time. He was not alone: drinking and smoking were common leisure activities all over the region. Public drinking was often coded as a masculine activity, especially in rural areas where women did not feel comfortable in male-dominated taverns. One resident of a Romanian village remembered that on paydays men flocked to the local tavern. It was so crowded, he said, that "people could not find seats inside and were forced to take their bottle and drink outside, on the side of the road or in the courtyard."[20] Smoking was also a common means of taking a break throughout the day. Along with the USSR and China, Eastern Europe had some of the highest rates of smoking in the world in the 1980s. More than 40 percent of Hungarians and Poles smoked, compared with 25 percent of Americans.[21] In Bulgaria, which grew most of the tobacco consumed in the Soviet bloc, half of the adult population identified as smokers and many of them smoked more than 20 cigarettes per day. The Bulgarian state cigarette manufacturer, Bulgartabak, catered to the tastes of newly prosperous East Europeans, creating distinct brands with different profiles for different countries and market segments and helping to identify smoking with leisure.[22]

In the name of public enlightenment, socialist governments subsidized culture, just as they subsidized the price of bread and milk. Books, newspapers and magazines were cheap, as were tickets to plays, concerts or the movies. Those in charge of cultural policy particularly wanted to make so-called high culture accessible to working people, so state budgets tended to privilege genres like ballet, classical music or the literary classics. During late socialism, these more traditional cultural forms increasingly competed with new genres like pop and rock music. While initially reluctant, state-controlled media gradually accepted popular music. Singers like the Czech Karel Gott became pop idols; Gott sold millions of records around the world and enjoyed the support of the Czechoslovak normalization government. In late 1960s and 1970s Hungary, rock bands like Kex, Omega and Illés played to large audiences at the Ifipark (Youth Park) entertainment complex in Budapest, although authorities sometimes censored the lyrics and initially refused to allow bands to perform in jeans.[23] In 1980s Poland, clubs associated with the Communist youth league and official houses of culture often hosted rock bands and popular groups were played on state-run radio and television.[24]

During late socialism, East Europeans became avid television viewers. According to research conducted by Czechoslovak sociologists in the early 1980s, watching television was the country's most popular cultural activity, followed by listening to the radio, reading and going to the movies.[25] Just like in the West, East European families gathered around their television sets most evenings to watch the latest programs. As in other realms of culture, state broadcasters promoted programming with a pedagogical emphasis, such as news or telecasts of ballets or symphony concerts, but audiences tended to prefer pure entertainment, such as scripted serials, pop music programs or game shows.[26] The most popular programs had very large audiences. The Czechoslovak medical drama *A Hospital on the Edge of Town*, which aired in 1977, was seen by 88 percent of television viewers. It was equally popular throughout the Soviet bloc and even imported into West Germany.[27] The East German police drama *Polizeiruf 110* (the emergency telephone number for the police) was perhaps the most successful of all East European TV serials. It began broadcasting in 1971 and continued even after the demise of the East German state in 1991. It was still in production in 2021, 50 years after its debut.

Like radio, television crossed borders. National broadcasters imported a considerable amount of programming, some from within the Soviet bloc, but often from the West. In their living rooms, East Europeans could see West German crime dramas like *Tatort* (Crime scene) or American shows like *Columbo* or *Dallas*. Some could tune in directly to Western television stations. Most East Germans—outside of one area around the city of Dresden dubbed the "Valley of the Clueless"—could receive West German television. Some Yugoslavs, Hungarians and Czechoslovaks could access West German, Austrian or Italian stations, although the programs would not be in their native languages. Others watched foreign stations from within the socialist world: when Romanian leader Nicolae Ceauşescu cut Romanian television broadcasts to only a few hours a day in the 1980s, those in range watched Bulgarian, Hungarian or Yugoslav television.[28] This exposure to a diverse array of television programs, even when they were edited for local consumption, gave East Europeans new exposure to the world, at least as portrayed on the television screen.

East Europeans also began to see more of the world through their own eyes. During late socialism, tourism became a mass phenomenon. Many East Europeans had at least four weeks paid vacation each year and growing numbers spent at least part of that time away from home. A majority vacationed domestically, taking advantage of local mountains, lakes or beaches, often using holiday facilities owned by trade unions or workplaces. In Poland's Bieszczady mountains, located on the eastern edge of the Carpathians, hostels built in the 1960s for workers constructing dams and hydroelectric plants on the San river were transformed into vacation hotels owned by different factories and unions for the use of their workers. Guests could swim, sail, hike or simply sunbathe and take in the fresh mountain air. The Bieszczady region received over one million tourists a year by the early 1970s. Demand was such that the number of

FIGURE 5.2 An East German man sits in a Mueller roof tent mounted on top of a Trabant 601, ca. 1985. © Sueddeutsche Zeitung Photo/Alamy Stock Photo RMJYP4.

tourists outstripped the available infrastructure, sometimes leaving those who had not planned in advance without a place to stay or get a hot meal.[29]

Camping was a popular vacation option, particularly among car owners. In 1967, over one million East Germans stayed at official campsites (this number does not include so-called wild campers who simply pitched tents in convenient woods or meadows). Many campers did not head to nature to "rough it." Instead, they wanted comfortable vacations in homelike surroundings. East German camping enthusiasts tied camping with consumerism, purchasing special cooking gear, sleeping bags, air mattresses and even plastic tea sets to make their vacations more pleasant. The more well-off bought deluxe tents that had multiple rooms or camping trailers large enough to qualify as weekend homes; others built permanent cabins or bungalows at campsites. Since state resources were limited, repeat campers helped to modernize the favorite campsites by installing electric hookups, toilets and shower facilities.[30] In Hungary, workers from the Budapest Hosiery Factory took the lead in fixing up the factory's campsite at Lake Balaton, adding a solar shower, a cooking area and handball courts. One of the workers later recalled, "It was wonderful... We put up tents and took our grandchildren. I made masses of pancakes, we bathed [swam] in Lake Balaton, and we had a good laugh. We'd grill bacon over a bonfire every night."[31]

In the 1970s, some urban dwellers built more permanent holiday cottages in the countryside as a place to spend vacations and weekends (this was also a popular practice in the Soviet Union during this period). Yugoslav leader Josip Broz Tito complained in 1968 that rows of illegally constructed weekend cottages along the Adriatic shore in Montenegro obstructed the view of the sea. Nonetheless, the trend continued. By 1986 there were more than half a million weekend cottages dotting the Yugoslav landscape. In 1970s Czechoslovakia, entire cottage colonies blossomed in the countryside. About one-third of Prague residents owned a cottage, while even more had access to one owned by a relative or friend. On weekends, the entire city emptied out as everyone retreated to the countryside.[32]

These second homes were usually do-it-yourself projects that involved significant time and effort on the part of their owners. Some were simple structures, lacking running water or electricity, but others became quite elaborate. Like camping enthusiasts, dedicated cottage owners invested considerable time and money in making their cottages comfortable places for their families to gather. Some historians have argued that camping and cottaging were ways that people resisted the collectivist impulse of the state by insisting on building their own private spaces for leisure. Yet most enthusiasts saw their activities in nonpolitical terms. Nor did socialist governments crack down on these practices; the Czechoslovak government even tacitly encouraged the mania for cottages by publishing a magazine devoted to cottage life, including articles on how to build additions or reinforce roofs, games for children and tips on how to pack for a successful weekend.[33]

FIGURE 5.3 Sunbathers on the beach at Varna (Bulgaria), 1963. © Photo by Chris Ware/Keystone Features/Getty Images.

International vacations also became possible for greater numbers of people during late socialism. Poles and Hungarians were increasingly able to travel to the West in the 1970s and 1980s, while other East Europeans gained greater mobility throughout the Soviet bloc. In the 1970s, East Germans, Poles, Czechoslovaks and Hungarians traveled fairly freely between each other's countries.[34] Popular vacation destinations within the socialist world included Hungary's Lake Balaton and Bulgaria's Black Sea coast, dubbed the "Red Riviera." In 1972 alone 2.4 million Soviet bloc tourists visited Bulgaria. Bulgaria's seaside resorts offered a range of experiences, from workers' hostels to luxury hotels. In addition to sea and sand, visitors could enjoy camel rides, folk dance performances, bars, discos, casinos and curiosities like the pirate-ship restaurant located on a boat perched in the sands of the Sunny Beach resort, where servers dressed in pirate costume.[35]

As they observed phenomena like weekend cottage colonies and pirate-ship restaurants, some Communists worried that their fellow citizens were not making the most of their free time. A 1964 article in a Bulgarian tourism magazine attempted to illustrate ideologically acceptable leisure practices. The article contrasted two fictional characters, Ivan and Dimitŭr. On his day off, Ivan took his family hiking in the mountains, where they enjoyed the fresh air and exercise. This left them refreshed for the coming week ahead. In contrast, Dimitŭr lagged in bed smoking cigarettes until 10 a.m. He then let his wife clean the house, while he joined a group of male friends for card games and *rakia*, a kind of plum brandy. At work on Monday, Dimitŭr felt as if he had not had a rest at all and struggled to complete his tasks.[36] The message here was clear: good socialists spent their leisure time productively. They rested and exercised to maintain their health or read books and went to cultural events to improve their minds. Yet messages like these had little impact on people's actual habits. Whether or not Communist ideologues approved, East Europeans continued to spend their free time watching television, hanging out at the pub, working on their cottages, plotting their next big consumer purchase or just doing as they pleased.

Kid or Car?

In 1964, the Hungarian magazine *Élet és Irodalom* published an article by novelist Ambrus Bor that lamented the country's low birthrate. Hungarians, Bor claimed, had become too focused on their own individual happiness, which they defined in material terms. Young people were putting their standard of living above their social responsibility to have children. They asked themselves "kid or car?" (*kicsi vagy kocsi*), meaning should we have a baby or save up to buy a car?[37] The answer was frequently in favor of the car. Bor's concerns about the moral failings of socialism's new consumerist generation were echoed across the region. In 1972, Czechoslovak television reported that several dozen families had responded positively to an advertisement that offered parents a car in exchange for giving up a child. As a reporter commenting on this story explained, "for many people it is first important to obtain an apartment, to furnish it with the best possible comforts, to get a car, to build a country getaway, and only then to consider perhaps having a child." Shortly after this incident, Czechoslovak leader Gustav Husák reprimanded couples for "attach[ing] greater importance to a car than to a child."[38]

Like Bor and Husák, many East Europeans worried about population decline and feared their countries were facing a demographic crisis. The fertility rate had been in gradual decline across Eastern Europe for much of the 20th century, just as it had been in the West. By the mid-1960s, birthrates across the region threatened to fall below replacement levels. Hoping to increase the birthrate, Communist governments developed a variety of strategies to encourage families to have more children. These pronatalist policies heralded a conservative turn in gender politics across the region. Whereas in the Stalinist 1950s governments had focused on women as workers, in the late 1960s they began to address them primarily as mothers, promoting maternity as women's most significant contribution to society. Resző Nyers, a prominent Hungarian official, exemplified this trend when he remarked in a 1970 meeting of the

Politburo, "I think women should be entrusted with more of the upbringing of children. And of course, the management of the household ... I believe women are better at these struggles."[39]

State policies assumed that women would always be the primary caregivers in the family. Rather than finding ways to allow both men and women to combine work and parenthood, governments encouraged women to take time off from work to concentrate on raising their families. They instituted generous maternity leaves that allowed women—but not men—to stay at home with their children for years. In Czechoslovakia, state-funded maternity leave was increased in 1968 from 18 to 26 weeks, and mothers were offered an additional year of childcare leave (in 1969 extended to two years). Beginning in 1976, East Germany offered women 26 weeks of maternity leave for their first child and a full year for each additional child. Benefits were similar elsewhere around the region. While many women welcomed these policies, they had the effect of shifting the burden of childcare from the state to women, particularly when children were small. They reinforced the notion that childcare and domestic work were women's responsibility, rather than the responsibility of both parents.[40]

Governments created an array of economic incentives to encourage larger families. Unmarried people and married couples without children faced income tax penalties, while couples with children were offered interest-free loans to help buy or furnish a home. Married couples with children were more likely to receive state housing than single or childless adults, who might be forced to live with their own parents well into maturity. Governments also offered monthly allowances and/or cash bonuses for each child, generally paid directly to mothers. East Germany offered 1,000 Marks per baby. The Bulgarian government tried to encourage women to have more than one child by awarding mothers 20 Leva for their first child, 200 Leva for the second and 5,000 Leva for the third (the average monthly wage was 114 Leva). The amount reverted to 20 Leva after the third child because officials did not want to encourage Bulgaria's minority Roma or Muslim families, who had higher fertility rates than the rest of the population, to have more children. Their desire to increase birthrates extended only to the country's white, Christian population.[41] Such attitudes toward Roma fertility were widespread. Local officials in Czechoslovakia coerced Roma women to agree to sterilization, a practice that continued well after the end of the Communist regime.[42]

Before the turn to pronatalism, most East European women were able to terminate a pregnancy if they wished. Abortion was legalized throughout most of Eastern Europe in the mid-1950s, well before it was legal in the West, albeit with some exceptions. In Czechoslovakia, women who wanted to end a pregnancy had to apply to a committee composed of doctors and public officials. These committees granted abortions only for specific medical or socioeconomic reasons, such as the age of the woman, her health, the number of children she already had or her financial situation. Abortion was never legalized in Albania and became widely available in East Germany only in 1972. While most East European women had access to abortion, other forms of contraception were often hard to find. One exception was in East Germany, where oral contraceptives were widely available after 1965. This lack of reliable access to contraception meant that abortion was the de facto method of birth control for many East European women.[43]

Beginning in the mid-1960s, some East European governments restricted access to abortion in order to increase the birthrate. After 1973, Hungary only permitted women who were either unmarried, had least two children, were over 35, lived in poverty or without access to adequate housing, or faced serious medical complications to terminate a pregnancy. Those who met these criteria had to apply to a committee for permission to have the procedure. About 3500–3600 applications (7–9 percent of the total) were denied each year. Even women who were successful found the process humiliating.[44] Bulgaria banned abortions for childless women in 1967 and extended the ban to women with one child in 1973; even women who met these qualifications had to apply to a commission for permission. According to the Bulgarian government, these laws were in women's best interest. The preamble to the 1973 abortion law declared that motherhood was a woman's "basic biological and social function and is an essential precondition for her happiness and survival." The law merely allowed women to achieve their true destiny. Some Bulgarians did not appreciate this assistance. As one woman remembered, "Thus, the Party and the government intruded in our beds, meddling in our personal sexual life and controlling its most precious part."[45]

Romania had Eastern Europe's most coercive population policy. Romania's drive to increase the birthrate was linked to the Ceaușescu regime's turn to nationalism. The Romanian government framed population decline as a national failure and exhorted Romanian women to become mothers for the sake of the nation's survival. According to Ceaușescu, it was "the highest patriotic citizens' duty for each family is to have and raise children." He claimed it was "inconceivable to imagine a family without children" and declared that "the greatest honor and social role for women is to give birth, to give life and to raise children."[46]

Ceaușescu's government pursued population increase at all costs. In 1966, Romania outlawed abortion except in cases of rape and medical emergency or if the woman already had four children or was at least 45 years old. Contraception was not illegal, but most Romanians found it impossible to obtain except on the black market. Yet even when told it was their patriotic duty, many Romanians did not want large families, particularly after the mid-1980s, when Ceaușescu's economic policy caused massive shortages of food and fuel. Faced with no other means to control their family size, Romanian women turned to self-induced or back-alley abortions. Between 1965 and 1989, approximately

9,500 Romanian women died from complications from illegal abortions; most of those who died already had at least two children.[47]

One Romanian woman, E.M., recalled that she had her first illegal abortion in 1981, one year after she had married and had her first child. She paid someone about twice her monthly salary to inject her uterus with a solution of vinegar and water. "From then on until 1987," she said,

> I had abortions approximately twice per year, with the exception of the year in which I had my second child. I became pregnant easily. On the one hand, I loved my husband and didn't want to deprive him of the right to a normal intimate life. At the same time, the only method we used to avoid my getting pregnant was the calendar and we didn't manage that with much rigor.

E.M. induced most of her own abortions and was hospitalized three times with complications. After the last hospitalization, she was interrogated by the police and sentenced to six months imprisonment for terminating a pregnancy. As E.M.'s story suggests, radical interventions like Romania's ban on abortion were not very effective. The Romanian birthrate quickly shot up shortly after the ban was instituted in 1966, but then swiftly decreased as women found ways to circumvent it.[48] Even when their governments offered substantial financial incentives, most East European couples preferred to have no more than two children.

Pronatalist policies in Eastern Europe were designed to promote the traditional family, but they also improved the position of single mothers. Single motherhood and divorce became less stigmatized in the 1970s and 1980s, although divorce was much more common in East Germany, Hungary and Czechoslovakia than in Poland or the Balkan countries. East Germany had the fifth highest divorce rate in the world.[49] East German photographer Eva Mahn described how state supports enabled women to raise children on their own. "[M]arriage? No. Why would we?" she said. "There were crèches, when they were little, kindergarten, after-school clubs… Women worked, the children were looked after. OK, two [children] would have been too many, but one was easy. And we never thought we needed men." Most East German women did marry at some point in their lives, but they felt free to leave relationships and live independently. In 1984, women initiated 68 percent of all divorces in the GDR. By the late 1980s, East Germans increasingly accepted cohabitation as a valid alternative to marriage. As one man remarked of his children, "They've all got a partner or a boyfriend, but none of them are married. Well, that's not so important nowadays."[50] Bulgaria was more socially conservative than East Germany on issues like single motherhood, but even here the government's constant emphasis on the need to have children decreased the stigma of illegitimacy. In 1989, 12.4 percent of the children born in Bulgaria were born to unwed mothers.[51]

Heterosexuality was assumed to be the norm in late socialist Eastern Europe, even in liberal East Germany. Homosexual sex was decriminalized in the GDR, Czechoslovakia, Bulgaria and Hungary in the 1960s (it had been legal in Poland since the 1930s), but legalization did not bring acceptance or even safety to gay people. Even in countries where homosexual sex was not against the law, the police frequently monitored the activity of gay men and lesbians. Homosexual life was largely invisible in popular media or confined to negative stereotypes. Homophobia was rampant. A gay Hungarian man recalled feeling like there was no way to change this environment. He said, "We accepted that homosexuals were secondary citizens... Perhaps not everybody, but the great majority, including myself, believed that this was self-evident."[52] Living in a society that so heavily privileged the heterosexual family, many gays and lesbians married people of the opposite sex, whether to please family members, to conform to social expectations or simply to be able to get their own apartment. A Czech lesbian, Dana, remembered,

> I knew that I am into girls since I was about 17 or so [...] Still, I started to date men and even got married. I thought about it and then decided why not? [...] Two years after we got married we got divorced, but my parents were happy because I was divorced and not single.[53]

Although they faced significant challenges, homosexuals in Eastern Europe were able to create lives for themselves. Despite discrimination, Kamila had a fulfilling life as a lesbian in late socialist Czechoslovakia. On the one hand, Kamila was careful not to call attention to her sexuality, particularly at work. Knowing that Czechoslovaks believed that lesbians appeared masculine or "butch," she always wore fashionable clothes and in the early 1970s even entered a televised talent contest called "the Perfect Girl." "Anything with a stupid title like that was a perfect opportunity to disguise that I'm into girls," she explained. In the early 1980s, Kamila lived with a female partner and her partner's young son. Neighbors and family did not question their relationship, accepting the useful fiction that Kamila was just helping out her "friend," who was raising her son alone. Kamila's life required subterfuge, but she was nonetheless largely able to live it as she wished.[54] Kamila's experience cannot be generalized to all gay people in Eastern Europe, but it does show how at least some people were able to live outside the parameters of heteronormativity during the era of late socialism.

The Black Triangle

In 1964, the popular East German magazine *Urania* published a set of alarming photographs. Next to an image of factory chimneys surrounded by ominous clouds of smoke was a picture of a stand of dying trees. The caption proclaimed,

"2.5 million tons of sulfur escape every year from the chimneys in our Republic. Through the exposure to sulfurous gases, forests in the Ore Mountains will soon die." The author of the accompanying article, Rudi Wetzel, warned that rapid industrialization was having a deleterious effect on the natural environment, putting East Germany's trees at risk.[55]

The forests Wetzel spotlighted were in a region known as the Black Triangle, an area that encompassed parts of East Germany, Czechoslovakia and Poland. The Black Triangle region was rich in deposits of lignite (brown coal). This ready source of energy had made the area an industrial center even before World War II. After 1945, it became a focus of socialist industrialization efforts. By the 1970s, the Black Triangle was a major industrial region and home to dozens of power plants, chemical factories, fuel refineries and other elements of heavy industry. This also made it a major source of industrial pollution. Brown coal is a particularly dirty form of fuel. When burned, it releases large amounts of soot and ash, as well as sulfur and nitrogen dioxides. In the Black Triangle, these pollutants fell back to the earth as acid rain, which devastated the region's forests.

By the late 1980s, the Black Triangle was considered one of the most polluted areas in the world.[56] This environmental damage had a significant effect on human health. In Czechoslovakia's coal-producing region of northern Bohemia, life expectancy in the 1980s was three to five years less than in other parts of the country.[57] Recognizing the problem, the Czechoslovak government began an initiative to send schoolchildren on study trips to places with cleaner air for several weeks at a time and even instituted a monthly cash subsidy to all residents of the most polluted areas. Recipients sardonically referred to it as their "burial bonus."[58]

During the decades after 1945, many parts of the world experienced increased pollution due to industrialization. While Eastern Europe was not unique in this respect, the region's policies on environmental issues were constrained by the competing demands placed on the socialist system. Many East Europeans recognized industrial pollution as a significant problem, but governments found it difficult to balance their commitment to an improved standard of living with the need to protect the environment.[59] In 1960 the Czechoslovak government enacted a series of environmental regulations, noting that maintaining a healthy environment was a necessary component of creating a better standard of living. Local town councils were empowered to assess air and water pollution and to fine enterprises that violated government standards. But in practice economic growth often took precedence over the environment. A 1967 proposal to lessen Czechoslovakia's coal dependency by importing cleaner burning Soviet natural gas was defeated by opposition from powerful mining interests, who argued that the socialist system needed to protect their jobs. This tendency to placate the mining industry continued after the Soviet invasion of 1968, when government officials stressed the need to maintain calm by keeping the miners happy.[60]

In northern Bohemia, even many local residents were more concerned with economic growth than environmental damage. In a study conducted in the town of Most in 1966—a town whose historic center was destroyed so that workers could mine the rich vein of coal that lay beneath it—90 percent of survey respondents said they were aware of environmental problems in the region. Yet 80 percent also said that this environmental impact was secondary to the economic importance of the mines and local industry, and 65 percent said that good jobs were worth the environmental damage that industry caused. Similar sentiments came out in another survey conducted in the town of Neštěmice in 1971: a majority of respondents saw the local factory's status as a significant polluter as secondary to its economic importance.[61]

The situation was similar across the border in East Germany. In the late 1960s and the early 1970s, East Germany was at the forefront of environmental policy in Europe. The GDR established a Ministry of Environmental Protection and Water Management in 1971 and empowered it to set standards for regulating emissions and other forms of pollution. However, the fines that could be levied on polluting factories were small, while remedies to lower their environmental impact, such as filtration systems to cleanse the sulfur dioxide from the exhaust of brown coal burning factories, were incredibly expensive. East Germany did not have the resources to install pollution remediation systems in its factories while still maintaining its levels of production. The result was that most polluters simply paid the fines and continued to pollute.[62]

East Germany hoped to transition away from its reliance on polluting brown coal by importing petroleum from the Soviet Union. However, East Germany's energy imports never came close to meeting its domestic needs. The situation worsened in 1981, when the USSR cut its annual oil exports to East Germany from 19 million tons to 17 million tons. This meant that if East Germany wanted to continue meeting its citizens' consumer expectations, it would need to not only maintain but increase its use of brown coal. East German leaders decided to privilege consumerism. This came at a pronounced environmental cost: pollution in the GDR increased rapidly throughout the 1980s.[63]

Not wanting to admit the scope of the problem, in 1982 the East German government began to restrict the publication of information about the environment. Yet East Germans could not help but notice the degradation of the environment around them. In some areas, the smoke from the burning coal was so thick that residents could not open their windows or hang laundry outside to dry, lest it turn black from the soot in the air.[64] Some East Germans angrily voiced concerns about the poor quality of the air and water. In 1983, a member of the Suhl district council spoke with some residents about a plan to deal with air pollution by planting pollution-resistant trees to replace the ones that had died. "Suddenly," he wrote in a report to GDR leaders, "a mother of three children stood up, angry, and asked the members of the council, if they wanted to offer the children some smoke-resistant lungs."[65] For East Germans like this woman, their quality of life was increasingly tied to the quality of the air, water and landscape. East German leaders, however, continued to privilege consumerism and housing construction over environmental protection, maintaining that it was economic growth that would lead to a better overall standard of living.

The Plastic People of the Universe

In April 1975, Václav Havel decided to act. Havel was a playwright who had been a prominent member of the Czechoslovak Writers' Union during the Prague Spring. Under normalization, Havel was blacklisted. He lost his ability to publish and his plays were no longer performed domestically, although they were produced abroad. For a time, he took a job in a brewery to make ends meet. While trying without success to work on a new play that he knew would never be published or performed in his own country, he felt the "need to stir things up, to confront others for a change." Putting the play aside, he wrote a letter to Gustav Husák, the general secretary of the Czechoslovak Communist Party, describing the problems he believed normalization had created in Czechoslovakia. After sending the letter to Husák's office, he also gave copies to representatives of the Western media. Within months, a translated version had been published in the West, and the original text was broadcast over foreign radio stations to Czechoslovak listeners.[66]

In his letter, Havel argued that normalization had created a profound moral crisis in Czechoslovakia. Most people, Havel claimed, did not support the regime. Yet, fear and apathy drove them to keep their opinions to themselves. Those who did what their leaders required of them were allowed to live undisturbed and concentrate on their cars and their cottages, while those who resisted might find themselves cast out of their profession. Consumer society, Havel charged, was really a form of mass bribery that compelled people to betray their real selves. By putting its citizens in this intolerable situation, the Husák regime had raised the standard of living at the cost of basic human dignity. It reduced people to "obedient members of the consumer herd," leaving a country that was intellectually and culturally barren. Havel challenged Husák to stop "deepening the spiritual and moral crisis of our society, and ceaselessly degrading human dignity, for the puny sake of protecting your own power."[67]

With his letter to Husák, Václav Havel became a public opponent of the Czechoslovak government. In the West, he would be called a *dissident*. Dissidents were well-known East European or Soviet writers and intellectuals who openly spoke out against their governments. Their work was often translated and published in the West. Prominent East European dissidents included the Polish writer Adam Michnik, the Hungarian novelist György Konrád, and Doina Cornea, a Romanian professor of French literature. Dissidents might suffer for their outspokenness: Havel, for example, lived under constant secret police surveillance and went to prison twice. Yet the notoriety dissidents en-joyed could also protect them, at least somewhat. Havel was released from both his prison sentences early because of international pressure.

These well-known writers were only the most famous faces in a larger world of oppositional activity that existed throughout late socialist Eastern Europe. Much of this activity centered around avoiding the strictures of censorship. Writers who wanted to get around the censors turned to underground publish-ing, also known as *samizdat* from the Russian term for "self-published." Banned literature had circulated in typescript in Eastern Europe since the 1950s, but samizdat networks became more organized in the 1970s. Czech writer Ludvik Vaculík, like Havel banned from publishing via official channels after 1969, founded the first samizdat publishing house, *Edice Petlice* or Padlock Editions, in 1973. Padlock Editions published 367 titles during its lifetime, including novels, plays, poetry, essay collections and works of history or philosophy. Vac-ulík assembled a crew of typists who "printed" each work on typewriters using layers of thin airmail paper and carbon paper, which allowed them to type between 8 and 12 copies at a time. Most samizdat books or journals circulated in editions of only a few dozen copies, but each copy typically went through many readers, passed clandestinely from one person to another. Often each person only had a few days to read a text before it was due to be passed onto the next person in line.[68]

Polish samizdat operations became the most extensive in the region in the aftermath of a new set of strikes in 1976. The impetus for the 1976 strikes was the same as in 1970: strapped for cash, the Polish government tried to suddenly raise the price of many basic foodstuffs by more than 50 percent. Protests broke out at more than 130 factories across the country. Within a day, the govern-ment withdrew the plan. Although it gave in to their demands, the Gierek government brutally punished some of the strikers. Thousands were arrested and as many as 20,000 lost their jobs. This cruel treatment pushed some Polish opposition intellectuals to set up a group to assist the persecuted workers. It was called the Committee for the Defense of Workers, but is often referred to by its Polish acronym, KOR.[69]

KOR's founders were interested in fostering a new Polish civil society, meaning a sphere of associational life that existed outside the parameters of the state. While their initial activity focused on providing legal and economic as-sistance to workers affected by the strikes, their larger goal was to develop links between workers and intellectuals and to inspire the growth of civil society. KOR inspired the formation of other organizations, including groups dedi-cated to helping the persecuted, groups of worker-activists, discussion groups and so on, and played an influential role in developing the underground press in Poland.

KOR created a network of donors, including Polish emigres and local priests who collected contributions from their parishioners, and used some of the funds to subsidize underground publishing. While Vaculík's Padlock Editions relied on typewriters and carbon paper, the largest Polish samizdat operations had their own printing presses. Some underground periodicals sprang directly from KOR, such as the newspaper *Biuleytn Informacyjny* (Information Bulletin) and the journal *Głos* (Voice), and dozens more were founded in its wake. In 1977, *Robotnik* (The Worker) debuted as a four-page newsletter in a run of 400 copies. In a year, it had expanded to 12 pages with new issues every two weeks in runs of approximately 20,000. The Warsaw-based Independent Publishing House (NOWa) was also founded in 1977. Between 1977 and 1989, NOWa published 294 books and 144 periodicals, many in runs of several thousand copies. Yet, even though the Polish underground press dwarfed its Czechoslovak counterpart, it still only reached a tiny percentage of the Polish population. Most underground books and journals were read primarily by the intelligentsia. Even publications aimed at workers, like *Robotnik*, were typically only distributed around large factories.[70]

Shortly after the founding of KOR, a group of opposition intellectuals in Czechoslovakia also organized to help those who had run afoul of their government. They were inspired by the trial of people involved with Czechoslovakia's underground music scene. In the 1970s, the Czechoslovak government began requiring musicians to make compromises in order to maintain their professional status, such as cutting their hair or not wearing scruffy clothes onstage. Some bands were not willing make these concessions. They lost their professional status and state subsidies but continued to make music. These underground bands had a somewhat ambiguous status, not precisely tolerated, but not exactly forbidden either. When their concerts started to become magnets for youthful nonconformists, the police became a more aggressive presence: in 1974, they violently halted a performance by the band the Plastic People of the Universe. After a few years of harassing concert goers, the police decided to arrest underground musicians and concert organizers instead. Several raids were conducted in March 1976: 19 people were arrested and over 100 were interrogated. In the end, seven people went to trial: three in July and four in September. All were charged with creating a public disturbance. They had, said the prosecutor, promoted songs that were indecently vulgar, displayed "an offensive disregard of society" and "had a negative effect on the lifestyle of young people."[71]

Václav Havel attended the September trial, which became widely known as the trial of the Plastic People of the Universe, although only two of the defendants were actually associated with the band. In a samizdat essay he wrote about the experience, Havel portrayed the defendants as innocent young people who took "responsibility for their own truth and [were] willing to pay a high price for it." Their courage made him feel challenged to follow their example.[72] In the weeks after the trial, Havel would be instrumental in getting together a disparate group of opposition Czechoslovak intellectuals to sign a statement demanding their government live up to its own commitments to uphold human rights. The 241 initial signatories pledged to chronicle Czechoslovakia's human rights abuses and to hold their government accountable for them. They called their group Charter 77, after their initial statement, which they released on January 1, 1977.

The founders of Charter 77 were inspired by the Helsinki Accords of 1975. The Helsinki Accords were the result of the loosening of tensions between the Soviet bloc and the West. For decades after the end of World War II, the West refused to recognize the existence of East Germany, hoping that Germany would eventually be reunited as a single country allied to the West. West Germany had no formal relationship with East Germany and never recognized the validity of its eastern borders. The situation only changed in 1969 with the election of a new West German chancellor, Willy Brandt, who was determined to strengthen West Germany's relations with its eastern neighbors. As Brandt pursued his policy of reconciliation, Western countries finally began to establish relations with East Germany. In this new environment, the Soviets renewed their calls for a general treaty that would recognize the existence of East Germany and all of Europe's post-World War II borders. This was the impetus for what became the Helsinki Accords. In addition to ratifying Europe's existing borders, the signatories agreed to respect their citizens' fundamental human rights and freedoms and to create new mechanisms for economic, cultural and scientific cooperation. The pact was signed by almost all European nations (Albania was an exception), the United States and Canada.

When the Helsinki Accords were signed, many observers were skeptical of its human rights guarantees, seeing them as meaningless pledges that would quickly be forgotten. But groups like Charter 77 latched onto Helsinki as a means of calling their governments to task for not adhering to their own laws and ideals. Charter 77 would work for the next 12 years to document human rights abuses in Czechoslovakia. Helsinki inspired similar activism all over Eastern Europe. A US-based group, Helsinki Watch, worked with East European activists to document violations of the Helsinki Final Act and publicize them in the West. Helsinki Watch would eventually become part of Human Rights Watch, which today monitors human rights abuses all over the world.

With the exception of the Polish Solidarity movement (which will be covered in Chapter 6), only a tiny fraction of the East European population was involved in opposition activity. The consequences of such involvement were very real. Ludvik Vaculík, for example, suffered constant surveillance. Every room in his apartment was bugged by the secret police; for decades, he and his wife, Madla Vaculíková, could only communicate important information in writing, which they did on a chalkboard, to avoid leaving a trace that could be found later. So often did agents clandestinely search his apartment after he had left for the day that Vaculík took to blaming them for every item that was misplaced. He and his wife were constantly followed by agents and interrogated many times. One officer forced Vaculíková to accompany him on walks or to coffee to persuade her to either divorce her husband or inform on him; at other times, officers informed her of her husband's infidelities. After Vaculík signed Charter 77, nude pictures he had taken with a girlfriend were published in a major magazine. The treatment of Vaculík was extreme, yet every signatory of Charter 77 could expect some level of harassment, including interrogations, house searches and vilification in the press.[73]

In a 1978 essay, "The Power of the Powerless," Václav Havel suggested that fear of this kind of retaliation was what held socialist regimes together. Afraid of losing a job, the possibility of higher education or the opportunity for a seaside holiday in Bulgaria, most people made whatever compromises their government asked of them. Their actions, Havel suggested, were crucial in maintaining the existing structure of power. In this view, ordinary people were both the victims of an oppressive government and an integral part of the very system that oppressed them. As Havel put it, with their everyday actions, "individuals confirm the system, fulfill the system, make the system, *are* the system."[74]

To illustrate this idea, Havel used the example of a greengrocer who receives a poster proclaiming "Workers of the World, Unite!" to place in his shop window next to the onions and carrots. He complies without thinking too much about it. After all, the greengrocer reasons, "what's wrong with the workers of the world uniting?" This seemingly insignificant act, Havel argued, was a public manifestation of the greengrocer's fear and subservience. When he placed the sign in the window, the greengrocer repressed his true self and agreed to "live a lie" in order to protect his comfortable life. In order to regain his human dignity, Havel claimed, the greengrocer should defy his fear, refuse to display the sign and accept the consequences. If he did so, he would find something more satisfying than a new car: intellectual authenticity. If more people followed this example and learned to "live in truth" instead of living the lie, then, Havel suggested, they might be able to transform the system itself.[75]

"The Power of the Powerless" was one of the most influential pieces of writing to come out of Eastern Europe during the late socialist period. Its impact has extended from the time of its initial publication through the work of scholars today. From Havel's perspective, consumer society was a trap that enticed people into becoming part of the system. In offering the possibility of a comfortable life, it set them up to be ruled by their own fear. Looking at it from another angle, however, we could see a better standard of living as something that East Europeans actively demanded from their governments and zealously protected. When the Polish government immediately buckled to strikers' demands in 1976, it admitted that it needed the consent of the population in order to function. Havel asked East Europeans to set aside their fear in the name of intellectual freedom, but he did not consider that many might be more prepared to take to the streets in pursuit of a different set of goals, such as a higher standard of living.

Notes

1 Brian Porter-Szűcs, *Poland in the Modern World: Beyond Martyrdom* (West Sussex: Wiley Blackwell, 2014), 277–278.

2 Televisions would become more affordable with every year but would still remain more expensive than in the West. Patrick Hyder Patterson, *Bought and Sold: Loving and Losing the Good Life in Socialist Yugoslavia* (Ithaca, NY: Cornell University Press, 2011), 42–43.

3 Ivan T. Berend, *Central and Eastern Europe, 1944–1993: Detour from the Periphery to the Periphery* (Cambridge: Cambridge University Press, 1996), 219.

4 György Péteri, "Alternative Modernity? Everyday Practices of Elite Mobility in Communist Hungary, 1956–1980," in *The Socialist Car: Automobility in the Eastern Bloc*, ed. Lewis H. Siegelbaum (Ithaca, NY: Cornell University Press, 2011), 48.

5 Mariusz Jastrząb, "Cars as Favors in People's Poland," in Siegelbaum, *The Socialist Car*, 35–38.

6 Jonathan Zatlin, "The Vehicle of Desire: The Trabant, the Wartburg and the End of the GDR," *German History* 15, no. 3 (1997): 358–380.

7 Jastrząb, "Cars as Favors in People's Poland," 36.

8 Luminita Gatejel, "Appealing for a Car: Consumption Policies and Entitlement in the USSR, GDR and Romania, 1950s–1980s," *Slavic Review* 75, no. 1 (2016): 141–142.

9 Paulina Bren, "Tuzex and the Hustler: Living It Up in Czechoslovakia," in *Communism Unwrapped: Consumption in Cold War Eastern Europe*, ed. Paulina Bren and Mary Neuburger (Oxford: Oxford University Press, 2012), 34.

10 Bren, "Tuzex and the Hustler," 33.

11 Rossitza Guentcheva, "Mobile Objects: Corecom and the Selling of Western Goods in Socialist Bulgaria," *Études Balkaniques* 45, no. 1 (2009): 3–28; Bren, "Tuzex and the Hustler," 28.

12 Guentcheva, "Mobile Objects," 20.

13 Miroslav Vaněk and Pavel Mücke, *Velvet Revolutions: An Oral History of Czech Society* (Oxford: Oxford University Press, 2016), 74.

14 Kristen Ghodsee, "Potions, Lotions and Lipstick: The Gendered Consumption of Cosmetics and Perfumery in Socialist and Post-Socialist Bulgaria," *Women's Studies International Forum* 30 (2007): 26–39.

15 Patterson, *Bought and Sold*, 271.

16 Patterson, *Bought and Sold*, 270.

17 Tamas Dobos and Lena Pellandini-Simanyi, "Kids, Cars or Cashews? Debating and Remembering Consumption in Socialist Hungary," in Bren and Neuburger, *Communism Unwrapped*, 332.

18 Paulina Bren, "Mirror, Mirror on the Wall… Is the West the Fairest of them All? Czechoslovak Normalization and Its (Dis)contents," *Kritika* 9, no. 4 (2008): 844–845.

19 Vaněk and Mücke, *Velvet Revolutions*, 152.

20 Narcis Tulbure, "Drink, Leisure and the Second Economy in Socialist Romania," in *Pleasures in Socialism: Leisure and Luxury in the Eastern Bloc*, ed. David Crowley and Susan E. Reid (Evanston, IL: Northwestern University Press, 2010), 268.

21 Berend, *Central and Eastern Europe*, 203.

22 Mary C. Neuburger, *Balkan Smoke: Tobacco and the Making of Modern Bulgaria* (Ithaca, NY: Cornell University Press, 2013), 197.

23 Alexander Vari, "Nocturnal Entertainments, Five-Star Hotels and Youth Counterculture: Reinventing Budapest's Nightlife Under Socialism," in *Socialist Escapes: Breaking Away from Ideology and Everyday Routine in Eastern Europe, 1945–1989*, ed. Cathleen Giustino, Catherine J. Plum and Alexander Vari (New York: Berghahn Books, 2015), 198–199.

24 Raymond Patton, "The Communist Culture Industry: The Music Business in 1980s Poland," *Journal of Contemporary History* 47, no. 2 (2012): 427–449.

25 Jarmila Horna, "Work Time, Non-Work Time, and Leisure in Czechoslovakia during the 1970s and 1980s: A Survey of Czech and Slovak Sources," *East Central Europe* 16, no. 1–2 (1989): 89–105.

26 Anikó Imre, *TV Socialism* (Durham, NC: Duke University Press, 2016), 10–12.

27 Paulina Bren, *The Greengrocer and His TV: The Culture of Communism after the 1968 Prague Spring* (Ithaca, NY: Cornell University Press, 2010), 145.

28 Imre, *TV Socialism*, 14–15, 200–201.

29 Patrice M. Dabrowski, "Encountering Poland's 'Wild West': Tourism in the Bieszczady Mountains Under Socialism," in Giustino, Plum and Vari, *Socialist Escapes*, 75–97.

30 Scott Moranda, "Camping in East Germany: Making 'Rough' Nature More Comfortable," in Crowley and Reid, *Pleasures in Socialism*, 197–218.

31 Eszter Zsófia Toth, "'My Work, My Family and My Car': Women's Memories of Work, Consumerism, and Lesiure in Socialist Hungary," in *Gender Politics and Everyday Life in State Socialist Eastern and Central Europe*, ed. Jill Massino and Shana Penn (New York: Palgrave Macmillan, 2009), 42.

32 Karin Taylor, "My Own Vikendica: Holiday Cottages as Idyll and Investment," in *Yugoslavia's Sunny Side: A History of Tourism in Socialism (1950s–1980s)*, ed. Hannes Grandits and Karin Taylor (Budapest: CEU Press, 2010), 171–210; Paulina Bren, "Weekend Getaways: The Chata, the Tramp and the Politics of Private Life in Post-1968 Czechoslovakia," in *Socialist Spaces: Sites of Everyday Life in the Eastern Bloc*, ed. David Crowley and Susan E. Reid (Oxford: Berg, 2002), 123–140.

33 Bren, "Weekend Getaways," 124–126.

34 Mark Keck-Szajbel, "A Cultural Shift in the 1970s: 'Texas' Jeans, Taboos and Transnational Tourism," *East European Politics and Societies* 29, no. 1 (2015): 212–225.

35 Neuburger, *Balkan Smoke*, 180–182.

36 Neuburger, *Balkan Smoke*, 167–168.

37 Dombos and Pellandini-Simanyi, "Kids, Cars or Cashews?" 333–334.

38 Bren, "Mirror, Mirror," 848.

39 Éva Fodor, "Smiling Women and Fighting Men: The Gender of the Communist Subject in State Socialist Hungary," *Gender and Society* 16, no. 2 (2002): 257.

40 Barbara Havelková, "The Three Stages of Gender in Law," in *The Politics of Gender Culture Under State Socialism: An Expropriated Voice*, ed. Hana Havelková and Libora Oates-Indruchová (New York: Routledge, 2014), 42–48; Josie McLellan, *Love in the Time of Communism: Intimacy and Sexuality in the GDR* (Cambridge: Cambridge University Press, 2011), 64–76.

41 McLellan, *Love in the Time of Communism*, 65; Ulf Brunnbauer, "'The Most Natural Function of Women': Ambiguous Party Policies and Female Experiences in Socialist Bulgaria," in Massino and Penn, *Gender Politics*, 88.

42 Věra Sokolová, *Cultural Politics of Ethnicity: Discourses on Roma in Communist Czechoslovakia* (Stuttgart: Ibidem Verlag, 2008).

43 Havelkova, "Three Stages," 35–41, MacLellan, *Love in the Time of Communism*, 60–64.

44 Susan Gal, "Gender in the Post-Socialist Transition: The Abortion Debate in Hungary," *East European Politics and Societies* 8, no. 2 (1994), 264; Julia Szalai, "Abortion in Hungary," *Feminist Review* 29 (Summer 1988): 98–100.

45 Brunnbauer, "'The Most Natural Function of Women,'" 90–91.

46 Gail Kligman, *The Politics of Duplicity: Controlling Reproduction in Ceaușescu's Romania* (Berkeley: University of California Press, 1998), 71.

47 Kligman, *Politics of Duplicity*, 207–218.

48 Kligman, *Politics of Duplicity*, 52–59, 191–193.

49 Eurostat, "Marriage and Divorce Statistics," https://ec.europa.eu/eurostat/statis-ticsexplained/pdfscache/6790.pdf (accessed October 8, 2019); Paul Betts, *Within Walls: Private Life in the German Democratic Republic* (New York: Oxford University Press, 2010), 88.

50 McLellan, *Love in the Time of Communism*, 66–81.

51 Brunnbauer, "'The Most Natural Function of Women,'" 93.

52 Anita Kurimay and Judit Takács, "Emergence of the Hungarian Homosexual Movement in Late Refrigerator Socialism," *Sexualities* 20, no. 5–6 (2017): 585–603 (quote on p. 597); Lukasz Szulc, *Transnational Homosexuals in Communist Poland* (New York: Palgrave Macmillan, 2018), 97–100.

53 Věra Sokolová, "State Approaches to Homosexuality and Non-Heterosexual Lives in Czechoslovakia during State Socialism," in Havelková and Oates-Indruchová, *Politics of Gender Culture*, 91–94 (quote on p. 92).

54 Sokolová, "State Approaches to Homosexuality," 94–103 (quote on p. 94).

55 Michel Dupuy, "Justifying Air Pollution in the GDR," in *Ecologies of Socialisms: Germany, Nature, and the Left in History, Politics, and Culture*, ed. Sabine Mödersheim, Scott Moranda and Eli Rubin (Oxford: Peter Lang, 2019), 120–121.

56 Don Hinrechsen and Tamas Revesz, "On a Slow Trip Back from Hell," *International Wildlife* 28, no. 1 (1998): 36.

57 Eagle Glassheim, *Cleansing the Czechoslovak Borderlands: Migration, Environment and Health in the Former Sudetenland* (Pittsburgh, PA: University of Pittsburgh Press, 2016), 113.

58 Eagle Glassheim, "Building a Socialist Environment: Czechoslovak Environmental Policy from the 1960s to the 1980s," in *Nature and the Iron Curtain: Environmental Policy and Social Movements in Communist and Capitalist Countries*, ed. Astrid Mignon Kirchhof and John R. Mitchell (Pittsburgh, PA: University of Pittsburgh Press, 2019), 149.

59 Raymond Dominick, "Capitalism, Communism and Environmental Protection: Lessons from the German Experience," *Environmental History* 3, no. 3 (1998), 311–332.

60 Glassheim, "Building a Socialist Environment," 141–142; Glassheim, *Cleansing the Czechoslovak Borderlands*, 116–117.

61 Glassheim, "Building a Socialist Environment," 143.

62 Eli Rubin, "The Greens, the Left and the GDR: A Critical Reassessment," in Mödersheim, Moranda and Rubin, *Ecologies of Socialisms*, 191–193.

63 Rubin, "The Greens, the Left and the GDR," 193–194; Tobias Huff, "Environmental Policy in the GDR: Principles, Restrictions, Failure and Legacy," in Mödersheim, Moranda and Rubin, *Ecologies of Socialisms*, 79.

64 Julia E. Ault, "Protesting Pollution: Environmental Activism in East Germany and Poland, 1980–1990," in Kirchhof and Mitchell, eds., *Nature and the Iron Curtain*, 154.

65 Dupuy, "Justifying Air Pollution," 134.

66 Václav Havel, "It Always Makes Sense to Tell the Truth," in *Open Letters: Selected Writings, 1965–1990*, ed. and trans. Paul Wilson (New York: Vintage, 1992), 84–101.

67 Václav Havel, "Dear Dr. Husák," in *Open Letters*, 50–83 (quote on p. 83).

68 Jonathan Bolton, *Worlds of Dissent: Charter 77, The Plastic People of the University and Czech Culture under Communism* (Cambridge, MA: Harvard University Press, 2012), 93–109.

69 Barbara J. Falk, *The Dilemmas of Dissidence in East-Central Europe: Citizen Intellectuals and Philosopher Kings* (Budapest: Central European University Press, 2003), 34–35.

70 Gale Stokes, *When the Walls Came Tumbling Down: Collapse and Rebirth in Eastern Europe*, 2nd ed. (Oxford: Oxford University Press, 2010), 27–33; Brian Porter-Szűcs, *Poland in the Modern World: Beyond Martyrdom* (Hoboken, NJ: Wiley-Blackwell, 2014), 287–288; Falk, *Dilemmas of Dissidence*, 40–42.

71 H. Gordon Skilling, *Charter 77 and Human Rights in Czechoslovakia* (London: Allen and Unwin, 1984), 7–15; Bolton, *Worlds of Dissent*, 115–124.
72 Václav Havel, "The Trial," in *Open Letters*, 106.
73 Bolton, *Worlds of Dissent*, 179–180, 239–243.
74 Václav Havel, "The Power of the Powerless," in *Open Letters*, 136.
75 Havel, "The Power of the Powerless," 125–214 (quote on p. 133).

6

DECADE OF CRISIS

The economic prosperity Eastern Europe enjoyed during the 1970s was short-lived. Throughout the 1980s, East Europeans saw their purchasing power decline as their governments struggled to figure out ways to restore economic growth. In Poland, popular frustration with the state of the economy led almost a quarter of the population to support the efforts of worker activists to create an independent trade union called Solidarity. Afraid of the challenge to its power, the Polish government declared martial law. This may have helped consolidate its power, but it did not help reverse the country's economic decline.

Throughout the 1980s, East European leaders searched for solutions to the economic slowdown. A growing number of socialist economists became convinced that market-based reforms were the key to fixing Eastern Europe's economic problems. After 1985, the efforts of these reformers were bolstered by new leadership in the Soviet Union. Soviet premier Mikhail Gorbachev hoped that his policy of perestroika, or restructuring, would help the USSR overcome its own economic difficulties. Unlike his predecessors, however, Gorbachev did not think the Soviet Union should determine policy in Eastern Europe. Leaders in Bulgaria, Czechoslovakia, East Germany (the German Democratic Republic or GDR) and Romania resisted the push to reform.

In 1989, the path toward economic reforms led Poland and Hungary to adopt plans for multiparty elections, putting an end to the Communist monopoly on power. In the rest of Eastern Europe, pressure built for similar changes. During the last months of 1989, millions took to the streets, and the remaining Communist governments in the Soviet bloc suddenly collapsed. After more than four decades, the Communist era in Eastern Europe was over.

DOI: 10.4324/9780813348186-7

A Revolution of the Soul

It was July 1980 and Edward Gierek was in trouble. Since coming to power in 1970, his government had built its legitimacy on its ability to provide stable supplies of consumer goods at consistent prices. But the brief period of prosperity Poland enjoyed during the early 1970s depended on loans from Western banks. Gierek and his advisors hoped that this influx of Western cash would spur Polish exports. Yet they did not institute the larger economic reforms that would have been necessary to make Polish goods more competitive in international markets. As a result, Polish exports did not improve, while Poland's debt to Western banks rose from $1.2 billion in 1971 to $23.5 billion in 1980, by which time the country's annual debt service nearly equaled its hard currency earnings. The Gierek regime's failure to raise food prices in 1976 only exacerbated the situation. By 1979, Poland had entered its biggest economic crisis since World War II.[1]

To reckon with this situation, the Gierek government tried once again to raise the price of meat, announcing that the cost of some products would increase by 90–100 percent. As had been the case in 1970 and 1976, the news sparked protests and strikes throughout the country. At first, these strikes seemed similar to their predecessors. Workers demanded pay raises and a return to the old prices. In 1980, however, strikers benefitted from the underground infrastructure that developed after the 1976 protests. Opposition activists gathered information about strikes in different locations and published it in underground periodicals such as *Robotnik*. Their reports were also broadcast over the radio by the BBC, Voice of America and Radio Free Europe. Strikers became aware that they were not acting in isolation but were part of a movement that stretched across the entire country. Their demands expanded, with some calling for better working conditions, changes to management, improvements in health care and a reform of the existing trade unions, which they claimed largely served the needs of the state rather than the needs of their members.[2]

The 1980 strikes were influenced by events within the Catholic Church. In 1978, Cardinal Karol Wojtyła, the bishop of the Polish city of Kraków, was elected pope, taking the name John Paul II. In June 1979, he made a triumphant visit to his native country. Millions of people gathered to see him at each stop on his trip. In his sermons and other public statements, John Paul articulated a powerful vision of Polish nationhood that was tied to a Christian embrace of the dignity of the human person and the dignity of labor. According to Jan Kubik, a scholar who was present during John Paul's stop in Kraków, the Pope's visit showed Poles that "the national community could be defined outside the Communist state." Those who were there described it as a deeply emotional experience that brought Poles together as a nation and underscored the distance between the Polish nation and its rulers. Reflecting on what had occurred in the underground journal *Robotnik*, the writer Jan Lityński urged his fellow

Poles to stay true to the community they had just forged. "Each of us was given a chance," he said.

> And it depends on us whether we can create a community of conscious people, honorable and brave, believers and nonbelievers, people living in the truth … The building of unity as it is propagated by John Paul II, unity without hatred, unity toward freedom, is very difficult. But after these nine wonderful days it seems to be possible.[3]

The strikes of July and August 1980 continued in the vein of the pope's visit by bringing together workers and activists from different locations and encouraging them to think beyond their own immediate demands. The Polish government initially tried to deal with the strikes as it had done before, by offering targeted concessions to workers at individual factories. In August 1980, however, workers at the Gdánsk Shipyard, led by the worker-activist Lech Wałesa, decided to refuse a deal. Instead, they continued their strike in solidarity with workers at other enterprises. They created an Interfactory Strike Committee to coordinate activity among the strikers and came up with a list of 21 demands for workers across the nation. The strikers insisted not only on better material conditions (pay raises, better health care, pensions and day care for children) but also on the right to form independent trade unions, guarantees of the right to strike and mechanisms to include the people in discussions of economic reform. Within two weeks, the Polish government had agreed to their demands, and the independent trade union known as Solidarity was born.[4]

Solidarity quickly became a mass phenomenon in Poland. In addition to blue- and white-collar workers, farmers, students, writers, academics and others rushed to create their own independent unions. At its height in 1981, ten million people—over a quarter of the population—had joined Solidarity, and even more were involved in affiliate groups. While Solidarity was formally a trade union, many described it in broader terms as a social movement or a form of independent civil society. In the spring of 1981, the British scholar Timothy Garton Ash asked factory workers in Poznań about how their lives had changed in the months since Solidarity came into existence. Their answer was less about the concrete gains they had achieved than a fundamental change in the atmosphere. People, they said, felt energized and newly empowered to speak their minds. They avidly read Solidarity newsletters and the mainstream Polish press, which had begun to report much more openly about current events. One of the workers, "a small man with a pale face and a dirty black jacket," described what had happened as "a revolution of the soul," in which everyone's fundamental outlook on life had changed. His sentiments were echoed by a historian at Kraków University who told Garton Ash, "It's simply that everyone feels better. I can't be more concrete than that."[5]

FIGURE 6.1 Solidarity members at a demonstration in Warsaw, 1980. © Photo by Keystone/Getty Images.

Solidarity leaders were careful not to challenge the Communist party's monopoly on political power. Nonetheless, Poland's socialist leaders were worried by what they saw. From its inception, Solidarity's goals had stretched beyond workers' pay and the standard of living. As Solidarity's program of October 1981 noted, "What we had in mind were not only bread, butter and sausage, but also justice, democracy, truth, legality, human dignity, freedom of convictions and the repair of the republic."[6] By internally modeling pluralist, democratic procedures, Solidarity set itself up as an alternative to the authoritarian socialist state through the very fact of its existence.[7]

For over a year, Communist officials allowed Solidarity to exist even as they threw obstacles into its path—harassing its activists, holding up its formal registration as a legal organization or dithering over whether Poland's independent farmers could establish their own branch of the union, dubbed "Rural Solidarity." As it tried to overcome these setbacks, Solidarity was often forced to call brief strikes to force the regime to adhere to its promises. As this went on, some currents within the union grew more radical, arguing that Solidarity should take on the role of a political opposition. The program developed at Solidarity's first congress, held in September 1981, did not go this far, but it did strike a confrontational tone, saying that the union must "take every possible step, *ad hoc* or long term, to save the country from downfall" and declaring that "there is no other way to that goal than by reforming the state and the economy on the basis of democracy and universal public initiative."[8]

After many tense months, General Wojciech Jaruzelski, who had taken over as the Polish Communist Party's leader in October 1981, decided that the situation required an extraordinary solution. With Soviet approval, he declared a "state of war" and introduced martial law. As tanks rolled out onto the streets on the night of December 12, Solidarity leaders were rounded up and taken into custody, preventing the union from offering an organized response. "Poles could not have been more taken aback if the Martians had just landed," said one inhabitant of Warsaw.[9] Another Solidarity activist remembered, "Nobody imagined that this seemingly weak government would prove strong enough to turn the police ... or the army ... on us."[10] There were some isolated strikes in response to the imposition of martial law, but Jaruzelski's harsh policies soon quelled most overt opposition. Yet even after it was eventually disbanded, Solidarity did not die. Many of its activists continued their work underground. And, perhaps even more crucially, the hopes and expectations that Solidarity awakened in Poland's population remained, just under the surface.

Turnabout and Reform

The economic woes that plagued Poland in 1980–1981 were felt throughout the socialist world, as the good times of the early 1970s gave way to a period of prolonged economic slowdown. As in Poland, governments throughout Eastern Europe found it impossible to maintain economic growth while simultaneously meeting the ever-growing material expectations of their citizens. These problems were compounded by growing foreign debt, particularly in Hungary and Poland. There was no clear or easy set of solutions for this increasingly precarious situation. Some countries tried to resist the need for change and simply worked to keep the existing system going for as long as they could. Others were forced into more active reform efforts.

Bulgaria hoped to improve its economic position by increasing the use of technology and the development of its computer and electronics industry. Inspired by the model of Japan, Bulgaria began to build its computer industry in the mid-1960s with the explicit goal of cornering the Comecon (CMEA) market. By 1985, Bulgaria produced 45 percent of all electronics traded within the Soviet bloc, including everything from mainframes and industrial robots to memory storage devices and personal computers. Yet while Bulgarian electronics were primarily purchased by other socialist countries, the industry developed in a global context. Bulgarian engineers learned from innovations in the West and Japan, via professional exchanges, formal cooperation and licensing agreements, and even industrial espionage. Eager to find additional customers, Bulgaria avidly pursued markets outside of the socialist world, particularly in developing countries like India, although Bulgarian sales to the rest of the world remained small in comparison with its exports within the Soviet bloc.[11]

Bulgarian leader Todor Zhivkov hoped that technology would help the country break out of economic stagnation without substantively changing the existing system of central planning. Mainframe computers would objectively analyze reams of economic data to make the centrally planned economy function more efficiently. Robots and automation would lower production costs, increase productivity and fix problems with quality control and worker error. The rise of the personal computers in the 1980s promised to bring innovation into even the smallest enterprises. Beginning in the 1980s, Bulgaria invested heavily in the personal computer, believing that widespread use of the PC could revitalize the entire economy. "With the help of personal computers," a Bulgarian party document claimed, "it will become possible to solve economic and technical tasks through cheap technology at the workplace of specialists, the engineer, the economist, the doctor, the economic director or supervising worker."[12] Bulgaria was not ultimately successful in creating this utopian technological revolution, but its economy was more robust than many other East European countries in the 1980s.

Romanian leader Nicolae Ceaușescu took a different approach. Romania faced a crisis in the late 1970s when global oil prices skyrocketed, forcing the country to take out high interest Western loans to buy fuel. By 1981, the country's debt had ballooned to $10.4 billion, 28 percent of Romania's GDP. To alleviate this burden, Ceaușescu declared that Romania would pay off its debts by 1990. In order to make this happen, Romania decreased Western imports and ramped up exports, siphoning goods away from Romanian consumers. The resulting shortages exceeded even the worst days of Stalinism. Gasoline was rationed beginning in 1979, and basic foods, including bread, meat, milk, oil and sugar, were rationed starting in 1981. By the mid-1980s, shoppers hoping to purchase meat or eggs waited for hours in line and sometimes came away empty-handed. Fuel shortages decreased tram and bus service so much that some passengers resorted to hanging off the sides of packed tram cars, while those that could walked instead. After 1982, electricity was rationed throughout the country: in some cities, there was simply no power after 10 p.m. each night, plunging entire communities into darkness. Heat and hot water were in short supply; thermostats across the country were frequently set as low as 57 degrees Fahrenheit.[13]

The Ceaușescu regime failed to recognize the painful sacrifices it demanded of its citizens. Instead, the government told Romanians that austerity was their patriotic duty and suggested that rationing would encourage healthy eating habits. Nicolae Ceaușescu privately defended the need to direct the state's resources toward production rather than to consumers, remarking to a group of regional party secretaries, "It is not a tragedy to wear a sweater around the house." His comment, which implied that austerity measures were no more than a mild inconvenience, stood in stark contrast to the experiences of many Romanians. One Bucharest resident remembered a period in the mid-1980s when the temperature inside her family's apartment was only 35 degrees Fahrenheit, forcing them to burn wooden crates for warmth. "We all slept in one room," she said. "We slept next to the fire with coats on. I remember I had to study for exams and I couldn't because it was so cold in the living room." A woman named Florina encapsulated the experience of the gas and electricity shortages this way: "It was so cold and dark. That is a pain I will never forget and which seems to me the most terrible... the cold and the horror of darkness, yes, that was the worst."[14]

Unlike in Poland, Romanians did not take to the streets to demand their government improve their standard of living. Instead, most people concentrated on doing what they could to make the situation better for their families. In order to improve their access to food, many turned to the informal economy. One woman, Tatiana, had family who lived in a village where they made cheese, one of the many staple foods that was in short supply in the 1980s. Every few months, one of Tatiana's connections would bring her a big bag of the village's cheese. She had so much of it, she later recalled, that she was inspired to learn how to make pizza. In a similar fashion, a dentist, Domnica, got scarce foodstuffs from her patients. As she explained it,

> For me, food was not a problem ... I had patients who were in commerce, and so whatever I wanted they would bring to me. In addition, I had relatives in the countryside where I could go and buy a calf or a pig.

Domnica and Tatiana, like those around them, did not see these kinds of exchanges as immoral or criminal; they were simply coping strategies that everyone engaged in. Even Communist elites participated in this kind of illicit trade, sometimes using their connections to substantially enrich themselves. A resident of the city of Botoşani complained in an anonymous letter to Elena Ceauşescu (Nicolae's wife and a high-ranking Communist official) that the town's former mayor had used her office to run a black market business selling imported refrigerators and televisions.[15]

In 1980s Romania, the informal economy took on a special significance, since it was used by many people just to acquire basic foodstuffs. But it was not a uniquely Romanian phenomenon. As discussed in Chapter 3, this shadow economy existed everywhere in Eastern Europe. By the 1980s, it was entrenched in everyday life throughout the region. To socialist planners and economists, the informal economy was a problem and a solution at the same time. It helped make up for deficiencies in state-sponsored systems of production and distribution, allowing consumers to get what they needed or wanted and preventing unrest. Yet it also helped to cause those very deficiencies: every bag of cheese that Tatiana received from her family meant that less was available for those waiting in line at their local market. Government officials were often reluctant to attack the informal economy. This might be because, like the mayor of Botoşani, they were profiting from it themselves. Yet they also feared the disruption that a systematic crackdown would cause, since these informal networks had become so deeply intertwined with the functioning of the state-sponsored economy.

In Hungary, reform economists decided that one way of dealing with economic crisis was to bring the informal economy into the light, creating more opportunities for private businesses and entrepreneurial activity within the framework of the socialist system. Hungary had a long history with market-based economic reforms, going back to the New Economic Mechanism (NEM) of 1968. Yet this did not insulate Hungary from economic slowdown. Like Edward Gierek in Poland, Hungarian leaders took on debt in the 1970s in order to avoid austerity measures. As in Poland, the Hungarians erroneously believed they would be able to increase hard currency exports to pay off these loans. By 1980, Hungary was facing a debt crisis.[16] Hungarian reform economists became increasingly convinced that the system of state planning was fundamentally flawed. They believed Hungary would only have a healthy economy if its firms were internationally competitive. This could only happen, they claimed, if Hungary moved to a fully market-based system, beyond the limited market mechanisms of the NEM, where individual firms were required to post profits and were allowed to set their own prices. Hungarians, reform economists argued, needed to develop a spirit of entrepreneurship that would encourage innovation and competition.

While they used terms often associated with capitalism—like markets, competition and entrepreneurship—many of these reform economists did not want Hungary to become more capitalist.[17] What they proposed instead was market socialism, where markets took on many of the functions of central planning (such as setting prices and production figures), but the means of production remained in public hands. Hungarian economist Tibor Liska, for example, advocated what he called "socialist entrepreneurship." Instead of guaranteeing employment, Liska said, the state should provide citizens with the means to be entrepreneurs, giving them the opportunity, but also the responsibility, to forge their own path according to their own talents. Unlike under capitalism, these socialist entrepreneurs would be developing state resources, not their own. Those who built successful ventures might earn a good living during their lifetime, but they would not be able to pass their advantages on to their children. In this way, socialism would create a truly level playing field that would encourage innovation and creativity.[18] Many other Hungarian economists believed Liska's proposals were unworkable, but his ideas helped to shape debates among economists about the right path for Hungarian economic reform.[19]

The Kádár government agreed with Hungarian economists about the need for change, but it was divided on how much reform was necessary. A reform faction within the Hungarian Communist Party thought the country should commit to market socialism, while other leaders remained leery of fully turning the state sector over to the market.[20] There was more consensus on the need to encourage entrepreneurship, although the changes that were implemented did not adhere strictly to the ideas of Tibor Liska. In 1981, Hungary legalized new forms of small business, including small cooperatives and different forms of work partnerships, which institutionalized the work many people had been doing informally (and sometimes illegally) as second jobs by allowing them to use state-owned facilities or equipment in their off-hours for their own projects. Throughout the 1980s, the number of privately owned small businesses increased dramatically as Hungarians were encouraged to regularize informal second jobs into licensed businesses. These measures were quite popular. The economist Gábor Révész estimated that by the mid-1980s four million Hungarians were involved in some way with a small business, and this burgeoning private sector was responsible for a quarter of the country's GDP.[21]

In 1985, Hungarian party leaders scaled back market-based reforms and partially stepped away from the austerity measures they had introduced in the wake of the debt crisis. As a result, Hungary's debt increased and economic growth faltered. Upset by what they perceived as their government's inaction, a group of reform economists from Hungary's Financial Research Institute issued a controversial report in 1986 called "Turnabout and Reform." In this document, they charged that Hungary would never recover economically as long as the state continued to have a significant hand in the economy, calling for "comprehensive, radical, democratizing, decentralizing and deregulating market reforms." These changes would, the authors admitted, create unemployment and lower living standards. Yet, they claimed, this kind of pain was necessary for the country's overall economic health. Significantly, "Turnabout and Reform" linked economic deregulation with democratization, advocating greater freedom of the press, more freedom to form associations and even a reduction of the Communist party's role in political life. This opened up a new arena in Hungarian debates over the country's future. Would moving toward a market economy mean changing the foundations of the socialist state? Reformers within the Hungarian Communist Party hoped that this would be the case. They championed "Turnabout and Reform" as a blueprint toward Hungary's future.

Brotherhood and Unity

The economic crisis that hit Eastern Europe in the 1980s was particularly devastating to nonaligned Yugoslavia. During the years between 1965 and 1978, Yugoslavia had the most developed consumer society in the socialist world, and its citizens enjoyed a continual increase in their standard of living. This period of prosperity came to an abrupt end in 1979, as the world was shaken by a new oil crisis. Like many other countries in the region, Yugoslavia had financed its boom with foreign loans that it spent propping up inefficient industries. Unlike them, it did not have the benefits of intra-Comecon trade and was more tightly integrated into the global economy. Yugoslavia's credit dried up as exports plunged.

Ordinary Yugoslavs felt the effects of this crisis keenly. Personal incomes tanked, inflation soared into the triple digits and unemployment rose dramatically, particularly in the poorer areas of the country. The price of essential basics like food and electricity rose 60 percent every six months.[22] There were shortages of coffee, gasoline, and even sugar and cooking oil. Ahmed Lemeš, a retiree living in Bosnia's capital, Sarajevo, told a reporter in 1984 that he couldn't afford to stock up on provisions for the winter. "Right now, everything is so expensive," he said, "I'm waiting until the prices go down." But the situation only worsened with each succeeding year.[23]

One of the factors that hindered the ability of Yugoslav leaders to solve the economic crisis was the country's federal structure. Yugoslavia was composed of six republics—Bosnia-Herzegovina, Croatia, Macedonia, Montenegro, Serbia and Slovenia—and two autonomous provinces, Vojvodina and Kosovo, both located within Serbia. Throughout its existence, the Yugoslav Communist Party had emphasized "brotherhood and unity," bringing Yugoslavia's different peoples together in pursuit of a common good. Yet, with the exception

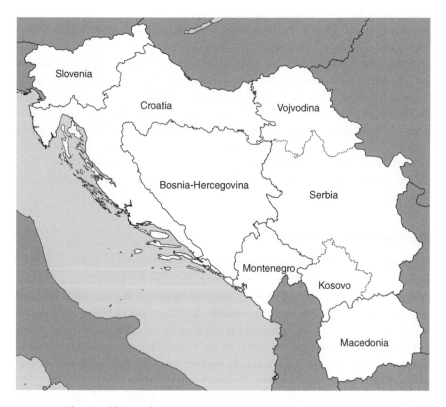

MAP 6.1 The republics and autonomous provinces of Yugoslavia.

of ethnically mixed Bosnia-Herzegovina, the population of each of the republics was dominated by one ethnic group. A new constitution, finalized in 1974, increased the autonomy of the republics and autonomous provinces, allowing each a veto on all federal legislation and a representative on the eight-person collective federal presidency. The leaders of each republic increasingly placed their own territory's interests above the needs of the country as a whole. This tendency increased after the death of Yugoslavia's leader Josip Broz Tito in 1980. Without Tito's strong centralizing hand, the republics frequently found themselves at an impasse, leaving the federal government unable to act.[24]

In the countries of the Soviet bloc, full employment was the norm. This was never the case in Yugoslavia. Unemployment was a long-standing problem in the country's less developed south and rates of joblessness increased substantially during the economic crisis of the 1980s. In 1980, the unemployment rate in Serbia proper swelled to 18.4 percent, while in Kosovo it was a staggering 39 percent. In contrast, the wealthier republics of Slovenia and Croatia had low unemployment rates. The problem was especially acute for young people; over half of the unemployed were under the age of 25.[25]

In March 1981, university students in the capital of Kosovo, Priština, rose in protest against inadequate living conditions and poor employment prospects. Demonstrations and riots quickly spread across the province. While it was located within the Serb republic, the Kosovar population was largely Albanian and Muslim.[26] Albanian protesters demanded that Kosovo be given the status of a republic, claiming that they faced discrimination at the hands of the Serb minority. The authorities reacted forcefully, shutting down the demonstrations and arresting many of the protesters. Federal officials claimed the riots were organized by Albanian counterrevolutionaries who wanted to separate from Yugoslavia and unite with Albania. Nothing was done to address the economic grievances that had sparked the protests.[27]

Following the March demonstrations, Kosovo's Serb minority felt under attack. The number of Serbs in Kosovo had been in decline for several decades, largely because of economic migration. Yet many claimed there was a concerted Albanian campaign to drive them out and "Albanianize" the region. The situation of the Kosovo Serbs became a flashpoint for some in greater Serbia. The region of Kosovo had a special place in Serb national mythology as the location of the 1389 battle that put Serbia under Ottoman rule. Some Serbs, therefore, interpreted Albanian calls for Kosovo to become its own republic as a challenge to their national patrimony. In 1986, Serb nationalist resentment burst into the open with the publication of a draft memorandum composed by some members of the Serbian Academy of Sciences (SANU) about the contemporary situation. The authors of this document emphasized Serb victimization and martyrdom, claiming that Serbs had frequently sacrificed themselves for the greater good of Yugoslavia. They alleged that Serb minorities throughout the other republics suffered systemic discrimination and claimed Serbs in Kosovo were victims of a "genocide." According to the memorandum, "No other Yugoslav nation has been so rudely denied its cultural and spiritual integrity as the Serbian people."[28]

The overt nationalism in the SANU memorandum was shocking to many Yugoslavs. Under Tito, the Yugoslav federal government had strongly discouraged the public expression of such ideas. It was roundly criticized throughout Yugoslavia, including in the Serb press. The president of the Serb republic, Ivan Stambolić, called it a "stab in the back of Yugoslavia, Serbia, socialism, self-management, equality, brotherhood and unity." Nonetheless, the memorandum brought widespread public attention to Serb nationalist grievances and gave them the imprimatur of an elite cultural institution. Serb journalist Milo Gligorijević remembered that everyone wanted to read the memorandum to see what all the fuss was about. The full text had not been published in the press, but illicit copies circulated. "In this way," Gligorijević wrote, "the Memorandum becomes a samizdat and achieves a mind-boggling number of copies and the largest circulation of any of the contentious books."[29]

As Yugoslavs debated the SANU memorandum, some Slovenian writers published a manifesto in which they complained Slovenia suffered from unequal treatment within the Yugoslav federation. Slovenia, they charged, was forced to financially subsidize the less developed south of the country, while the Slovenian language was not given the same status as Serbo-Croatian. In 1988, these views moved into the mainstream of Slovenian public life during the trial of three Slovenian journalists arrested for revealing military secrets. The journalists were convicted in a military tribunal that took place in the Serbo-Croatian language. Opposition Slovene intellectuals claimed the trial was a violation of the journalists' basic human rights. The incident galvanized Slovenia's burgeoning alternative scene. Half a million people, accounting for a quarter of the Slovenian population, signed a petition calling for the release of the journalists, and tens of thousands gathered to protest on their behalf. Even Slovenia's Communist leaders supported the protests, aligning themselves with the Slovenian opposition rather than the Yugoslav state.[30]

As the Slovenian Communists began to distance themselves from Yugoslavia, a Serb Communist official, Slobodan Milošević, decided to capitalize on Serb nationalist feeling to expand his own power. In 1987, Milošević was newly installed as the head of the Serbian Communist Party when he traveled to Kosovo to attend a rally of local Serbs. He arrived to see a boisterous crowd of thousands eager to complain about Kosovo's Albanian population. The crowd suddenly surged toward the building where the rally was to take place, and the police began to beat them back with their batons. Milošević stopped them and told the crowd, "No one should dare to beat you." He emphasized the importance of their presence in Kosovo and vowed that Serbia would help them to remain there. Milošević then began to receive delegates from the crowd, staying up all night to hear their stories. By the morning, the Kosovar Serbs embraced him as their champion. He was, some later said, the only politician "unashamed of his own people, unburdened with guilt, and ready to right some self-evident wrongs."[31]

After that night in Kosovo, a friend said that Milošević "was like a heated stove. He was full of emotions. He could not control his feelings. He could not calm down."[32] Back in Belgrade, Milošević embraced his role as a nationalist champion and began to use the power of the crowd to build his influence and eliminate those who opposed him. His primary weapons were an astute use of the media (much of which he controlled) and mass protest rallies. These rallies brought together tens of thousands of people to sing nationalist songs, wave flags and express their support of Milošević and his policies. Within a year, Milošević had extended his control over the Serb media and managed to purge his greatest opponents from within the Serb Communist Party, replacing them with his supporters. Having consolidated his hold on the Serb republic, Milošević used similar methods to put his supporters in power in Vojvodina, Montenegro and Kosovo. The Albanian population of Kosovo protested with mass demonstrations and strikes, but they were quelled by the military. In March 1989, the government of Kosovo agreed to constitutional changes that would put it back under Serbian authority. Albanian protests were crushed by the police, causing the deaths of 28 people.[33]

With Milošević, nationalism traveled from the margins of Yugoslav politics to the very center. Milošević's embrace of nationalism made him immensely popular in Serbia, even with many of the country's opposition intellectuals. Unlike the moribund federal government, Milošević seemed to be a man of action with strong plans for the future. Serbs argued that the changes spurred by Milošević represented an "anti-bureaucratic revolution" that removed ineffective leaders who had been incapable of solving Yugoslavia's many problems. They characterized the mass rallies that had sprung up all over Serbia in 1988 as an outpouring of popular democracy. Yet non-Serbs, like the Slovene sociologist Tomaž Mastnak, wondered if it might be better to call them "mass raids of the chauvinistic mob."[34] As the 1980s came to an end, these opposing interpretations of the same events showed the peoples of Yugoslavia moving farther and farther away from any common understanding of either their country's problems or the possible solutions.

While Yugoslavia was the most ethnically mixed country in Eastern Europe, it was not the only one to have difficulties integrating different communities into socialist society. Bulgaria was home to approximately 800,000 Turkish-speaking Muslims, as well as 200,000 Bulgarian-speaking Muslims (sometimes referred to as Pomaks). Together these groups composed about one-ninth of the total population. Bulgarian Communists made efforts to assimilate these communities, but many resisted. After several decades, Bulgarian Muslims retained some of their cultural distinctiveness, including modes of dress, given names and, in the case of the Turks, language. In 1984, spurred on by high birthrates among Muslims, a fear of Muslim ties to Turkey and global Islam, and the 1981 Albanian protests in nearby Kosovo, the Bulgarian government launched what it called the Rebirth Process, a radical program to forcibly assimilate the country's Turkish-speaking Muslim population (the Pomaks had already been subjected to similar programs in the 1960s and 1970s). Bulgaria's Turks, Communist leaders claimed, were not really Turks at all: they were Bulgarians who had been forcibly assimilated to Islam and Turkish culture when Bulgaria was part of the Ottoman Empire. Unlike Bulgaria's Christians, they had never fully escaped this oppressive Ottoman past. Now, they would be "reborn" and become fully Bulgarian at last.[35]

The Rebirth Process did not ban Islam, but it did try to remove all aspects of what Communists considered to be Turkish culture from Bulgarian life. The government banned the use of the Turkish language in public, closed down Turkish-language newspapers, prohibited traditional Muslim forms of dress—such as fezzes, headscarves and the baggy pants known as *shalvari* worn by women—and forbade other Muslim cultural practices, including circumcision and burial rites. Most dramatically, the state forced Bulgarian Muslims with Turco-Arabic names (such as Mustafa or Ali) to adopt new Slavic names (like Iordan or Kiril). Some Muslim villages were surrounded by police who forced the whole population to change their names on the spot. In other areas, officials went from house to house and confiscated identity documents, replacing them with new ones. Some had their names changed at work, or at school, or in government offices. Those who refused found that without a new identity card they could no longer access public services, including health care, or even be paid their salaries.[36]

Despite these draconian measures, the Bulgarian government found that Turkish practices were hard to eradicate. While they might cooperate when they felt it was necessary, Bulgarian Turks often continued to use their original names, speak Turkish and wear Muslim dress, both at home and in public. Some demonstrated publicly and were arrested, beaten and even killed by police. While Bulgarian leader Todor Zhivkov claimed the policy was a success in 1985, resistance continued and Bulgarian Turks arguably moved closer to a Turkish identity than before. In one incident, the world-champion weight lifter Naim Suleimanov defected during a competition in Australia in 1986 to protest being forced to adopt a Bulgarianized version of his name (Naum Shalamanov).[37] Things came to a head in May 1989, when Bulgarian Turks launched a series of demonstrations that spread all across the country. After brutally crushing their protests, Zhivkov pushed those Muslims who identified as Turkish to apply for exit visas and leave the country. Between June and August 1989, 350,000 Muslims fled Bulgaria for Turkey. Unlike in Serbia, where measures against Kosovar Albanians were widely popular, Zhivkov's attacks on the Turks diminished public trust in his regime, causing some Bulgarians to question the legitimacy of the socialist state.[38]

A New Face in Moscow

In 1985, the Polish general Wojciech Jaruzelski was the youngest leader in the Soviet bloc. He was 62. Gustav Husák, János Kádár, Todor Zhivkov and Erich Honecker had all been born before World War I. Along with Nicolae Ceauşescu, all four had been in their jobs since the 1960s. But when the ailing Konstantin Chernenko died after less than a year in power, the Soviet Union decided to go in a different direction. Mikhail Gorbachev was only 54 when he took over as General Secretary of the Soviet Communist Party in March 1985. Beyond the mere fact of his age, Gorbachev came to power determined to shake up what he believed was an ossified Soviet system.

When Gorbachev took office, the Soviet Union was not facing an economic crisis fueled by debt like Poland, Hungary or Yugoslavia. Yet Soviet economic growth had been anemic for years. Like many East European economists, Gorbachev believed the Soviet Union needed to shift from relying on extensive growth—fueled by infusions of new resources, such as raw materials and labor—to intensive growth, which meant increasing worker productivity and efficiency. He hoped to achieve this through a reform program called *perestroika* or "restructuring." Perestroika was a wide-ranging attempt to reinvigorate Soviet socialism by encouraging people to rededicate themselves to socialist ideals. The crucial element in perestroika was what Gorbachev called the "human factor" or the potential that existed inside every Soviet citizen. As he said in a speech shortly after taking office, the economic picture would improve if "we activate the human factor, striving for each [person] to carry out his position at work voluntarily and with full effect."[39]

As it evolved over the years between 1985 and 1989, perestroika incorporated several different elements. At the center of perestroika was a plan to incorporate market elements into the centrally planned economy, as the Hungarians and Yugoslavs had done. Yet Gorbachev believed that for economic reform to be effective, it had to be accompanied by political reform. This was represented by the idea of *glasnost* or openness. While it was often taken in the West to mean freedom of speech, Gorbachev used glasnost to indicate greater transparency on the part of the state. A third element of perestroika was democratization. Again, Gorbachev used this word differently from the ways Western observers might assume. For him, democratization meant increasing popular participation in socialist politics, not challenging the Communist party's hold on power. Eventually, this came to include the formation of new institutions, such as the creation of the USSR Congress of People's Deputies in 1988, where delegates would be selected via contested elections. These elections were not meant to challenge Communist power—although a few independents made it onto the ballot, most candidates were Communist party members—but they allowed voters to choose representatives on the basis of their ideas and past record rather than simply accepting the candidates the Communist party had selected for them.[40]

Gorbachev wanted to encourage his East European colleagues to embark on their own programs of perestroika. His ideas were most warmly received in Hungary, where a cohort of reform-minded Communist officials had already been moving in a similar direction. In addition to its various market-oriented economic reforms, Hungary had introduced multicandidate elections in 1985, several years before the Soviets. In May 1988, Hungarian reformers decisively took over the government, pushing János Kádár into retirement and removing many of his closest allies from the Central Committee. Kádár was replaced by Károly Grósz, whose government swiftly moved ahead with plans to create a market economy. Some of the more radical Hungarian reformers also advocated what they called "socialist pluralism," which went well beyond Gorbachev's ideas for democratization in the Soviet Union. While Grósz remained skeptical, the reformers were convinced that the only way for the Hungarian Communist Party to maintain its power was to share it.

After 1988, Hungarian Communists began steps to integrate the non-Communist opposition into public life. A few leading Hungarian Communists, particularly Imre Pozsgay, had cultivated contacts with opposition intellectuals for years. Pozsgay had especially close relations with Hungary's populist writers, a group whose nationalism sometimes put them at odds with Communist orthodoxy. Pozsgay even spoke at a 1987 conference that brought together dozens of these populist intellectuals in the town of Lakitelek, where he held out the possibility of increased populist participation in a more pluralist Hungary. After the Lakitelek conference, the populists were allowed to form an organization, the Hungarian Democratic Forum, to meet and discuss ideas. In late 1988, more new political associations began to spring up, including the Alliance of Free Democrats—composed of people associated with the non-populist, liberal opposition—and the Alliance of Young Democrats, known by its Hungarian acronym, Fidesz, whose members needed to be under the age of 35. In mid-1989, each of these groups only had a few thousand members, but their existence showed Hungary slowly moving toward a more democratic political system.[41]

In the beginning of 1989, the Hungarian Communist Party announced it would allow multiparty elections the following year, although all participants would need to accept socialism as a guiding principle.[42] In 1956, the Soviet Union sent in troops to prevent Hungary from creating a multiparty system. Yet in 1988 and 1989, as Hungary's Communists began to dismantle the leading role of the Communist party in Hungarian politics, the Soviets did nothing. Gorbachev had a different approach to Soviet security than his predecessors, preferring to promote arms control and a new rapprochement with the West. In a speech at the United Nations on December 7, 1988, he declared "force and the threat of force can no longer be, and should not be, instruments of foreign policy," strongly suggesting that the Soviet Union would not militarily interfere again in Eastern Europe.[43] Whatever policies they chose, the Communist governments of Eastern Europe would now be on their own.

As the Hungarian Communists embarked on their path toward a multiparty system, the leaders of Bulgaria, Czechoslovakia, East Germany and Romania did their best to ignore perestroika. Yet even in these countries, where leaders strongly resisted political change, there was growing support for market-based economic reforms, particularly among technocrats, economists and other experts. In Czechoslovakia, government experts drew up a plan for economic restructuring in 1987, proposing a package of measures to reduce the state's role in the economy and force state enterprises to become more self-sufficient. For some Czechoslovak economists, these proposed reforms did not go far nearly enough. In an influential article published in August 1988, economists Václav Klaus and Dušan Tříska argued that no centrally planned economy could set prices as well as a market. Drawing on the Austrian school of economic ideas associated with men such as Ludwig von Mises and Friedrich von Hayek, whose work circulated in Czech translation via samizdat in the late 1980s, Klaus and Tříska proposed moving completely to a market economy.[44] While economists like Klaus and Tříska emphasized the need for radical change, elsewhere in Communist party circles there was little support for even the government's modest reform program. Officials at all levels of the party's hierarchy were more concerned with maintaining their own power than with economic efficiency.[45] Lacking enthusiasm from the top, this tepid Czechoslovak perestroika floundered.

After it declared martial law in 1981, Poland also seemed unlikely to welcome perestroika. However, the Polish government was pragmatic. The enormous response to Solidarity in 1980–1981 had revealed widespread discontent with the regime. At the same time, the economic problems that had led to Solidarity's rise persisted, and Poland's debt to Western banks continued to grow. Polish leaders hoped to offer concessions that would increase their support both at home and with their Western lenders. In 1986, Poland issued an amnesty to those who had been arrested under martial law and substantially eased censorship. Formally banned authors were published in the mainstream press, interviews with opposition activists appeared in major newspapers and a prominent samizdat journal, *Res Publica*, was given legal status. The effects of the new press freedom were so striking that *Res Publica*'s editor, Marcin Król, remarked in 1987 that Poland was "a changed country. A different country."[46] Solidarity itself, however, remained banned.

Poland's leaders hoped that this liberalization would encourage the population to support economic reform measures, even if this meant a hit to the standard of living. In November 1987, the Polish government optimistically organized a referendum on economic and political reforms, betting that half the electorate would vote yes. Shockingly, voters failed to approve the proposals.

This very public repudiation of the government's program made it clear to all that the regime did not have the public's support. This became even more apparent when a wave of strikes broke out the following year. These strikes were not called by underground Solidarity leaders but organized by a younger generation of workers who had come of age after the imposition of martial law. The strikers opposed austerity measures that even Solidarity leaders had come to see as necessary, but which nonetheless hit younger and poorer workers hard.[47] Even though the strikes were much more limited than they had been in 1980, the effect was potentially devastating for the practically bankrupt Polish government. Polish leader Wojciech Jaruzelski was desperate to get the strikers back to work, but his comrades in the Polish Politburo had no ideas on how to do so. "We must square the circle of impossibility to reform socialism," he said to fellow party leaders. "How long can people's power hang on just by threatening workers with tanks and police truncheons?"[48]

Knowing that neither Gorbachev nor his Western creditors would approve of a return to martial law, Jaruzelski proposed opening a dialogue with Solidarity. Hardliners within the party leadership protested, but ultimately capitulated after Politburo member Alfred Miodowicz rashly offered to debate Solidarity leader Lech Wałesa on television. Miodowicz believed he would eviscerate the less educated Wałesa, showing the public that the opposition was not prepared to participate in politics. Instead, over 20 million Poles watched Wałesa persuasively make the case for a more democratic Poland.[49] As Polish interior minister Czesław Kiszczak ruefully noted the next day, "Wałesa presented himself as a politician of great stature, with a clear and convincing vision of the country's future. He turned out to be a man with a constructive attitude, motivated by a will toward real dialogue and understanding."[50] A few months later, Polish Communist leaders began a series of roundtable talks with Solidarity activists.

The negotiations between the Polish government and Solidarity lasted from February to April 1989. Solidarity leaders did not go into the talks intending to challenge the Communist hold on political power; their goal was Solidarity's relegalization. Paradoxically, it was the Polish Communists who now wanted Solidarity to enter politics, only seven years after they had initiated martial law to prevent it from doing so. In this new era of perestroika, Polish leaders believed that if they could bring Solidarity into government, it would legitimate their austerity measures in the eyes of the population and help them to stabilize the economy. Communists would, they reasoned, be able to shift some of the blame for unpopular but necessary economic policies onto Solidarity. Therefore, the Communists insisted that in return for allowing Solidarity to legally exist, it would have to participate in elections for a newly reorganized Sejm (the Polish parliament). Solidarity would only be allowed to contest a limited number of seats in the Sejm's lower house, theoretically guaranteeing that it would not actually gain power. The agreement also created new senate, where all seats would be freely contested. Solidarity leaders reluctantly agreed to these conditions. "None of us want these elections," Lech Wałesa complained, "They're the terrible price we have to pay to get our union back."[51]

The elections took place on June 4, 1989, less than two months after the final roundtable agreement was concluded. The results surprised everyone. Solidarity took almost every seat it was allowed to contest, while the Communists failed to achieve an outright majority of the votes cast in most of their races, including those contests where their candidates ran unopposed (voters were allowed to cross off the names of the candidates they did not want). Due to the election's complicated procedural rules, the Communists would eventually win all of the seats that had been set aside for them in the Sejm's lower house during a second round of voting. But the result was still a stunning Communist defeat. Voters had taken matters into their own hands and used the election as an opportunity to show their utter disapproval of Communist rule. Communist leaders were dumbfounded. As one of the Communist negotiators during the roundtable talks, Mieczysław Rakowski, later wrote in his memoir, "Somehow, in the depth of our brains, we were convinced that we would win the elections, because, after all, we had always won elections."[52] What would happen once it was clear this was not the case?

Solidarity leaders had gone into the elections intending to respect the terms of the roundtable agreement, but the government's enormous defeat made them rethink their position. A month after the elections, as the Communists struggled to put together a government that would be approved by the new Sejm, the dissident Adam Michnik proposed a radical solution in a newspaper editorial entitled "Your President, Our Prime Minister." Just a few months earlier, the prospect of a Solidarity prime minister sharing power with a Communist president was an unthinkable outcome. Now, facing defections from within their own coalition, Communist leaders realized that, unless they wanted to return to martial law, they had no other option. On August 24, 1989, Catholic activist and Solidarity stalwart Tadeusz Mazowiecki was elected prime minister, and the era of one-party rule in Poland was over. However, the Communists had won in one crucial respect: Poland's economic crisis would now be Solidarity's problem.

We Are the People

In the middle of 1988, East Germany faced a meat shortage. Fearing the discontent that such shortages could arouse, the country's leaders scrambled to increase supply by cutting exports and directing meat processors and retailers to make greater use of all parts of the animal, including tails and heads. Yet these measures could not compensate for the larger systemic issues that lay behind the bare spots on store shelves. An earlier campaign to increase the weight of East German hogs had primarily increased their fat content, resulting in poor quality meat that many consumers refused to buy. Faulty infrastructure meant that it was hard to get the animals that were produced to consumers. After decades of neglect, over half of East Germany's slaughterhouses were deemed public health hazards, although party officials insisted that they be used anyway. The country lacked sufficient refrigerated trucks or railway cars to distribute what was slaughtered. Aged equipment at meat processing plants could not deal with the larger carcasses of the fatty hogs, so grocery stores often received whole animals instead of smaller sections. These stores had neither the personnel nor the equipment to properly butcher what they were delivered. Rather than spending nights and weekends working overtime to cut and pack meat, poorly paid shop assistants quit. By the summer of 1989, meat counters across the country suffered from a shortage of employees, forcing some stores to reduce their hours or even shut down entirely.[53]

The factors that prevented East Germans from finding cutlets to serve at summer barbecues illustrated the increasingly intractable economic problems the country faced. Beginning in the 1970s, East German leader Erich Honecker, like his counterparts across the region, prioritized consumer spending and maintaining full employment, even if this required taking out Western loans. This debt tied the country to the global economy, where it was unable to compete, leading to ever-greater debt as exports could not raise enough hard currency to meet the payments. In Poland and Hungary, this unrelenting cycle pushed Communist leaders toward marketization and persuaded them of the need to work with the non-Communist opposition. To Honecker, however, the changes occurring in Poland and Hungary represented a betrayal of socialism.

Frustrated with their government's open disdain for perestroika and its inability to improve the economic situation, some East Germans decided to take matters into their own hands. As it moved forward with its own reforms in May 1989, Hungary decided to demilitarize its border with Austria, rolling back the barbed wire that had separated the two countries since the beginning of the Cold War. A few East Germans vacationing in Hungary took advantage of the disappearance of the border fence to illegally cross over to Austria. From there, they continued to West Germany, where, per longstanding policy, they were granted citizenship. As word of this new hole in the Iron Curtain spread, tens of thousands of East Germans resolved to leave for the West. Many of them gathered in makeshift camps in Hungary, hoping to make it over the newly opened border. Over 3,000 crowded into the garden of the West German embassy in Prague to ask for asylum; others did the same at the West German embassies in East Berlin, Warsaw and Budapest.[54]

With the inducement of one billion Deutsche Mark (DM) in loan credits from the West Germans, the Hungarian government decided to open the border for East Germans on September 10. Within 24 hours, 8,000 had left for the West. "I can't believe that it actually worked," exclaimed the driver of the first East German car to cross into Austria. A few weeks later, as the situation in the vastly overcrowded embassy garden in Prague threatened to become a humanitarian crisis, West German officials persuaded Honecker to allow the people camping there to board special sealed trains bound for West Germany. When thousands more took their place within a few days, East Germany suspended visa-free travel to Czechoslovakia. The urge to leave did not abate, however. After the Czechoslovak border was reopened on November 1, the flow of emigrants resumed.[55]

The spectacle of this exodus, which many viewed on West German TV, inspired East Germans to protest the policies that had driven so many of their fellow citizens to leave. The Monday afternoon peace service at the Nikolai Church in Leipzig was a focal point for this swelling East German opposition that quickly ballooned into a mass movement. On September 4, 1,200 people turned up at the service to demand "an open country with free people." By October 2, the number of attendees had grown to 10,000. They marched through the city chanting "we're staying here!" While their fellow citizens had chosen emigration, they demanded the regime create the conditions under which they could remain. On October 4 and 5, 30,000 people demonstrated in Leipzig. On October 7, protests in several cities disrupted events marking the 40th anniversary of the GDR. The police reacted with brutal force, clubbing demonstrators and arresting approximately 1,000 people.[56]

Mikhail Gorbachev, in Berlin to attend the anniversary celebrations, counseled East German leaders to accept the need for change, saying "If we fall behind, life will punish us immediately."[57] Erich Honecker was not inclined to follow Gorbachev's advice. A few months earlier, the Chinese government had used tanks and armed soldiers to bloodily crush pro-democracy protests in Beijing's Tiananmen Square. Although Gorbachev made it clear that the Soviet Union would not help put down unrest in the GDR, many feared East Germany would resort to this "Chinese solution." Yet while the East German government did mobilize thousands of armed soldiers and police officers in anticipation of a planned demonstration in Leipzig on October 9, local leaders in the city were determined to defuse the situation. The march of 70,000 people went off peacefully and no shots were fired.[58] After October 9, the threat of violence receded and demonstrations spread across the country. Hundreds of thousands of people marched and chanted "We are the people!" With this slogan, the marchers suggested that they, not the East German Politburo, had the power to shape the country's future.

East German leaders scrambled to respond. Erich Honecker, who had so strongly resisted the pull of perestroika, was ousted as party leader on October 17. He was replaced by Egon Krenz, who tried to style himself as a reformer. But few were satisfied with this change. In the estimation of one observer, Krenz, whose most distinguishing feature was his enormous teeth, "looked more like a used car salesman than a statesman whom one could trust."[59] Instead of dying down, the protests expanded. On October 30, over a million

FIGURE 6.2 East German demonstrators with a picture of Mikhail Gorbachev, April 1989. © Sueddeutsche Zeitung Photo/Alamy Stock Photo DYTFT9.

people demonstrated in cities all across the country. Their demands included free elections, free travel and free speech. On the night of November 4, between 500,000 and 1 million people marched in East Berlin, and coverage of the protest appeared on East German TV.[60]

A few days later, on November 9, the new East German leadership met to discuss ways of appeasing the ever-increasing crowds. The Politburo had intended to address the issue of travel and emigration, but, through a series of miscommunications, it approved a much more radical policy than had originally been intended. The new regulation would allow all East Germans to easily apply to travel to the West through all border points, including Berlin, beginning on November 10.[61]

That evening, East Berlin party chief Günter Schabowski was tasked with announcing the new travel regulations at a news conference. Schabowski, who had not been at the meeting where the matter was discussed, was confused by what he was reading. He failed to emphasize that applications were supposed to be required for travel. Even more fatefully, asked when the new rules would take effect, he replied, "right away."[62] Fueled by Schabowski's words, rumors started to spread that the border checkpoints in Berlin were open. By 11 p.m. a crowd of 20,000 had gathered at one of the border crossings, demanding to be let through. The border guards had not been given any instructions, and their frantic calls to their superiors did not receive a response. Not wanting to resort to violence and fearing the restive crowd, they opened the gates and let the people pass. For the next few days, Berlin was the site of an enormous party, as West Berliners greeted the surprise arrival of their neighbors from the East with applause and sparkling wine.[63]

While the East German government had intended to liberalize travel to the West, the way it happened—with jubilant crowds bursting through the border gates in the middle of the night—made it seem like a revolution, not a concession. Within weeks, the Communist hold on power had completely collapsed. Opposition leaders began to meet with Communist officials in roundtable talks. Free elections were scheduled. The entire leadership of the East German Communist party was replaced. Yet, even as plans were made for a newly democratic GDR, some wondered: if there was no socialist dictatorship in the East, why should there be two Germanies? Within a few months, the prospect of a unified Germany, which had been unthinkable for decades, started to look like an inevitability.[64]

From the day it was erected in 1961, the Berlin Wall had symbolized the bitter divisions of the Cold War. The Wall's sudden and unexpected collapse shocked the entire world. The impact was most immediate, however, in the rest of the Soviet bloc, where the fall of the Berlin Wall acted as a catalyst for further revolutionary events. In Bulgaria, changes had been afoot well before November 9. For decades, Todor Zhivkov had managed to circumvent any challenges to his hold on power. In 1989, this changed. Zhivkov's expulsion of the Turks created an economic crisis that sparked discontent. The Bulgarian intelligentsia, inspired by Gorbachev's perestroika, began to create opposition groups. More significantly, high-ranking members of the Bulgarian Communist Party began to see Zhivkov as a liability. As events heated up in Berlin, they persuaded Zhivkov to resign. His departure was announced on November 10, the day after the Berlin Wall came crashing down. His successor, Petŭr Mladenov, quickly initiated a democratic transformation, ending the party's monopoly on power, initiating discussions with the opposition and calling for free elections in spring 1990.[65]

Bulgaria followed the Hungarian model, where the driving impetus for change came from within the Communist party itself. In Czechoslovakia and Romania, the momentum came from the streets. In Prague, Czechoslovak police brutally broke up a peaceful march of university students on November 17, beating the participants with clubs and menacing them with dogs. This exhibition of cruelty was the catalyst that quickly brought the masses to the streets. Within days, opposition groups had formed around the country. Demonstrations, rallies and happenings sprang up everywhere. On November 27, half of the population joined in a general strike. There was an intoxicating atmosphere of joy and possibility; one participant described it as a "beautiful fever." Faced with this massive outpouring of public disapproval, the Czechoslovak regime began to negotiate with the dissidents it had previously jailed. Before the year was over, the Czechoslovak parliament had elected the dissident Václav Havel as the country's new president. The Czechoslovak Communist regime collapsed so swiftly and peacefully that the events leading to its demise would be called the "Velvet Revolution."[66]

As Eastern Europe's Communist regimes evaporated in the fall of 1989, Romania's Nicolae Ceaușescu hoped to escape their fate. He would not succeed. Demonstrations began in Romania on December 15 in the city of Timișoara, when a few elderly parishioners gathered to protest the removal of their outspoken pastor, László Tőkés. As they stood vigil, others began to join them. The next day, the crowd had grown and people began to chant "Freedom!" and "Down with Ceaușescu!" By December 17, crowds were circulating around the center of the city. The local party headquarters was ransacked as rioters smashed windows and looted stores. Ceaușescu, convinced that the demonstrators were really foreign provocateurs, sent in the army to crush the protests. Security forces shot into the crowd, killing 60 people. Yet the demonstrations continued, moving into the factories. By December 20, the protesters had taken over the city, and the army, wary of more violence, decided to withdraw.[67]

As the protests started to spread to other towns, Ceaușescu decided to hold a massive rally in the capital city of Bucharest on December 21. The event, to be broadcast live on television, was supposed to show the country that the Communist regime had the support of the masses. The opposite happened. As the cameras rolled, viewers suddenly heard noise and cries of "Ceaușescu dictator." On the screen, a frightened-looking Ceaușescu appeared confused and was unable to silence the crowd. The broadcast was abruptly terminated for several minutes. When the picture came back, the demonstrators were gone, but it was too late: Romanians had seen their supposedly mighty leader looking small and vulnerable. That night, protesters swarmed Bucharest. The next day, Nicolae Ceaușescu imagined that he would address and quiet the crowd, but instead he and his wife Elena were forced to flee by helicopter, escaping just as a horde of protesters entered party headquarters. They were caught within hours. On December 25, a hastily convened military tribunal tried, convicted and immediately executed both Ceaușescus.

For a few days, chaos reigned in Bucharest. A group of Communist officials led by a known Ceaușescu opponent, Ion Iliescu, created a new government, which they branded the National Salvation Front (NSF). Fighting broke out, ostensibly between the army—which supported the NSF—and Securitate (secret police) forces defending the old regime. In the confusion, however, it was hard to conclusively determine precisely who was fighting and for what purpose. Doubts still exist about exactly what happened during these chaotic days, when over 1,000 people were killed in violent clashes. Some in Romania consider the events of 1989 to be a revolution. Others believe what happened was a coup d'etat, where one group of Communists merely displaced another. Former Communist elites would indeed retain a great amount of influence in Romania, as they would all over Eastern Europe. Yet the essential elements of the Communist system, including the centrally planned economy, state ownership of the means of production and one-party rule, would all be eliminated.

While the Communist regimes in Albania and Yugoslavia nominally survived for a few more years, 1989 marked the symbolic end of Communist governments in Eastern Europe. Strikingly, the wave of regime change felled those governments that had actively pursued perestroika as well as those that had resisted it. In 1991, the Soviet Union itself disintegrated. In the euphoria that surrounded this surprise end to the Cold War, many East Europeans imagined that a transition to capitalism would create the bright future that Communism had promised but never delivered. The reality turned out to be much more painful than they expected.

Notes

1 Grzegorz Ekiert, *The State Against Society: Political Crises and Their Aftermath in East Central Europe* (Princeton, NJ: Princeton University Press, 1996), 222–226.
2 Jan Kubik, *The Power of Symbols Against the Symbols of Power: The Rise of Solidarity and the Fall of State Socialism in Poland* (University Park, PA: Penn State University Press, 1994), 184–185.
3 Kubik, *Power of Symbols*, 129–152, 274–276.
4 Timothy Garton Ash, *The Polish Revolution: Solidarity* (New York: Scribner, 1983), 37–67.
5 Garton Ash, *The Polish Revolution*, 278–279.
6 "Solidarity's Program of October 16, 1981," in *From Stalinism to Pluralism: A Documentary History of Eastern Europe since 1945*, 2nd ed., ed. Gale Stokes (Oxford: Oxford University Press, 1996), 209–213.
7 Arista Maria Cirtautas, *The Polish Solidarity Movement: Revolution, Nationalism Human Rights* (New York: Routledge, 1997), 4–5.
8 "Solidarity's Program of October 16, 1981," 212.
9 Garton Ash, *The Polish Revolution*, 264.
10 Gale Stokes, *The Walls Came Tumbling Down: Collapse and Rebirth in Eastern Europe*, 2nd ed. (Oxford: Oxford University Press, 2012), 46.
11 Victor Petrov, "A Cyber-Socialism at Home and Abroad: Bulgarian Modernization, Computers, and the World, 1967–1989," Ph.D. diss, Columbia University, 2017.
12 Petrov, "A Cyber-Socialism at Home and Abroad," 253–316 (quote on p. 304).
13 Jill Massino, *Ambiguous Transitions: Gender, the State and Everyday Life in Postsocialist Romania* (New York: Berghahn Books, 2019), 335–355.
14 Massino, *Ambiguous Transitions*, 350.
15 Massino, *Ambiguous Transitions*, 339–341 (quote on p. 341).
16 Adam Fabry, "The Origins of Neoliberalism in Late-Socialist Hungary: The Case of the Financial Research Institute and 'Turnabout and Reform,'" *Capital and Class* 42, no. 1 (2018): 87–88.
17 Johanna Bockman, *Markets in the Name of Socialism: The Left-Wing Origins of Neoliberalism* (Stanford, CA: Stanford University Press, 2011), 160–164.
18 J. Bársony, "Tibor Liska's Concept of Socialist Entrepreneurship," *Acta Oeconomica* 28, no. 3/4 (1982): 422–455.
19 Ivan Berend, *The Hungarian Economic Reforms, 1958–1988* (Cambridge: Cambridge University Press, 1990), 254.
20 Berend, *The Hungarian Economic Reforms*, 246–249.
21 Gábor Révész, *Perestroika in Eastern Europe: Hungary's Economic Transformation, 1945–1988* (Boulder, CO: Westview Press, 1990), 113–118.

22 Jasminka Udovički and Ivan Torov, "The Interlude: 1980–1990," in *Burn this House: The Making and Unmaking of Yugoslavia*, ed. Jasminka Udovički and James Ridgeway (Durham, NC: Duke University Press, 2000), 81.
23 Marie-Janine Calic, *The Great Cauldron: A History of Southeastern Europe*, trans. Elizabeth Janik (Cambridge, MA: Harvard University Press, 2019), 520.
24 Stokes, *Walls Came Tumbling Down*, 209–214.
25 Susan L. Woodward, *Socialist Unemployment: The Political Economy of Yugoslavia, 1945–1990* (Princeton, NJ: Princeton University Press, 1995), 384–387.
26 According to the 1981 census, 77.4 percent of the Kosovar population was Albanian and 13.2 percent was Serb. Most Kosovar Albanians are at least nominally Muslim, while its Serbs are Orthodox Christians.
27 Momčilo Pavlović, "Kosovo Under Autonomy, 1974–1990," in *Confronting the Yugoslav Controversies: A Scholars' Initiative*, ed. Charles Ingrao and Thomas A. Emmert (West Lafayette, IN: Purdue University Press, 2009), 49–80.
28 "Memorandum of the Serbian Academy of Sciences (SANU)," trans. Dennison Rusinow, in Stokes, *From Stalinism to Pluralism*, 279.
29 Jasna Dragović-Soso, *Saviours of the Nation: Serbia's Intellectual Opposition and the Revival of Nationalism* (Montreal: McGill-Queen's University Press, 2002), 177–189 (quotes on p. 186 and 188).
30 Dragović-Soso, *Saviours of the Nation*, 189–195 and 214–216; Wachtel and Bennet, "The Dissolution of Yugoslavia," 32–34.
31 Udovički and Torov, "The Interlude," 87–88.
32 Stokes, *Walls Came Tumbling Down*, 218.
33 Wachtel and Bennet, "The Dissolution of Yugoslavia," 30–33, Udovički and Torov, "The Interlude," 90–91.
34 Dragović-Soso, *Saviours of the Nation*, 207–227.
35 Mary Neuburger, *The Orient Within: Muslim Minorities and the Negotiation of Nationhood in Modern Bulgaria* (Ithaca, NY: Cornell University Press, 2004), 3, 76–80.
36 Neuburger, *The Orient Within*, 77–81, 162–168.
37 After applying for Turkish citizenship, Suleimanov changed his name to the more Turkish Süleymanoğlu. He went on to win Olympic gold medals competing for Turkey in 1988, 1992 and 1996.
38 Neuburger, *The Orient Within*, 82.
39 Courtney Doucette, "Perestroika: The Last Attempt to Create the New Soviet Person," Ph.D. diss, Rutgers University, 2017 (quote on p. 9).
40 Doucette, "Perestroika."
41 While it began as a youth-oriented party, Fidesz would transform itself into a rightist party in the 1990s. Rudolf L. Tőkés, *Hungary's Negotiated Revolution: Economic Reform, Social Change and Political Succession, 1957–1990* (Cambridge: Cambridge University Press, 1996).
42 Tőkés, *Hungary's Negotiated Revolution*, 298–305.
43 "Address by Mikhail Gorbachev at the UN General Assembly Session (Excerpts)," December 7, 1988, History and Public Policy Program Digital Archive, CWIHP Archive. http://digitalarchive.wilsoncenter.org/document/116224.
44 Rudolf Kučera, "Making Standards Work: Semantics of Economic Reform in Czechoslovakia, 1985–1992," *Zeithistorische Forschungen/Studies in Contemporary History* 12, no. 3 (2015): 427–447.
45 Michal Pullmann, "Planning, Efficiency and Socialist Entrepreneurship: Economic Reform and Elite Transformation in Late Socialist Czechoslovakia," *Prague Economic and Social History Papers* 11, no. 1 (2010): 86–95.
46 David Ost, *Solidarity and the Politics of Antipolitics* (Philadelphia, PA: Temple University Press, 1990), 176–177.
47 Ost, *Solidarity*, 182.

48 Stephen Kotkin, with Jan T. Gross, *Uncivil Society: 1989 and the Implosion of the Communist Establishment* (New York: Modern Library, 2010), 124.

49 Ost, *Solidarity*, 185.

50 Kotkin, *Uncivil Society*, 125–126.

51 Stokes, *The Walls Came Tumbling Down*, 147.

52 Kotkin, *Uncivil Society*, 130.

53 Jonathan R. Zatlin, *The Currency of Socialism: Money and Political Culture in East Germany* (Cambridge: Cambridge University Press, 2007), 149–155.

54 Charles S. Maier, *Dissolution: The Crisis of Communism and the End of East Germany* (Princeton, NJ: Princeton University Press, 1997), 120–131.

55 Konrad H. Jarausch, *The Rush to German Unity* (New York: Oxford University Press, 1994), 16–25.

56 Maier, *Dissolution*, 135–149; Jarausch, *Rush to German Unity*, 45.

57 Jarausch, *Rush to German Unity*, 53.

58 James Mark, Bogdan C. Iacob, Tobias Rupprecht and Ljubica Spaskovska, *1989: A Global History of Eastern Europe* (Cambridge: Cambridge University Press, 2019), 101–107.

59 Jarausch, *Rush to German Unity*, 60.

60 Jarausch, *Rush to German Unity*, 46–48.

61 Mary Elise Sarotte, *The Collapse: The Accidental Opening of the Berlin Wall* (New York: Basic Books, 2014), 105–115.

62 Sarotte, *The Collapse*, 115–118.

63 Maier, *Dissolution*, 160–167.

64 Maier, *Dissolution*, 173–185.

65 Stokes, *Walls Came Tumbling Down*, 168–174; Tomasz Kamusella, *Ethnic Cleansing During the Cold War: The Forgotten 1989 Expulsion of Turks from Communist Bulgaria* (New York: Routledge, 2019).

66 James Krapfl, *Revolution with a Human Face: Politics, Culture and Community in Czechoslovakia, 1989–1992* (Ithaca, NY: Cornell University Press, 2013), quote on p. 39.

67 The next few paragraphs are drawn from Peter Siani-Davies, *The Romanian Revolution of December 1989* (Ithaca, NY: Cornell University Press, 2005).

7

FROM COMMUNISM TO NEOLIBERALISM

After Eastern Europe's Communist governments suddenly collapsed in 1989, most East Europeans imagined that their lives would rapidly improve. Many would be disappointed. In the years after 1989, Eastern Europe's democratically elected governments moved to dismantle the socialist system and create capitalist market economies. Their neoliberal economic policies ushered in a prolonged period of economic pain. Some prospered in the new capitalist economy, finding new opportunities and new prosperity. For others, however, capitalism brought only impoverishment and uncertainty.

The end of socialism had the most devastating consequences in Yugoslavia. Economic collapse fueled the dissolution of the country, leading to a bloody civil war in which approximately 140,000 people died.[1] During the conflict, combatants engaged in ethnic cleansing, using violence in an attempt to create ethnic homogeneity in a region that had been characterized by its diversity. As a result, millions of civilians were forced to flee their homes. Many never returned.

East European leaders hoped to find a new place in the world by reorienting themselves toward the West and becoming members of the North Atlantic Treaty Organization (NATO) and the European Union (EU). The path to EU membership would be long and hard. Between 2004 and 2007, the former countries of the Soviet bloc joined the EU, signaling the end of their transition to democratic government and a market economy. Yet while some celebrated this "return to Europe" as a moment of possibility, others saw little to cheer in a newly capitalist society that had left them behind.

Shock Therapy

In "The Power of the Powerless," his influential essay from 1978, Czechoslovak dissident Václav Havel argued that both socialist and capitalist societies faced a

DOI: 10.4324/9780813348186-8

crisis of authenticity. Western liberal democracies might seem more free than socialist dictatorships, Havel wrote, but this freedom was in many ways an illusion. In the West, he said, "people are manipulated in ways that are infinitely more subtle and refined than the brutal methods used in the post-totalitarian societies." As Havel portrayed it, Western-style parliamentary democracy and its attendant capitalist consumer society did not represent much of an improvement from the socialist system. Rather than aspiring to ape the West, Havel imagined a system he called "post-democracy," a form of participatory democracy that lodged power in local communities rather than in professional political parties and global corporations.[2]

During Czechoslovakia's Velvet Revolution of November 1989, many of those who took to the streets echoed Havel's ideas. These idealistic protesters envisioned themselves building a new society, which would be, as one group of activists put it, "pluralist, tolerant, brighter, more universal, more effective, more blissful, more human, constantly adapting to new circumstances."[3] While some protesters advocated market capitalism as the way forward, greater numbers called for a rejuvenated socialism, along the lines of the failed reforms of 1968. All demanded a democracy in which ordinary people would be heard and respected. In a televised debate on November 24, Slovak activist Milan Kňažko pictured an "enormous round table, around which 15 million people can sit. And," he continued, "we must reckon with everyone's opinion, so that everyone might freely express himself without fear, that he might express his own substance and vision of our society."[4] Similarly idealistic sentiments were expressed all over Eastern Europe in the waning days of 1989.

Within the space of a few months, however, these dreams of participatory democracy and rejuvenated socialism had been pushed to the margins. During the 1990s, the countries of Eastern Europe successfully replaced their one-party dictatorships with multiparty parliamentary systems. At the same time, the dissident-led citizen's collectives of the revolutionary period faded away and were replaced by a new cadre of professional politicians who fronted Western-style political parties. In the 1990s, these newly minted politicians made creating a capitalist market economy their primary task. Eastern Europe swiftly became part of a growing global neoliberal consensus which promoted economic growth above all else and advocated minimal government intervention in the economy. Throughout the region, economists and policy makers espoused radical economic reforms based around the ideals of deregulation, privatization, free trade, lower taxes and a smaller social safety net.

Some have claimed that Western advisers and Western financial institutions, such as the IMF and World Bank, forced Eastern Europe to accept neoliberal economic policies. Many East European economists, however, had been avid supporters of marketization well before 1989. The fall of socialist governments allowed them to openly embrace free market ideals and use their influence to shape state policies. The Czech economist Václav Klaus, who served as Czechoslovakia's finance minister from 1990 to 1992 and was prime minister of the independent Czech Republic after 1993, was his country's loudest voice in favor of neoliberal reforms. Klaus, a devotee of Margaret Thatcher, firmly rejected the idea of market-based socialism (often referred to as the "third way") as an insufficient half measure, arguing "the third way leads to the Third World."[5] Klaus painted the capitalist market economy as the "normal order" and socialism as an irrational, failed experiment. Only an "unconstrained, unrestricted, full-fledged, unspoiled market economy," he said, would lead to success. Soon, even Václav Havel felt compelled to agree, writing in 1992,

> The only way to the economic salvation of this country … is the fastest possible renewal of a market economy … It is in our common interest that the reforms be fundamental and quick. The more half measures we take, and the longer they drag on, the greater the sacrifices will be.[6]

All the countries of the former Soviet bloc eventually accepted the need for neoliberal economic reforms, but the specifics of how these reforms were managed and when they were implemented varied considerably by country. In the early 1990s, there was considerable debate over whether it was better to implement the changes needed to move to a market economy all at once—termed "shock therapy"—or more gradually. In practice, however, the dividing line between these approaches was blurry. Poland, for example, began as a vocal proponent of shock therapy but shifted to a somewhat more gradual approach after 1993. In 1989, Polish Finance Minister Leszek Balcerowicz proposed a radical plan for marketization that involved rapidly lifting of state subsidies on food, fuel, rent and other necessities, privatizing state-owned businesses, deregulating prices and opening the country to foreign investment. Balcerowicz, who was an economist by training, theorized that this shock therapy would create an intense but short recession, after which markets would adjust themselves and Poland would move toward prosperity. The pain turned out to be far greater than he had envisioned. In 1990–1991, the Polish gross national product fell by 18 percent, while unemployment and inflation spiked dramatically.[7] In these first years of shock therapy, the average monthly income per person in Poland was only $89, and average levels of consumption decreased. After a few years of pronounced recession, the Polish economy began to improve, but this growth was not felt evenly throughout the population. In 2003, real wages in Poland had increased to 131 percent of their 1989 level, yet one quarter of all Polish households fell below the poverty line.[8]

Despite the economic havoc they caused, the Balcerowicz reforms did not spark popular protests like those Poland had seen in 1970, 1976 or 1980. This lack of protest was typical throughout Eastern Europe in the 1990s: even when economic reforms caused great hardship, people rarely took to the streets to demand change. They did, however, make their feelings known at the ballot box. In 1993, the Solidarity-backed government that had promoted the Balcerowicz plan was voted out of office in favor of a left alliance led by former Communists turned into Social Democrats. In a sign of how completely and rapidly the political environment in Poland had changed since 1989, this "post-Communist" Polish left did not renounce their predecessor's neoliberal program once they took office. Under ex-Communist Aleksander Kwaśniewski, who was elected president in 1995 and continued in office until 2005, the government largely continued the same policies, although it did attempt to alleviate some of the economic dislocation they caused by implementing reforms more gradually and devoting more resources to welfare programs.[9]

East Germany's transition to a market economy was particularly abrupt, largely due to political circumstances. When East German demonstrators took to the streets in 1989, they did not do so to demand the end of the East German state. Before 1989, the geopolitical realities of the Cold War had made a united Germany almost unimaginable. But after the fall of the Berlin Wall, momentum for the unification of East and West Germany increased rapidly. The first freely elected East German government—chosen in March 1990—vowed to pursue unification with the West. While the Soviet Union was initially skeptical of a single German state as part of NATO, Soviet leaders were eventually persuaded to agree to German unification, largely on Western terms. On October 3, 1990, the new Germany came into existence.

Given East Germany's inferior economic position, the merger of the two states took place largely under West German offices. While the German government tried to safeguard the livelihood of former East Germans, the economic consequences of unification were devastating. Even before formal unification, on July 1, 1990, East Germany adopted the West German currency, the Deutsche Mark (DM). In a bid to protect East German savings, the East German currency was exchanged with the DM at a rate of one to one. While it temporarily gave East Germans more purchasing power, this exchange rate made it much harder for East German firms to compete with their Western counterparts. East German goods became substantially more expensive just as demand for them decreased. The result was that East Germans kept their savings but found their jobs in jeopardy. By 1991, industrial production in the former East had fallen by two-thirds, and some four million were unemployed or in make-work positions. As businesses in the former East Germany contracted or failed, 1.4 million people migrated west in search of economic opportunity. While a few areas gradually recovered, many towns in eastern Germany remained economically bereft even three decades later.[10]

As part of its bid to restructure the socialist economy, the former East German state created a holding company trust, the Treuhand. The Treuhand was initially supposed to help thousands of socialist enterprises make the transition to a market economy. After German reunification, the Treuhand's emphasis switched to the rapid privatization of East German firms. Instead of helping East German firms become more competitive and then looking for buyers, the Treuhand now hoped to sell them off as quickly as possible. Its new West German chairman, Detlev Rohwedder, declared, "privatization is the best restructuring." But few investors wanted to purchase polluting East German factories badly in need of modernization. Many enterprises, like the Wartburg automobile factory in Eisenach, which employed 20,000 people, were simply closed. Others had their most productive pieces sold to Western firms at fire sale prices. By 1994, when the Treuhand announced it had completed its work, over four million industrial jobs had disappeared.[11]

The East German experience reveals some of the difficulties inherent in moving from a socialist to a capitalist economy, particularly in privatizing large state enterprises. So-called small privatization—meaning the sale of retail shops, restaurants, bakeries and other small businesses—generally proceeded smoothly. These kinds of businesses had a local clientele and could find local buyers. In Poland, Hungary and Czechoslovakia, most retail stores were successfully privatized by 1993.[12] The privatization of large enterprises ("large privatization") was much more problematic. Socialism had typically created a tightly linked industrial landscape built around large combines. It was impossible to sell off individual enterprises without disrupting the entire industrial ecosystem.

Finding potential buyers for large firms was another issue. East European governments hoped that foreign investment would save their industries and the jobs attached to them, but few Western companies wanted to invest in crumbling socialist factories. There were some success stories, such as the Czechoslovak automaker Škoda, which became a subsidiary of Volkswagen in 1991, and the Romanian car manufacturer Dacia, bought by Renault in 1999. Both firms improved their products, found new markets and are still producing today. Yet the glut of firms on the market in the 1990s meant that Škoda and Dacia were the exception rather than the rule. Most socialist firms were unable to attract foreign capital. Many simply failed.[13]

Large privatization offered many opportunities for corruption. This was most famously the case in the former Soviet Union, where a few well-connected men—the so-called oligarchs—were able to make enormous fortunes by purchasing Soviet energy companies and the rights to other natural resources at rock bottom prices. Eastern Europe had its own share of dubious transactions. One of the most notorious was the case of the Czech-American Viktor Kožený, known as the "pirate of Prague." In the early 1990s, Václav Klaus developed a plan to privatize Czechoslovak industries by giving all citizens the opportunity to cheaply purchase books of vouchers that could be turned into shares of Czech companies. His goal was to keep companies in local hands rather than sell them to foreign buyers. This "voucher privatization" spawned the creation of investment funds that promised impressive returns to those who turned over their vouchers. Many, although not all, of these funds were fraudulent. Kožený's fund, Harvard Capital and Consulting, promised a tenfold return and attracted hundreds of thousands of investors with an effective television marketing campaign. Kožený fled the country a few years later, having used the vouchers to make $200 million for himself. His investors were left with nothing.

Despite allegations of fraud in Prague, Kožený continued to present himself as a legitimate businessman. He became known for his lavish lifestyle, which included paying over £13,000 (about $20,000) for a single meal at a London restaurant in 1997. In 1999, he was indicted on fraud charges for a similar scheme involving oil privatization in the former Soviet republic of Azerbaijan, but this time involving American investors. Kožený escaped to his estate in the Bahamas, where he successfully avoided extradition despite warrants for his arrest from both the United States and the Czech Republic. In 2011, a Czech court sentenced him in absentia to ten years in prison for his financial malfeasance.[14]

The chaotic economic environment of the 1990s also contributed to the growth of organized crime, particularly in the Balkans, which experienced greater poverty and less economic opportunity than countries like Poland or the Czech Republic. In Bulgaria, real wages decreased by 50 percent between 1989 and 1993. As late as 2001, they remained at half of their 1989 level.[15] Bulgaria had little organized crime before 1995, but criminal gangs expanded rapidly after the country faced a major financial crisis in 1996. The country's currency lost 25 percent of its value and two-thirds of its banks went bankrupt.[16] This Bulgarian mafia had its roots in groups of men familiar with violence who were left without economic security after the end of the socialist system: former police officers, ex-Communist officials and former athletes, particularly wrestlers. They began with protection rackets and then moved into drug and cigarette smuggling, human trafficking and contract killing. Similarly, organized crime in Albania exploded after the country experienced a severe financial crisis in 1997. Albanian gangs smuggled arms to nearby Kosovo during the 1999 war and later expanded into drugs and human trafficking.[17]

A particularly poignant symbol of Eastern Europe's unruly transition to market capitalism in the 1990s was the rise of pyramid schemes. In a pyramid scheme, people deposit money into a fund and are promised an extravagant return (perhaps eight to ten times their original stake) within a set period, usually a few months. While they might pretend to be based on smart investments, pyramids are scams; they simply pay out the cash their "investors" have put in until the pool of money they owe exceeds their receipts and they collapse. Those early to the scheme can make money, but the more numerous latecomers at the bottom of the pyramid lose everything. Pyramid schemes sprang up all over Eastern Europe in the 1990s. Some countries banned them quickly after they appeared (they were already illegal in most capitalist countries), but in Romania and Albania, they continued for years before any legal action was taken against them.

In Romania, the pyramid scheme called "Caritas" was estimated to have had between two and eight million depositors. While the precise amount of cash placed in Caritas will probably never be known, it is likely that over a trillion Romanian lei were funneled through it between 1992 and 1994. Anthropologist Katherine Verdery hypothesized that profits from pyramid schemes played a major role in consolidating Romania's post-Communist political and economic elite; these insiders used pyramid schemes to raise substantial capital for themselves, allowing them to establish businesses or fund political parties. But why would so many ordinary Romanians give their money to pyramids? One reason is that they had little understanding of capitalist economics and did not realize that the incredible returns Caritas promised could never have come from legitimate investments. But the popularity of pyramids was not simply the result of ignorance. A "mutual-aid game"—which was how Caritas billed itself—did not seem irrational at a moment when inflation in Romania was over 300 percent, people had experienced a 40 percent drop in their real income, and banks failed to provide adequate credit for those who did want to start a new business. Caritas might have been a gamble, but at a moment when money in a savings account lost value with each passing day, there were few alternatives.[18] There was a similar dynamic at work in Albania, where two-thirds of the population invested in pyramid schemes in 1996–1997. When Albania's pyramids collapsed in 1997, the devastation was so great that it caused widespread rioting, leaving the country in chaos.[19]

After a decade of reforms, Eastern Europe's neoliberal leaders had achieved a mixed record of results with their economic policies. The countries of East-Central Europe—Poland, Hungary, the Czech Republic, Slovakia and Slovenia—endured inflation and unemployment, but eventually began to achieve sustained economic growth. The countries of the Balkans lagged considerably behind, and their inhabitants faced great economic uncertainty. But even within Eastern Europe's pockets of prosperity, the transition to the market was more traumatic that most people had imagined it would be. As East Europeans discovered, their experiences under socialism had not always prepared them for the realities of life in the capitalist world.

If People Want Coffee, They Won't Buy Tea

One day in 1996, Jarek, a salesman for Alima, a Polish baby food company, was trying to convince a grocery store manager in Lublin to purchase more creamed turkey, one of the company's most popular offerings. The manager refused, saying that she would not purchase any turkey until she sold the jars of lamb she already had on the shelves. Jarek argued that if customers wanted turkey, they wouldn't buy lamb instead, but she was not convinced. He left without making a sale. "Stupid Communist, that's what she is!" he exclaimed as he left the store. "If people want coffee, they won't buy tea! They'll go to another shop! Doesn't she know that there are other shops around the corner?"[20] Jarek and the grocery store manager were both Polish, but, for Jarek, they represented two different worlds. The grocery store manager embodied a supposedly rigid and inflexible socialist world that was not capable of adapting to changing times. In contrast, Jarek saw himself as part of a new, dynamic, capitalist Poland.

Jarek's company, Alima, had been purchased by the American company Gerber in 1992. Gerber's managers believed that making Alima viable in a market economy required its employees to break former socialist habits by adopting new values, such as flexibility, individualism and innovation. In fact, the socialist economy of shortage had always required Alima workers to operate very flexibly. If there was no fruit to make into baby food or juice, Alima retooled its production line to work with whatever was available. If they got tomatoes, Alima workers could make ketchup. If they found cabbage, they could make stuffed cabbage rolls. If there was no sugar and fruit delivered to the factory started to rot before it could be processed, they could make schnapps with the fermenting fruit. Yet this kind of flexibility was specific to the socialist economy: Alima's managers needed to fill quotas, not satisfy consumers. Gerber's American managers found it hard to translate Alima's socialist work practices into their capitalist idiom. In their world, it was not an advantage for a baby food company to be able to make schnapps from rotting fruit. They believed new products should result from marketing research, not necessity.[21]

One American Gerber executive recalled how Polish workers proposed making apple juice concentrate. To the workers, this seemed like a good decision because it would give Alima an additional product, and it would provide a market for the apples local farmers grew. The American manager objected, noting that the apples grown in the region were too sour to make good juice. The manager was accustomed to working in an environment where customers had choices and where a company's priority was making a profit. Why, he asked, should Alima make juice no one wanted to buy? The Alima workers, however, had a different perspective. They saw Alima as embedded in a community. For them, the plant's purpose was to support local farmers and to provide jobs. If making apple juice concentrate did those things, who cared if it was sour? Customers could add sugar if they needed to.[22]

Gerber's American executives believed Alima's success depended on having managers who understood the capitalist worldview. They fired Alima's socialist management team and hired young people like Jarek in their place. As firms around Eastern Europe tried to rapidly adjust to market conditions, young, urban professionals like Jarek, particularly those with university degrees and a knowledge of Western languages, were well poised to take advantage of the moment. Herma, a Czech sales manager who was in her early 20s when the socialist regime fell, was one of the young people who used the transition to the market to forge a promising new career. As she recalled in 1999, "before 1989, with the same education and same knowledge, opportunities were few. Now we have lots of opportunities." Like Herma, Irena, a 1987 graduate of the Prague University of Economics with excellent English, had the right skills to succeed in the capitalist job market. With only a few years of work experience at a Czech academic research institute, in 1990 Irena answered a newspaper job ad to be an administrative assistant at a new multinational company. The firm grew quickly and Irena was soon promoted to human resources manager, despite having no experience in this field. By the end of the 1990s, both Herma and Irena had become successful members of the managerial elite.[23]

Some who initially lost jobs in the transition were able to successfully transform themselves and forge new careers. In 1989, 38-year-old electrical engineer Vladimír Vaněk worked at the Research Institute of the Czechoslovak Ministry of the Interior. After being fired in the early 1990s, Vaněk forged a career as an IT expert and tax consultant. He admitted that under the capitalist system he had to work much harder than before. Yet, he enjoyed the challenge, remarking, "The roughness today suits me."[24] Vaněk's experience was echoed by the Romanian Valeria R. During the socialist period, Valeria worked at a research institute. After 1989, she lost her job and fell into a deep depression. Ultimately, however, she was able to reinvent herself and become the manager of a printing company. In 2003, Valeria declared,

> Yes, I can say it [life] has changed for the better. If you want to you can plan things; you have many more opportunities in your life; the fact that you can travel, you have access to information, there is no basis for comparison.[25]

Vladimír, Valeria and others like them had the skills and the luck to take advantage of the opportunities that the turn to capitalism created. Yet many others, particularly older people, industrial workers and rural dwellers, faced new hardships under the market economy. Unemployment, virtually unknown under socialism, became a constant threat. State support for health care, childcare, and higher education was slashed. Income inequality increased enormously. A survey conducted in Hungary in 1991–1992 reported that 9 percent of households had suffered significant loss of income in the previous two years, and 37 percent had seen a moderate loss. The income level of 22 percent of those surveyed remained the same, while 16 percent reported a modest gain and 16 percent a significant gain. These gaps tended to solidify with time. A 2005 study reported that the average life expectancy in the posh second district of Budapest was six years higher than that in the impoverished tenth district just across the river. Around the same time, Poles with incomes in the top 20 percent of the population earned six times more than those in the bottom 20 percent. On a

FIGURE 7.1   A homeless man sleeps in front of a well-stocked grocery store, Budapest, 2013. © Vladimir Pomortzeff/Alamy Stock Photo DRMW9H.

global scale, this is relatively moderate level of inequality, but it was nonetheless a significant change from the more egalitarian socialist period.[26]

While the transition's winners celebrated their new wealth, its losers acutely felt the injustice of winding up on the bottom. People who had grown up in a society where full employment was the norm were despondent at the loss of a job. Jaroslava Pavezová, a Czech cook, recalled,

> Four years ago I actually experienced myself what it's like to be without a job and, at nearly fifty-three, to be begging and scrounging for work … you work in a kitchen for thirty-five years, you're never on sick leave, and then to be looking for a new job at my age … It's painful and humiliating. It's more than a human being can take.[27]

Retired people were particularly subject to impoverishment, as inflation reduced the buying power of their pensions and governments cut benefits. Valeria P., a retired nurse in Romania, lamented,

> It does not matter that we have plenty in the stores, I cannot afford anything. As a retired woman, I must be very careful. There was no electricity before, now we have it, but I use only 40-watt bulbs if necessary. There was no hot water before, nowadays, hot water is so expensive that we only use cold water and we have water meters.[28]

When Lada, a worker in a Czech cosmetics factory, joined the crowds on the streets of Prague in November 1989, she was sure the protests would bring a better life for everyone. "It's going to be fabulous," she thought,

> Finally we're going to have it good, we're going to have more money,
> we're going to be able to travel … Finally those of us at the bottom—be-
> cause I am a worker—we're going to have it better.

She and her fellow workers at the factory—all women—reckoned that change
would require sacrifice, but they believed that they would eventually reap the
rewards. Instead, their lives became a "hunt for money." Jirka, who was 51
years old in 2000, described how her standard of living had fallen since the end
of socialism:

> I can't afford a vacation, which before I could afford. Before we could af-
> ford to buy a new car. Now it is absolutely, simply not possible any longer
> … What I earn is enough for us, for the family's subsistence and for the
> necessary expenses [i.e., electric, gas, phone] … and it's enough so that
> the children can study, but in no way for anything else.

Her coworker Daša agreed, saying, "I thought that after these ten years that we
would truly be somewhere else."[29]

When Communist-era industries failed, whole towns and regions could fall
from security into precarity. The Rhodope mountains of Bulgaria had been
home to a thriving network of lead and zinc mines. Under socialism, the mines
had provided well-paid jobs for the region's men and fueled the modernization
of local towns and villages. After 1989, however, Bulgarian mines found it hard
to compete on the open market. The Rhodope mines continued under state
ownership until 1998, when they were split up and privatized under somewhat
dubious circumstances. Most closed soon after; the workers were fired and the
machinery sold for scrap. After the mines failed, there were few employment
opportunities in the area. Those who could fled to find jobs elsewhere, while
those who stayed lived a hand-to-mouth existence. Donka worked as a seam-
stress and had a side job selling Avon products, but her earnings of approximately $165 per month were not enough to adequately support her unemployed
husband and two teenage sons. Donka's family subsisted mostly on bread, sup-
plemented with vegetables and yogurt she produced herself on plot of land
owned by her mother. Donka's husband, like many of the local men, turned
to alcohol as a comfort. Vesela, a waitress at a bar frequented by unemployed
miners, sympathized with their despair, saying, "They have nothing else. They
used to have so much money, and everyone respected them. But it is hard for
a man to be without work. There is nothing for them to do. What can miners
do without mines?"[30]

Statistical data show that by 2004 living standards had improved on average
throughout Eastern Europe. But even those who had greater purchasing power
were not always sure their lives had improved under the market economy. The
American anthropologist Kristen Ghodsee, who conducted extensive research

on Bulgaria's transition to a market economy in the 1990s and 2000s, remarked that people often "complained to me that life is faster now, that they must run everywhere to get everything done, and that they lead exhausting, multitasking lives with no time for friends or family or lovers." Yet, Ghodsee noted, sociological data from 1969 showed that Bulgarian women spent an average of 14.5 hours a day on their jobs, housework and childcare; they had little free time. Nonetheless, the daily toil they experienced under socialism felt less burdensome to Ghodsee's interlocutors than the existential pressures of capitalism. Ghodsee concluded,

> maybe the comparison is not about the actual amount of time spent at home or at work or waiting in line for toilet paper, but about the stress one feels about the passing of time, the anxiety produced by living in a society where time is money.[31]

The move to a market economy had erased socialism's shortages, but it had not necessarily brought happiness.

We'll Have to Take to the Woods Again and Fight

On June 4, 1990, a few months after his party won Hungary's first multiparty elections since the 1940s, Prime Minister József Antall declared, "in spirit, I consider myself to be the prime minister of 15 million Hungarians." While it sounded innocuous to the uninitiated, Antall's statement was a provocation: Hungary only had 10.5 million inhabitants. The larger figure could only be derived by including the Hungarian-speakers who resided in other countries. Significantly, Antall made this claim on the 70th anniversary of the Treaty of Trianon, the agreement that had awarded pieces of what had been Hungary to neighboring Romania, Czechoslovakia and Yugoslavia after World War I. Even after seven decades, Antall suggested, the Hungarian communities in these countries still belonged to a unified Hungarian nation.[32]

In the early 1990s, Antall's embrace of Hungarian minorities abroad did not bear much fruit. Western governments did not support Hungarian irredentist dreams and Hungary's open support of possible border revisions antagonized its neighbors. Antall may have hoped that nationalist rhetoric would increase his popular support at home, but most Hungarians cared more about his government's economic performance than its solidarity with ethnic Hungarians abroad. At the same time, radical elements within Antall's own party took advantage of the new political climate to promote views that were overtly racist. One, party vice-chairman István Csurka, wrote an article in 1992 in which he invoked antisemitic conspiracy theories that posited Jews as the force behind both international financial institutions and Communism, two forces he saw as inimical to the Hungarian nation. Csurka was later dismissed from his post as a result of Western pressure. In 1994, voters rejected Antall's party and elected a new government from the socialist left.[33]

Antall's turn to nationalism was part of a broader trend in East European politics after 1989. Nationalist politicians throughout the region turned to ethnic conflict, xenophobia and other populist themes to gain votes. Slovak Vladimir Mečiar was a political opportunist who used nationalism to stay in power for much of the 1990s. As prime minister of the region of Slovakia under the federal Czechoslovak system, Mečiar argued that the neoliberal policies of Václav Klaus benefitted Czechs at the expense of Slovaks. Rather than working out their differences, Klaus and Mečiar decided to split Czechoslovakia apart, despite polls showing that a majority of Czechs and Slovaks wanted to keep the country together. The Czech Republic and Slovakia separated peacefully in 1993 in what has been called the "Velvet Divorce."[34]

As prime minister of an independent Slovakia, Mečiar presided over a corrupt privatization process that rewarded his friends and party loyalists, allowing them to purchase state assets at a fraction of their value. The level of corruption discouraged foreign investors, hobbling the Slovak economy. Mečiar's party—Movement for a Democratic Slovakia (HZDS)—flouted democratic institutions and used state radio and television services to brand opponents as enemies of the Slovak nation. To escape responsibility for the country's poor economic performance, Mečiar encouraged Slovaks to blame their economic problems on the machinations of outsiders, including Czechs, Slovakia's Hungarian minority, the Roma, opposition politicians and journalists. Mečiar was finally ousted by a coalition of opposition parties in 1998.[35] After he was gone, Slovak leaders began to implement neoliberal policies, including privatizing health care and a flat tax rate for individuals and businesses. This brought greater foreign investment and increased economic growth, but at the expense of high unemployment and reduced social benefits.[36]

Mečiar's demonization of the Roma community was echoed across the region. Racist invective about the Roma became commonplace in Eastern Europe's newly free media. Roma people were almost invariably characterized as lazy and prone to criminality, and they became popular scapegoats for the pain of the transition to a market economy. In reality, the Roma were disproportionately among those who suffered downward mobility after 1989, quickly losing the economic gains they had made under socialism. Unemployment rates among the Roma community rose as high as 90 percent, and many Roma families became mired in grinding poverty. One result of this newly visible anti-Roma racism was a wave of violent attacks on Roma people and property. In one infamous attack in 1993 in the Romanian town of Hădăreni, three Roma men were killed by a mob and 14 Roma homes were destroyed. Among the perpetrators were several policemen who were never put on trial, despite clear evidence against them. The situation of the Roma across the region of Eastern Europe drew the attention of international human rights organizations like

Human Rights Watch and Amnesty International and eventually led to the establishment of the European Roma Rights Center, an NGO dedicated to helping Roma victims of human rights abuses. Anti-Roma racism, however, remained common in much of Eastern Europe.[37]

Nowhere did nationalist politics have more fateful consequences than in Yugoslavia. Nationalism began to dominate Yugoslav politics in the late 1980s, as figures like Slobodan Milošević used nationalist grievances as a way to consolidate power. In 1990, each of the country's six republics organized multiparty elections for their own regional governments. Nationalists of various stripes won power in all of them. These elections set the stage for the republics of Slovenia and Croatia to declare independence in 1991. After a brief standoff, Slovenia was able to secede without incident. In contrast, Croatia's declaration of independence sparked a civil war. In 1992, the fighting spread to Bosnia-Herzegovina. The war in Bosnia and Croatia ended in 1995, with the internationally brokered Dayton Accords. Conflict then spread to Kosovo in 1998–1999 and Macedonia in 2001.[38]

The violence in Yugoslavia, which sometimes pitted neighbor against neighbor, was driven by the fear that if Yugoslavia's republics became independent, their governments would attack the ethnic minorities in their midst. This fear was carefully nurtured by politicians like Slobodan Milošević. Slovenia escaped the war because it was a small, remote and ethnically homogeneous republic without significant ethnic minorities. In contrast, 582,000 Serbs lived in Croatia.[39] After the nationalist Franjo Tudjman was elected president of Croatia in 1990, Milošević began warning Croatian Serbs that they would never be safe in an independent Croatia. Tudjman's actions gave some credence to Milošević's claims. His government wrote a new constitution, named Croatia the "state of the Croatian nation" and officially marked Serbs as a minority. It also rehabilitated a Croatian national emblem (the red and white checkerboard or šahovnica) that had been used by the Ustaša, the Croatian fascists from World War II. These actions became fodder for sensationalist reporting on Serb television, which warned of a possible genocide of Croatian Serbs. Extremist Serb groups, such as Vojislav Šešelj's Chetniks (named for Serb World War II-era paramilitaries), began to visit Croatian Serb villages to urge the inhabitants to arm themselves.[40]

Ejub Štitkovac, a Bosnian Muslim journalist, visited Croatia shortly before the war began in 1991 intending to see two friends, one Serb and one Croat. He was amazed at how ethnically polarized the environment had become. His Croatian friend refused to accompany Štitkovac to see their Serb friend, even though this man had been the Croat's friend since childhood and served as the best man at his wedding. "'We'll leave that visit for better times,' he said. 'If Serbs like him don't wake up and realize Milošević is trying to push them into war with us, all hell will break loose.'" The Serb friend had precisely the opposite view: he was convinced the Croats were getting ready to murder the Serbs and claimed Tudjman's party had drawn up lists of Serbs to be shot. "We'll have to take to the woods again and fight," he said. Two days later, he went and joined a paramilitary group.[41]

The distrust that had grown between ethnic groups before the war began increased exponentially once the conflict had begun. Serb and Croat television stations constantly ran images of brutal killings to emphasize the savagery of the other side and justify the war. Accuracy was not as important as the political message. According to Serb journalist Milan Milošević, "It was not unusual for Croatian and Serbian television to borrow each other's victims. The same victim would be identified on a Zagreb screens as a Croat and on Belgrade screens as a Serb."[42] Each side would spin its own stories about how the deaths had occurred at the hands of the other side. The spectacle of death convinced many viewers that people who had just months before been their compatriots were now their sworn enemies.

Bosnia-Herzegovina was at the heart of the violence. Bosnia was a multi-ethnic republic: 43 percent Bosnian Muslim, 31 percent Serb and 17 percent Croat.[43] After Croatia and Slovenia seceded from Yugoslavia, the Muslim and Croat populations of Bosnia also favored independence, reluctant to remain in a Serb-dominated Yugoslavia. Bosnian Serbs, however, believed that they would become an oppressed minority in an independent Bosnia. In an interview with an American journalist in September 1990, Bosnian Serb leader Radovan Karadžić declared, "The most direct danger to the Serb people is that there will be a breakup of Yugoslavia and that part of the Serb nation will become a minority in a new foreign country. This would mean their destruction." Bosnian Serbs, said Karadžić, were willing to go to war to protect their national sovereignty.[44] When the Bosnian government proceeded with its plans for secession, Bosnian Serb paramilitaries, bolstered with arms and personnel from the Serb-dominated Yugoslav National Army, moved to secure part of Bosnia for their use alone. In just over half a year, more than two million people would be forced to flee their homes.

The Yugoslav wars of secession were the bloodiest and most destructive conflict in Europe since World War II. Approximately 140,000 people were killed; about 100,000 of those deaths occurred in the Bosnian war. Roughly five million people were displaced, including over half of the 4.4 million inhabitants of Bosnia-Herzegovina. This mass displacement of civilians was the result of conscious policies on the part of the combatants, which became known internationally as *ethnic cleansing*. In ethnic cleansing, perpetrators aimed to create an ethnically pure territory by violently expelling all members of other ethnic groups. The use of violence in the process of ethnic cleansing was deliberate and purposeful, designed to intimidate, terrify and humiliate the victims. This violence included mass killings of civilians and unarmed detainees. The United Nations International Criminal Tribunal for the former Yugoslavia documented hundreds of cases of mass killings committed during the conflict.

While all ethnic groups engaged in these murders, a majority of the victims were Bosnian Muslims. In the most notorious massacre of the war, between 6,500 and 8,800 unarmed Muslim men and boys were systematically murdered by Bosnian Serb forces outside the town of Srebrenica in 1995. Sexual assault was another weapon used in ethnic cleansing to terrorize and humiliate victims. It is difficult to determine how many sexual assaults occurred during the Yugoslav conflict, particularly since many rape victims did not want to speak publicly about their experiences. According to one estimate, there were approximately 25,000 cases of rape, torture and sexual abuse of Bosnian Muslim women at Serb-run detention camps during the war.[45]

The destruction of property was an essential component of ethnic cleansing. Perpetrators burned down the houses of the unwanted population in order to prevent their return. They destroyed mosques, churches and other cultural sites, hoping to annihilate the heritage of the victim group and erase it from the landscape. Personal gain was an additional motive for property crimes: many engaged in looting and theft as they rousted their victims from their homes.[46] Some paramilitaries joined the fighting expressly for this purpose. Kenan Trebinčević, whose Muslim family was one of the last to remain in the Bosnian town of Brčko after it had been cleansed by Serbs, remembered the day a Serb couple from Belgrade armed with Uzis knocked on the door of his family's apartment. After looking around, the Serbs decided to take a chandelier as payment for not inflicting any further violence on the family. Kenan was drafted to help them take the chandelier to their newly acquired home in town. He was stunned to see that the garage of their commandeered house was teeming with televisions, video cassette recorders, stereos, furniture, paintings and other objects confiscated from the Muslim community.[47]

The story of the Kozić family exemplifies the brutal violence of ethnic cleansing. Adem Kozić was a poor Muslim living in a tiny village in eastern Bosnia. Some of his neighbors fled to escape the Serbs and urged him to join them, but Adem, his wife Hanifa and two of their children stayed behind. Two weeks after the others had left, a group of armed Serb men showed up in a van and ordered the Kozić family and all the other Muslims left in the village to leave immediately. They hurriedly packed a few things and fled. After spending the night in a meadow, they were forced onto buses going into the town of Višegrad. When they arrived at the town's firehouse, Serb gunmen strip-searched the women and took all of their valuables. That night, amid gunshots, the male detainees were taken away. None returned. Some days later, the body of Adem Kozić was fished out of the Drina river by Muslim refugees who had clustered in a town downstream. His body was one of dozens that floated down the river that month.

Without being told the fate of their men, the women and children were held at the firehouse for 15 days. Every night, some of the women were raped by their captors. Then they were loaded onto buses and, after a long and torturous journey, dumped on the border between Serbia and Macedonia. Denied entry into either place, they spent months trapped in the no-man's land between them, living off food donated by local Albanians. Eventually the Red Cross was informed of their plight, and the survivors finally wound up at refugee camps in Turkey.[48]

When the war broke out, many people of all ethnicities opposed it. By one estimate, 50–80 percent of Serbian army reservists called up in 1991 refused to serve. Some Serb men went into hiding, and as many as 200,000 fled the country rather than fight. Others deserted the battlefield in droves.[49] Shortly before the violence began, tens of thousands marched in Bosnian towns, proclaiming, "We want to live together," while protestors in the capital city of Sarajevo held banners reading, "Yugo, We Love You!" Throughout the conflict, many tried to help neighbors and friends of different ethnicities escape harm.[50] Yet these opposing voices were marginalized and silenced, sometimes via harassment and threats of violence. This systematic silencing of the peaceful majority was paradoxically assisted by Western observers, who became convinced that the conflict in Yugoslavia was due to supposedly ancient and unstoppable ethnic hatreds that had naturally erupted once an authoritarian Communist government was no longer there to contain them. Rather than seeing the conflict as orchestrated by elites who hoped to use nationalist war to keep power, many Western leaders blamed it on supposedly backward "Balkan" mentalities that, they believed, prevented the Yugoslav peoples from ever living together peacefully.[51]

The belief that the conflict was inevitable shaped Western policy. Western governments quickly accepted that dissolution was the only possible solution to the Yugoslav crisis. The United States and its West European allies refused to intervene militarily in the conflict, declining to do anything to stop the ethnic cleansing in Bosnia until after the massacre at Srebrenica. A NATO bombing campaign on Bosnian Serb positions eventually brought all parties to the negotiating table. The resulting Dayton Accords ended the war, but at the cost of hardening ethnic divisions rather than overcoming them. Independent Bosnia's complicated and byzantine governmental structure, which included 13 parliaments and 180 ministries for a country of only four million people, allocated political power by ethnicity, assigning parliamentary seats to Muslims, Serbs and Croats. Politicians had little incentive to cooperate, creating a system one scholar described as "parasitic, unrepresentative, and unresponsive," dominated by "red tape, bureaucracy and corruption."[52] There were few economic opportunities for those without political connections; in 2015, 44 percent of the population was officially unemployed. Most educated young people emigrated to find better lives elsewhere, leaving the less skilled and the elderly behind.[53]

As they gradually emerged from the wreckage of Yugoslavia, the newly independent countries of Slovenia, Croatia, Serbia, Bosnia, Montenegro, Northern Macedonia and Kosovo have all struggled to develop democratic

MAP 7.1 Eastern Europe in 2021.

institutions and functional market economies.[54] They have had widely varying degrees of success. Kosovo, which declared independence from Serbia in 2008 and whose sovereignty is still not recognized by many nations, has lagged far behind Slovenia, which escaped the war blessed with Yugoslavia's most highly developed economy. To achieve stability and prosperity, the countries of the former Yugoslavia set their sights on becoming part of the EU. This was something that also inspired the other countries of Eastern Europe.

From Global Socialism to Fortress Europe

In many accounts of 1989, the fall of the Berlin Wall was the moment that Eastern Europe emerged from a 40-year period of isolation. Yet this powerful image of trapped East Europeans suddenly breaking free of an oppressive Iron Curtain neglects the fact that Eastern Europe had been part of a socialist world that spanned the globe. With the exception of nonaligned Yugoslavia (and after 1961, Albania), the countries of Eastern Europe had close economic and security ties to the Soviet Union via the Council for Mutual Economic Assistance (CMEA) and Warsaw Pact. They also enjoyed close relations with other socialist and socialist-leaning countries in Asia, Africa and Latin America. The East European experience of this wider socialist world was not limited to elite foreign relations and commercial trading contacts. Being part of a global socialist community inspired Hungarian students to demonstrate in support of the Cuban Revolution and Salvador Allende's Chile. It allowed Bulgarian women's activists to organize workshops for African and Asian women who wanted to learn about UN procedures and share strategies for change. It brought Polish economists to lecture in India, tens of thousands of Vietnamese workers to Czechoslovakia and over 600 students from Angola to study at East German universities.[55]

This global socialist world collapsed after 1989. Eastern Europe's new neoliberal regimes had little desire to continue former relationships built on the foundation of socialist solidarity. The economic and military alliances that bound Eastern Europe to the Soviet Union, the CMEA and the Warsaw Pact, were dissolved in 1991, shortly before the Soviet Union ceased to exist. In their place, Eastern Europe's new leaders hoped to reorient their countries away from Russia and the Global South and turn them toward the West. They framed this reorientation as a "return to Europe," implying that Eastern Europe's more global outlook under socialism had been an aberration and a mistake.[56] East European governments hoped to achieve this "return" by joining the EU and NATO. Membership in these organizations would become Eastern Europe's foremost foreign policy goal after 1989.

The EU formally came into existence with the Maastricht Treaty of 1992, but its beginnings lay in the 1950s. After the end of World War II, some of the countries of Western Europe began to explore greater economic cooperation between them as a means of preventing future conflicts. What began as a free trade zone among six countries had by 1992 become a group of 12 nations committed to an unprecedented level of economic integration, including a single market, a common currency (the Euro), a common central bank and the free movement of capital and labor throughout all member countries. The Maastricht Treaty laid the groundwork for deepening political integration between EU member states, including a common commitment to democratic institutions and common foreign policy and security aims. Eastern Europe's desire to join the EU was both symbolic and practical. Membership offered development aid and integration into a larger European economy. It also represented a definitive break with the Communist past. The existing countries of the EU could see a similar range of possible advantages. Admitting the countries of Eastern Europe into the union would aid the EU's mission of promoting peace and stability across the continent. It would also open new markets to West European companies and help the EU to become a bigger player on the world stage.[57]

However, the EU would not make it easy for the countries of Eastern Europe to join. According to the 1993 Copenhagen criteria, which spelled out the requirements for EU membership,

> Membership requires that the candidate country has achieved stability of institutions guaranteeing democracy, the rule of law, human rights and respect for and protection of minorities, the existence of a functioning market economy as well as the capacity to cope with competitive pressure and market forces within the Union.[58]

In addition to proving that they had established stable democratic institutions and implemented the legal basis for capitalism, aspiring member states needed to adopt the *acquis communautaire*, or the existing body of EU laws and regulations. This body of law was enormous, comprising up to 100,000 pages of text. It dealt with everything from environmental standards and food safety practices to banking regulations and intellectual property laws. While it is easy to satirize the incredibly detailed provisions of many EU regulations—which require, for example, that bananas be "free of abnormal curvature" or that animals only be slaughtered in rooms tiled from wall to wall—the point of common standards was to enable the EU to function as a single economic unit. Having the same standards theoretically meant that no country could undercut another by skimping on safety or quality.[59]

The process of meeting these requirements was long and arduous, requiring what amounted to a legal revolution.[60] Each candidate country's entire body of law and administrative practice had to be changed to conform with EU standards. While West European candidates for EU membership, such as Finland

FIGURE 7.2   A woman in Wrocław rides her bike next to a billboard urging Poles to vote "yes" in the referendum to join the EU, 2003. © Photo by Sean Gallup/Getty Images.

and Austria, also needed to conform to the *acquis* before they could be admitted, only applicants from Eastern Europe were required to prove that they had met democratic norms and human rights standards. While some grumbled, most East Europeans supported EU membership. In 2003, 77 percent of Czechs voted in favor of joining the EU. Vladimir Spidla, the Czech prime minister at the time, acknowledged the difficulty of the process, noting, "We will have to comply with all kinds of EU regulations, and that will cause a lot of headaches for Czech firms." Yet, he said, "It will open the door for them to the European market." Zdenka Kobilková, a 57-year-old lecturer at a school for tour guides, concurred, telling a reporter, "It's for my children and my grandchildren, so that they will have a better life."[61] The Czech Republic, Hungary, Poland, Slovakia and Slovenia finally became members of the EU in 2004, 15 years after they began their transition away from socialism. Bulgaria and Romania joined in 2007. Croatia became an EU member state in 2013, while in 2021 Albania, Montenegro, Northern Macedonia and Serbia were still preparing to meet the *acquis*.

One tenet of EU membership is that the citizens of EU nations have the right to work in any EU country. However, East Europeans had to wait for up to seven years after accession to fully enjoy this freedom. The delay was due to West European fears of a deluge of poor East Europeans seeking employment in the rich West. "We can't just open the floodgates," argued German trade unionist Roland Issen. France was equally suspicious of East European labor migration. In 2005, a successful campaign to persuade French voters to reject a proposed EU constitution rested on the specter of an army of "Polish plumbers" who would take away French jobs.[62] This army did not appear, but millions of Poles did migrate in search of work after 2004. In 2011, there were 2.1 million Poles living abroad, mostly in Western Europe. In 2016, Poles were the one of the largest immigrant groups in the United Kingdom, second only to India.[63] The numbers were even greater from impoverished Romania. Between 2009 and 2011, 2.4 million Romanians—over 10 percent of the population—left the country.[64]

Having the freedom to travel, study or work anywhere in the EU has allowed East Europeans to live in ways that were unimaginable for most under socialism. Today, some who emigrate leave permanently, but others stay abroad for a few years and return home. Some East European workers take part in annual seasonal labor migrations, picking asparagus in Germany or tomatoes in Spain. Others navigate complicated circular trajectories related to their professional and personal situations, such as an unexpected job offer, a new romantic relationship, the death of a parent or the birth of a child. The new ease of mobility EU membership has provided means emigrants can stay connected to their home countries as never before. For Gosia, a Polish emigrant who grew up in the United Kingdom, an EU passport and budget airlines made it possible for her to take weekend jaunts to Kraków just to have lunch and see

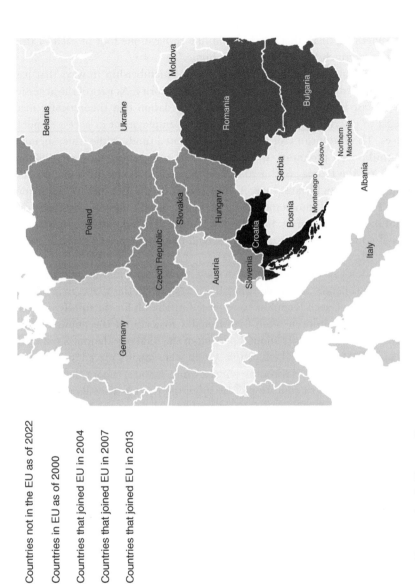

MAP 7.2 EU expansion in Eastern Europe.

Countries not in the EU as of 2022

Countries in EU as of 2000

Countries that joined EU in 2004

Countries that joined EU in 2007

Countries that joined EU in 2013

a play. Gosia relished her ability to live simultaneously in a Polish world and a British one. When asked if she would prefer to live in either Poland or the United Kingdom, she said, "I would not want to decide–I would not want to have something final, that's it. I would like to have one foot in each of these countries in which I feel very much at home."[65]

Gosia was able to enjoy the benefits of EU membership in ways that have not been available to Eastern Europe's Roma minority. As part of the accession process, East European countries adopted legislation that theoretically made it illegal to discriminate against the Roma in employment or access to public services. The European Commission also devoted funds to the issue, spending €100 million on programs to improve Roma integration between 1998 and 2008.[66] Yet the Roma continued to face unequal access to employment, education, housing and health care. A 2009 report by the European Commission against Racism and Intolerance about Hungary noted a number of possible factors for the lack of progress, including the failure of local authorities to translate national policies into workable practice and the persistence of racist discourse in the public sphere.[67]

The issue of school segregation in the Czech Republic illustrates the difficulties Roma people faced even after EU accession. In the 1990s, many Roma children in the Czech Republic were placed in schools for the mildly mentally disabled. Roma children often constituted a majority of the pupils in these schools, despite being only about 3 percent of the total population. Roma children outside of this special education system were usually placed in segregated schools (or segregated classrooms within white schools) where they typically received a substandard education.[68] In 2000, the parents of 18 Roma children who had been sent to schools for the mentally disabled sued the Czech Republic for discrimination at the European Court of Human Rights. In 2007, they won their case in a landmark judgment that Roma rights advocates compared to the *Brown v. Board of Education* ruling in the United States. Yet even with this win, change was slow to arrive. In 2011, the European Roma Rights Center worried that new legislation in the Czech Republic merely perpetuated the problem by allowing "disability and socio-economic status to be used as a proxy for race."[69] A 2015 investigation by the human rights organization Amnesty International found that Roma children were still being systematically placed into newly renamed "practical" schools or segregated institutions.[70]

The EU's efforts to encourage East European governments to improve the situation of Roma citizens were not altruistic. West European governments were afraid that if conditions for the Roma did not improve, Roma communities would try to migrate to the West. Their fears were realized after 2007, when thousands of Roma from Romania and Bulgaria used their new EU citizenship to look for greater opportunity elsewhere. They did not receive a warm welcome. In 2008, Italy unveiled a plan for a "Roma census" that required fingerprinting all Roma, including children, as if they were criminals.

Local officials in Italy bulldozed Roma campsites and deported the residents. France conducted large-scale deportations of Roma in 2009 and 2010, expelling around 10,000 people each year. While the European Commission protested the French deportations as against EU law, France altered its policies to comply but continued to deport or evict Roma with foreign passports anyway. In 2013, France evicted 19,000 Roma living in shantytowns on the outskirts of French cities and deported 11,000.[71]

The continued plight of the Roma illustrates the multifaceted and sometimes unexpected effects of the fall of Communism in Eastern Europe. In 1989, most East Europeans thought that the future would bring them more freedom and a better standard of living. They discovered that these two things did not always go hand in hand. While freedom might bring opportunity, it could also be cruel. After 1989, some prospered, but many suffered. The pain and the fear they experienced sometimes found its expression in racism, intolerance and violence. Given that one of the goals of the EU was to promote peace and stability in Europe, some hoped that EU membership might help address these issues. After 2008, however, the EU itself would become the target of nationalist politics.

Notes

1 This number is from Catherine Baker, *The Yugoslav Wars of the 1990s* (New York: Palgrave Macmillan, 2015), 1.
2 "Post-totalitarian" was the adjective Havel used to describe Communist governments in Eastern Europe after 1968. Václav Havel, "The Power of the Powerless," in *Open Letters: Selected Writings 1965–1990*, trans. Paul Wilson (New York: Vintage, 1992), 208–211 (quote on 208).
3 James Krapfl, *Revolution with a Human Face: Politics, Culture and Community in Czechoslovakia, 1989–1992* (Ithaca, NY: Cornell University Press, 2013), 76.
4 Krapfl, *Revolution with a Human Face*, 90–100 (quote on p. 90).
5 James Mark, Bogdan C. Iacob, Tobias Rupprecht and Ljubica Spaskovska, *1989: A Global History of Eastern Europe* (Cambridge: Cambridge University Press, 2019), 64.
6 Elaine Susan Weiner, *Market Dreams: Gender, Class and Capitalism in the Czech Republic* (Ann Arbor: University of Michigan Press, 2007), 58–60.
7 Philipp Ther, *Europe Since 1989: A History*, trans. Charlotte Hughes-Kreutzmüller (Princeton, NJ: Princeton University Press, 2016), 77–83.
8 Ivan T. Berend, *From the Soviet Bloc to the European Union: The Economic and Social Transformation of Eastern Europe Since 1973* (Cambridge: Cambridge University Press, 2009), 187–188, 209.
9 Mark et al., *1989*, 83–84.
10 Charles S. Maier, *Dissolution: The Crisis of Communism and the End of East Germany* (Princeton, NJ: Princeton University Press, 1997), 290–293; Ther, *Europe Since 1989*, 85–89.
11 Rohwedder was killed by Red Brigade terrorists in 1991. Maier, *Dissolution*, 293–303 (quote on p. 294).
12 Berend, *From the Soviet Bloc to the European Union*, 16.
13 Ther, *Europe Since 1989*, 95–96.
14 Steve Levine, "Investor Is Accused of Fraud Over Azerbaijan Venture," *New York Times*, December 22, 1999, https://www.nytimes.com/1999/12/22/world/international-business-investor-is-accused-of-fraud-over-azerbaijan-venture.html

(accessed May 14, 2020); "Co dnes dělá Viktor Kožený?" *Dotyk*, October 28, 2019, https://www.dotyk.cz/magazin/viktor-kozeny-20191023.html (accessed May 14, 2020).

15 Berend, *From the Soviet Bloc to the European Union*, 187.
16 Kristen Ghodsee, *Muslim Lives in Eastern Europe: Gender, Ethnicity and the Transformation of Islam in Postsocialist Bulgaria* (Princeton, NJ: Princeton University Press, 2010), 74.
17 Leslie Holmes, "Organised Crime in—and from—Communist and Post-communist States," in *30 Years since the Fall of the Berlin Wall: Turns and Twists in Economies, Politics, and Societies in the Post-Communist Countries*, ed. Alexandr Akimov and Gennadi Kazakevitch (Singapore: Palgrave Macmillan, 2020), 83–113.
18 Katherine Verdery, *What Was Socialism and What Comes Next?* (Princeton, NJ: Princeton University Press, 1999), 168–203.
19 Christopher Jarvis, "The Rise and Fall of Albania's Pyramid Schemes," *Finance and Development* 37, no. 1 (March 2000), https://www.imf.org/external/pubs/ft/fandd/2000/03/jarvis.htm (accessed May 15, 2020).
20 Elizabeth C. Dunn, *Privatizing Poland: Baby Food, Big Business and the Remaking of Labor* (Ithaca, NY: Cornell University Press, 2004), 89.
21 Dunn, *Privatizing Poland*, 16–17, 84.
22 Dunn, *Privatizing Poland*, 96.
23 Weiner, *Market Dreams*, 72–74.
24 Miroslav Vaněk and Pavel Mücke, *Velvet Revolutions: An Oral History of Czech Society* (New York: Oxford University Press, 2016), 142, 217.
25 Jill Massino, *Ambiguous Transitions: Gender, the State and Everyday Life in Socialist and Postsocialist Romania* (New York: Berghahn Books, 2019), 392.
26 Berend, *From the Soviet Bloc to the European Union*, 193, 209.
27 Vaněk and Mücke, *Velvet Revolutions*, 141.
28 Massino, *Ambiguous Transitions*, 389.
29 Weiner, *Market Dreams*, 95–101.
30 Ghodsee, *Muslim Lives*, 56–108 (quote on p. 107).
31 Kristen Ghodsee, *Red Hangover: Legacies of Twentieth-Century Communism* (Durham, NC: Duke University Press, 2017), 106–107.
32 Myra Waterbury, "The State as Ethnic Activist: Explaining Continuity and Change in Hungarian Diaspora Policy," Ph.D. diss, New School University, 2007, 186–187.
33 László Valki, "Hungary: Understanding Western Messages," in *Democratic Consolidation in Eastern Europe Volume 2: International and Transnational Factors*, ed. Jan Zielonka and Alex Pravda (Oxford: Oxford University Press, 2001), 281–310.
34 Krapfl, *Revolution with a Human Face*, 208–216.
35 Milada Anna Vachudova, *Europe Undivided: Democracy, Leverage, and Integration after Communism* (Oxford: Oxford University Press, 2005), 25–62.
36 Ther, *Europe Since 1989*, 115–118.
37 István Pogány, "Pariah Peoples: Roma and the Multiple Failures of Law in Central and Eastern Europe," *Social and Legal Studies* 21, no. 3 (2012): 375–393; Celia Donert, *The Rights of the Roma: The Struggle for Citizenship in Postwar Czechoslovakia* (Cambridge: Cambridge University Press, 2017), 247–270; David M. Crowe, "The Roma in Post-Communist Eastern Europe: Questions of Ethnic Conflict and Ethnic Peace," *Nationalities Papers* 36, no. 3 (2008): 521–552.
38 Marie-Janine Calic, *The Great Cauldron: A History of Southeastern Europe*, trans. Elizabeth Janik (Cambridge, MA: Harvard University Press, 2019), 529–536.
39 Paul Robert Magocsi, *Historical Atlas of Central Europe* (Seattle: University of Washington Press, 2002), 162.
40 Ejub Štitkovac, "Croatia: The First War," in *Burn This House: The Making and Unmaking of Yugoslavia*, ed. Jasminka Udovički and James Ridgeway (Durham, NC: Duke University Press, 2000), 155–158.

41 Štitkovac, "Croatia," 154–155.

42 Milan Milošević, "The Media Wars: 1987–1997," in Udovički and Ridgeway, *Burn This House*, 120–121.

43 In the 1991 census, 5.4 percent of the Bosnian population identified as "Yugoslavs" and 2.2 percent as "other." Magocsi, *Historical Atlas of Central Europe*, 165.

44 Chuck Sudetic, *Blood and Vengeance: One Family's Story of the War in Bosnia* (New York: Penguin, 1999), 84.

45 Estimates of the dead in the Yugoslav wars can vary widely. I have used the conservative figures adopted by the multinational group of scholars who took part in the Scholars' Initiative. See Marie Janine Calic, "Ethnic Cleansing and War Crimes, 1991–1995," in *Confronting the Yugoslav Controversies: A Scholars' Initiative*, ed. Charles Ingrao and Thomas A. Emmert (West Lafayette, IN: Purdue University Press, 2009), 114–152.

46 Calic, "Ethnic Cleansing and War Crimes."

47 Kenan Trebinčević, *The Bosnia List: A Memoir of War, Exile and Return* (New York: Penguin, 2014), 115–123.

48 Sudetic, *Blood and Vengeance*, 118–124.

49 V.P. Gagnon, *The Myth of Ethnic War: Serbia and Croatia in the 1990s* (Ithaca, NY: Cornell University Press, 2006), 2–5.

50 Jasminka Udovički and Ejub Štitkovac, "Bosnia and Herzegovina: The Second War," in Udovički and Ridgeway, *Burn This House*, 183–184.

51 Mark et al., *1989*, 208–209.

52 Eric Gordy, "Dayton's Annex 4 Constitution at 20: Political Stalemate, Public Dissatisfaction and the Rebirth of Self-Organisation," *Southeast European and Black Sea Studies* 15, no. 4 (2015): 611–622.

53 Larisa Kurtović, "'Who Sows Hunger, Reaps Rage': On Protest, Indignation and Redistributive Justice in Post-Dayton Bosnia-Herzegovina," *Journal of Southeast European & Black Sea Studies* 15, no. 4 (2015): 639–659; Azra Hromadžić, "Disillusioned with Dayton in Bosnia-Herzegovina," *Current History* 117 (March 2018): 102–107.

54 The former Yugoslav republic of Macedonia agreed in 2019 to change its name to Northern Macedonia to resolve a dispute with Greece.

55 James Mark and Peter Ápor, "Socialism Goes Global: Decolonization and the Making of a New Culture of Internationalism in Socialist Hungary, 1956–1989," *Journal of Modern History* 87, no. 4 (2015): 852–891; Kristen Ghodsee, *Second World, Second Sex: Socialist Women's Activism and Global Solidarity during the Cold War* (Durham, NC: Duke University Press, 2018); Małgorzata Mazurek, "Polish Economists in Nehru's India: Making Social Science for the Third World in an Era of De-Stalinization," *Slavic Review* 77, no. 3 (2018): 588–610; Alena K. Alamgir, "Socialist Internationalism at Work: Changes in the Czechoslovak-Vietnamese Labor Exchange Program, 1967–1989," Ph.D. diss, Rutgers University, 2014; Marcia C. Schenk, "Negotiating the German Democratic Republic: Angolan Student Migration during the Cold War,1976–9," *Africa* 89, suppl. 1 (2019): 144–166.

56 Mark et al., *1989*, 125–154.

57 Berend, *From the Soviet Bloc to the European Union*, 84–85.

58 Berend, *From the Soviet Bloc to the European Union*, 89.

59 Zsuzsa Gille, *Paprika, Foie Gras and Red Mud: The Politics of Materiality in the European Union* (Bloomington: Indiana University Press, 2016), 21.

60 Berend, *From the Soviet Bloc to the European Union*, 94.

61 Peter S. Green, "In Binding Ballot, Czechs Give Landslide Approval to 2004 Membership in European Union," *New York Times*, June 15, 2003, https://www.nytimes.com/2003/06/15/world/binding-ballot-czechs-give-landslide-approval-2004-membership-european-union.html (accessed May 18, 2021).

62 Ther, *Europe since 1989*, 308–309.

63 G.C., "Poland's Emigration Headache," *The Economist*, November 5, 2013.

64 Massino, *Ambiguous Transitions*, 384.

65 Gosia's life will undoubtedly be complicated by the UK's departure from the EU, which took effect in 2021. Marta Bivand Erdal and Aleksandra Lewicki, "Moving Citizens: Citizenship Practices among Polish Migrants in Norway and the United Kingdom," *Social Identities* 22, no. 1 (2016): 112–126.

66 Will Guy, "Roma: Living Conditions, Social Perception and State Policy in the Macro-Region of 'Eastern Europe' Before and After 1989," *Südosteuropa Mitteilungen* 2 (2009): 61–62.

67 István Pogány, "Pariah Peoples: Roma and the Multiple Failures of Law in Central and Eastern Europe," *Social & Legal Studies* 21, no. 3 (2012): 384.

68 These practices have been observed all over the region, not only in the Czech Republic. Vera Messing, "Differentiation in the Making: Consequences of School Segregation of Roma in the Czech Republic, Hungary, and Slovakia," *European Education* 49 (2017): 89–103.

69 Pogány, "Pariah Peoples," 385–386.

70 Amnesty International, *Must Try Harder: Ethnic Discrimination of Romani Children in Czech Schools*, 2015, https://www.amnestyusa.org/files/musttryharder_embargoed_report.pdf (accessed June 10, 2020).

71 Jacqueline S. Gehring, "Free Movement for Some: The Treatment of the Roma after the European Union's Eastern Expansion," *European Journal of Migration and Law* 15, no. 1 (2013): 7–28; "Hounding the Roma in France," *New York Times*, January 8, 2015, https://www.nytimes.com/2015/01/08/opinion/hounding-the-roma-in-france.html (accessed May 18, 2021).

8

EASTERN EUROPE IN THE 21st CENTURY

Joining the European Union (EU) was supposed to mark the end of Eastern Europe's transition away from Communist dictatorship to capitalist democracy. In the 21st century, however, democratic governments in Eastern Europe faced new challenges. After the Great Recession of 2008, populist parties surged in popularity all over Europe, including Eastern Europe. In Hungary and Poland, populist parties won power and quickly began to flout EU democratic norms. While claiming to still respect democracy, these populist governments worked to limit the independence of the judiciary and to take control of the media, marginalizing their opponents.

East European populists have demonized the EU as the source of what they deemed to be pernicious "Western" values, like multiculturalism, feminism and respect for LGBTQ+ people, which they claimed were alien to Eastern Europe. In Poland in 2019 and 2020, the ruling Law and Justice Party (PiS) used the threat of what it called "LGBT ideology" as a campaign tool, promising to protect the traditional family from this foreign danger. Similar agitation against "gender ideology" led Bulgaria and Poland to reject the Istanbul Convention, an international treaty aimed at stopping domestic violence.

The populists' fervent nationalism and staunch anti-Communism fueled longstanding debates over the memory and meaning of the Communist past. Many East Europeans prefer to view the Communist era through the lens of totalitarianism, which paints Communist governments as all-powerful dictatorships that ruled primarily through fear. Others, however, insist that this model does not adequately represent their memories. As Eastern Europe faces the challenges of the 21st century, East Europeans have not agreed on how to write the history of the Communist era into their national stories.

DOI: 10.4324/9780813348186-9

Illiberal Democracy

In the years just after EU accession, the East European economy was booming. Growth rates were high and foreign investment increased dramatically. Many expected that within a few years Eastern Europe would have caught up economically with the rest of the EU. Encouraged by this optimistic forecast, some East Europeans decided it was a good time to invest in their personal futures by taking out mortgages to purchase new homes. Banks, eager to pursue this new market, urged people to take on more debt. In Hungary, a 2007 television advertisement for Raffeisen bank featured a mortgage broker telling potential home buyers that they could qualify for a loan whatever their income—their ability to pay was portrayed as inconsequential. To get a better interest rate, many Hungarian mortgage seekers were persuaded to take out loans in foreign currency, like the Swiss franc. As long as the exchange rate was stable, they would pay less per month. But if the value of the Hungarian forint went down, their payments could go up dramatically. Many were willing to take the risk. Between 2003 and 2010, the Hungarian mortgage market experienced spectacular growth, fueled primarily by foreign currency loans.[1]

In 2008, a global financial crisis spurred by predatory lending practices stunned the world. Hungary was one of its early victims. Like many of its citizens, the Hungarian government had also borrowed in foreign currency. It was forced to seek a bailout by the IMF and to institute austerity measures at home. In a similar fashion, many Hungarian mortgage holders saw their monthly payments increase by as much as 80–90 percent. Some lost their homes and others fell into poverty trying to maintain their payments. Eva and Miklos Kertész saw their mortgage payments triple, forcing them to endure great hardship. Eva later told a reporter, "Imagine, we couldn't pay our electricity bills. We had to borrow money to survive, we could not even buy bread. We didn't have enough to buy even a piece of bread! The bank robbed us of everything."[2] Their distress was shared by many Hungarians. A survey conducted in 2009 found that only 6 percent of Hungarians were satisfied in the current economy. Seventy-two percent believed that Hungarians were worse off in 2009 than they had been under Communism.[3]

The financial crisis discredited Hungary's ruling Social Democratic Party, which was already burdened by scandal. In 2006, the party's leader, Hungarian Prime Minister Ferenc Gyurcsány, was caught on tape claiming that party officials had shamelessly lied about the country's economic situation in order to win that year's parliamentary elections. Support for the Social Democrats tanked, allowing the rightist Fidesz Party to win 53 percent of the vote in Hungary's 2010 elections. Due to the intricacies of the country's election laws, this bare majority of the vote gave Fidesz a two-thirds majority in the Hungarian parliament, allowing it to pass legislation and even rewrite the constitution without the consent of any other parties. This election marked the beginning of the populist turn in East European politics.

Populist parties can come from any part of the political spectrum and can advocate very different policies. What they share is a similar way of looking at the world. Anti-elitism and anti-pluralism are at the core of the populist worldview. Populists portray themselves as the moral voice of the people, who they see as oppressed by self-serving elites. They believe that only they can truly represent the "real" people who, they often insist, have been bludgeoned into silence by the elitist political class. Since they claim to represent the authentic nation, populists do not recognize their opponents as having legitimate viewpoints. Instead, they see them as enemies who do not even deserve to be heard. Populists may claim to support democracy, but they typically reject liberal democratic norms of compromise. If they gain power, populist parties usually seek to exclude those with opposing views from participation in government.[4] After the financial crisis of 2008, populist parties gained support all over the European continent. In Eastern Europe, they were most successful in Hungary and Poland.

After winning the 2010 elections, Hungary's Fidesz Party took a decisive turn toward populism. In defiance of EU norms, Fidesz leader Viktor Orbán openly rejected liberal democracy. The term *liberal democracy* is defined as a representative system of government that protects individual freedoms and respects the rule of law. The word "liberal" in this context refers to individual liberties, not progressive politics. Orbán, however, tried to twist this meaning, linking liberal democracy to progressive causes like multiculturalism, immigration and gay marriage. For Orbán, these causes were Western impositions foreign to the Hungarian nation. Instead, Orbán has endorsed *illiberal democracy*. As Orbán defined it in 2018, illiberal democracy aligns with conservative ideals. It promotes "Christian culture" and the traditional family while opposing immigration.[5] Some, however, have argued that Orbán's embrace of the term "illiberal democracy" only obscured the extent to which Hungary has effectively become one-party state. The Fidesz government, they charge, has ceased to be a democracy at all.

Shortly after taking power in 2010, Orbán began to use his party's supermajority in the Hungarian parliament to weaken Hungary's democratic system of checks and balances, putting Fidesz in control of the entire state apparatus. The Orbán government took formerly independent, nonpartisan branches of the Hungarian government—such as the Central Bank or the Office of the Public Prosecutor—and filled them with its supporters. It attacked the independence of the judiciary and packed the Constitutional Court with its allies. It wrote a new Hungarian constitution without input from other parties and had it approved only by the Fidesz-dominated parliament without a popular vote.[6] To further protect its hold on power, Fidesz engineered election reforms and gerrymandered districts to make it almost impossible for it to lose future elections. With these changes, Fidesz was able to maintain its supermajority in the 2014 and 2018 elections despite earning less than 50 percent of the total vote.

Fidesz's push to promote its own supporters and marginalize those who disagreed was not limited to the upper levels of government. Under the cover of austerity measures, the Fidesz government fired thousands of civil servants believed to not be loyal to Fidesz, including many of the workers at Hungarian public television, most of the staff of the National Development Agency (the arm of the government that distributes EU funds to local projects), and ordinary teachers and school principals. Private businesses seeking government contracts felt pressured to show their loyalty to the government by sacking employees who were identified with the opposition. Fearing for their livelihoods, hundreds of thousands of people, largely educated professionals, left the country to find work elsewhere.[7]

Fidesz also moved to control the media landscape, stacking media regulatory bodies with its allies and encouraging its wealthy supporters to buy up news outlets. By 2019, all Hungarian daily newspapers and almost all daily radio and television news programs were considered pro-Fidesz.[8] The ramifications of this were clear in a 2018 election for a local office in Budapest's Eighth District. The government-funded, free local paper featured the Fidesz candidate in 22 articles. The name of his opponent, Péter Győri, was not mentioned at all.[9]

Fidesz justified its antidemocratic actions by claiming that it spoke for all true Hungarians. Fidesz came to power inveighing against international banks and EU elites who, it claimed, had led Hungary into economic crisis. Its nationalist rhetoric grew even more virulent during the migrant crisis of 2015. In the summer and autumn of that year, over a million people flooded into Europe hoping to be granted asylum. Many were refugees from the Syrian civil war. Others were fleeing poverty and oppression in countries like Iraq and Afghanistan. Few of them wanted to apply for asylum in Hungary, but hundreds of thousands hoped to travel through Hungary on their way to Germany or Austria. Viktor Orbán equated the refugees with terrorists and claimed that this influx of Muslim immigrants would destroy Europe's Christian civilization. Rather than allowing the refugees passage through Hungary, his government built a 110-mile razor wire fence along the border with Serbia to keep them out. Orbán became a leading critic of the EU's immigration policy, heading a coalition of other East European countries who refused to allow Muslim refugees to settle on their territory. As Orbán remarked in 2016, "For us migration is not a solution but a problem, not medicine but a poison, we don't need it and won't swallow it."[10]

After 2015, immigration became a central element of Fidesz's domestic politics. According to Orbán, the sudden rush of Muslim asylum seekers was the work of a cabal of Hungary's enemies, led by EU bureaucrats and the financier George Soros. Orbán claimed that these foes had plotted to flood Europe with

Muslims in a bid to weaken Hungarian national sovereignty. He called this the "Soros plan."[11] This supposed "Soros plan" had no basis in fact. Soros, an American citizen, was a Hungarian émigré who left the country after surviving anti-Jewish persecution during World War II and became a billionaire investor. Soros has devoted much of his considerable fortune to philanthropic causes, particularly in the realm of intellectual freedom and building democracy. Despite his Hungarian origins, Soros was not a major public figure in Hungary until Orbán and his political consultants decided to make him into Hungary's biggest enemy.[12]

The Fidesz-led disinformation campaign against Soros was often blatantly antisemitic, pointing at mysterious shadowy conspiracies and the power of international finance. Soros, Fidesz claimed, used his billions to control the EU and the liberal media. Soros money, Fidesz alleged, was behind anyone who protested against the Orbán government and its policies, including activists who organized street protests, NGOs who tried to help asylum seekers and left-wing political parties. In 2017, posters appeared on billboards around Budapest with pictures of Soros and the slogan, "Don't let him get the last laugh." In 2018, the Fidesz government passed a package of laws it dubbed the "Stop Soros" bill which restricted the ability of NGOs to offer assistance to asylum seekers and made helping an illegal immigrant to seek asylum into a crime. According to Hungarian Interior Minister Sándor Pintér, the point of the "Stop Soros" bill was "to stop Hungary from becoming a country of immigrants."[13]

Assisted by its control over the news media and by the continuing disorganization of the Hungarian left, Fidesz enjoyed the support of a substantial number of Hungarians, particularly those who live in rural areas. Some liked its nationalism, its support for traditional values and its strong stance against immigration.

FIGURE 8.1 Posters saying "Don't let Soros have the last laugh" inside the Budapest metro, June 2017. © REUTERS/Alamy Stock Photo 2CNCBHH.

Others appreciated its ability to provide jobs: under Fidesz, unemployment fell and wages increased. Despite Orbán's frequent demonization of the EU, some of this job growth was enabled by EU development funds, which Fidesz funneled into large state construction projects.[14] Orbán also forced banks to renegotiate foreign currency mortgages into Hungarian forints, lowered utility prices and instituted tax policies that favored middle-class families.[15]

Support for populist parties increased all over Eastern Europe after 2008. This phenomenon was driven by voter frustration with the political parties that had governed Eastern Europe since 1989. Whether they hailed from the left or from the right, these parties all advocated similar policies, such as neoliberal economic reforms and EU accession. In the minds of many voters, these ruling parties became a self-serving and corrupt elite that neglected their concerns. Populist parties tapped into this growing discontent by offering a clear alternative to the status quo, feeding on real weaknesses in the existing spectrum of political choices. Support for populists was strongest among groups that had not benefited from the transition to a market economy, such as rural dwellers, older people and people without university degrees. This was the case in Poland, where the populist Law and Justice Party (known by its Polish acronym PiS) came to power in 2015. Although it won just 38 percent of the vote, PiS gained 52 percent of the seats in the Polish parliament, giving it sole control of the legislative branch. In 2016, the PiS candidate, Andrzej Duda, won the presidency, extending the party's hold on power.

Once it gained office, the PiS government defied the constitution and assaulted the system of safeguards that was supposed to protect Poland's liberal democracy. Like Fidesz had done in Hungary, PiS attacked the autonomy of the Polish judiciary, refusing to seat judges appointed by its predecessor and proposing a package of laws that would allow the government to pack the courts with PiS supporters. The leader of PiS, Jarosław Kaczyński, said openly in a television interview that his party focused on the courts because they were a venue where "all our actions could be questioned for whatever reason." With similar motives, the PiS government changed the civil service law in 2016 to make it easier to fire state employees and replace them with PiS supporters. PiS also moved to curtail the independence of the Polish news media. Critical journalists who worked at state-owned television and radio stations were fired, and the stations were transformed into government mouthpieces. News broadcasts on state-owned Polish public television routinely praised the PiS government while painting its opponents in outrageously disparaging terms, like "defenders of pedophiles" and "absentee parents."[16]

According to PiS leaders, these actions were justified because PiS alone represented the "true Poland," which it defined as Catholic and conservative. PiS, in their estimation, had a moral right to rule that absolved it of any need to respect democratic institutions. Its adherents were patriots and its opponents were former Communists who had profited off of 1989 to the detriment of everyone else. According to PiS leader Jarosław Kaczyński, those who supported PiS were the "better sort of Poles" and those who opposed it were "the worst sort." Kaczyński accused leaders of the largest opposition party, the Civic Platform, of conspiring with Russia to mastermind a plane crash in 2010 that killed his twin brother, Lech, who was president of Poland at the time. While there was no evidence to support this theory, Kaczyński asserted it as the truth. PiS leaders also supported conspiracy theories about Polish civil society groups and NGOs that protested their policies, claiming that these groups were artificial creations funded by political opponents or foreigners like George Soros rather than authentic community organizations. With these kinds of tactics, PiS hoped to delegitimize those who opposed its policies by painting them as traitors to the "real" Polish nation.[17]

PiS combined social conservatism and vehement nationalism with redistributive economic policies often associated with the left. PiS leaders claimed that the transition of the 1990s was a corrupt enterprise that primarily benefited former Communist elites. According to Mateusz Morawiecki, the prime minister of the PiS government after 2017, the goal of the PiS "revolution" was to "repair all the flaws of the post-Communist period" by helping those who had suffered most since 1989. The PiS government worked to redirect state funds away from major urban centers and toward neglected parts of eastern Poland and to lift the wages of working- and middle-class families. One of its most popular policies, the 500+ program, gave parents monthly payments of 500 złoty (about $125) for each child under 18. The PiS government also eliminated income taxes for people under 26 years old and increased pension payments for retirees.[18]

These policies were crucial for Agnieszka and Adam Kowalczyk, a middle-aged couple from the town of Zamość in eastern Poland. The Polish economy as a whole had boomed after 2004, but that wealth passed by towns like Zamość. The Kowalczyks had jobs but found it hard to support their four children. "We mostly bought poor quality food and cheap clothes," Adam recalled, adding, "we could not invest in our children." They decided to take a chance and vote for PiS in 2015, calling the party "the lesser of two evils." They were pleased to find that under PiS their income more than doubled. As Agnieszka described it, "We still couldn't go on a crazy shopping spree, but we could buy better food, nicer clothes and we could send our children to math lessons, guitar lessons, English and dance lessons. We started really investing in their education." The Kowalczyks voted for PiS again in 2019, helping the party to maintain its parliamentary majority.[19]

Critics of the Fidesz and PiS governments have charged that their policies have weakened the foundations of democracy in their countries. The EU agreed. The Treaty of the European Union requires EU member states to respect "EU values," including democracy, the rule of law, human rights and the protection of minorities, but it provides only limited mechanisms for sanctioning those who fail to do so. In 2017, the EU instituted proceedings against Poland for undermining the independence of the judiciary. In 2018, it began a similar process with Hungary, citing concerns about the independence of the judiciary, freedom of the press and the rights of minorities and refugees.[20] Both governments have claimed that these charges are baseless and the work of those want to harm their nations; in Hungary, some declared they were orchestrated by George Soros.[21] In 2021, both cases were still tied up in legal proceedings. Regardless of their outcome, however, these cases have helped to change the story of Eastern Europe's trajectory since 1989. Before 2010, scholars characterized Eastern Europe's path after 1989 as a triumphant march toward democracy. In the years since 2010, they have questioned that narrative and wondered if this period of democratic backsliding will lead Eastern Europe back to authoritarianism.[22] Only time will tell.

Stop Gender?

In 2013, Polish scholar Agnieszka Graff unexpectedly found herself in the middle of a culture war. Before 2013, Graff recalled, "gender" was an obscure word in Polish, mostly used by academics in the humanities and social sciences. Then that summer, Bishop Tadeusz Pieronek remarked in a public debate, "And I would also like to add that gender ideology is worse than Communism and Nazism put together." This was the beginning of a concerted campaign by the Polish Catholic Church to paint "gender ideology" as a danger to the heterosexual family and public morality. In November, Graff, a professor at the University of Warsaw and a feminist activist, was invited to take part in a public debate in Warsaw on the topic of "Gender: Blessing or Curse?" To her surprise, "the event was interrupted by angry demonstrators bearing signs like 'Gender 666' and 'Stop Gender,' who detonated a smoke bomb and fled the room shouting 'Shame on you!' and 'This is Poland!'"[23]

Renewed support for the traditionally gendered family—where women took on the roles of childcare and housework and men served as the family's primary breadwinners—actually extended back into the Communist period. While Communist governments formally embraced gender equality, they did not do much to promote changes in the gendered distribution of labor within the household. Beginning in the 1960s, pronatalist policies encouraged many mothers to leave the workforce to care for their young children (as detailed in Chapter 5). These policies suggested that women's most important contribution to society was as mothers rather than as workers. After 1989, these trends continued but were now characterized as anti-Communist. Gender equality was frequently portrayed in the media as something that was foreign to Eastern Europe, imported either by Communists in the 1940s or by Western feminists after 1989. In reality, the countries of Eastern Europe had their own domestic feminist traditions that existed before, during and after Communism.

During the transition to a market economy, East European governments were forced to cut spending for many programs that supported families, including funding for day-care facilities and monthly payments to parents. In Czechoslovakia, the number of nursery school places for children under three declined from 78,555 in 1989 to 17,210 in 1991.[24] Most assumed that it was women's responsibility to fill this gap, usually by leaving the workforce to take on the demands of full-time childcare. In 1992, a World Bank report suggested that Hungary limit its maternity leave benefits as a cost-cutting measure and put more funding into state-supported childcare facilities. The Hungarian parliament ignored this advice and continued to allow up to three years of childcare leave, which was primarily used by women.[25] In the years since the 1990s, the Hungarian economy has not adapted its policies to accommodate working mothers. In a 2010 study, Hungarian mothers complained that a lack of part-time work, flexible schedules and childcare made it impossible for them to go back to their original jobs after having children, forcing them to take informal or under the table work well below their skill level instead. As one woman said,

> I used to talk to all these mothers on the playground and many of them did not go back to work in their profession but started working for a pizzeria, or cleaning houses, or whatever... I never understood why they would [do that]... but now I'm starting to get it. It's the schedule that forces mothers to do this.[26]

After 1989, many of Eastern Europe's new political parties shared Communist concerns about decreasing birthrates and population decline. In the 1990s, these concerns coalesced around the issue of abortion. In the immediate aftermath of 1989, Romania quickly liberalized its restrictive and widely hated Ceaușescu-era laws to make abortion accessible to all women within the first trimester of pregnancy; Bulgaria quietly did the same. Elsewhere, however, the trend was toward making abortion less accessible. In Germany, women from the former GDR had to accept the more restrictive laws of West Germany when the two countries were united in 1991. In the early 1990s, conservatives and religious groups in Croatia, the Czech Republic, Hungary, Poland, Serbia, Slovenia and Slovakia proposed making abortion illegal.[27] Most of these efforts were ultimately not successful. In Hungary, however, a 1992 law made it much more difficult for women to obtain an abortion. Things were most contentious in Poland, where the attack on abortion was led by the Catholic Church and supported by the Solidarity government. In 1993, Poland passed one of the most restrictive abortion laws in Europe. Abortion remained legal only in cases where the mother's life was in danger, in instances of rape or incest, or when the fetus had life-threatening defects. This law was dubbed a "compromise" because it was not the complete ban that Church leaders demanded.[28]

The 1993 controversy over abortion in Poland helped spark the creation of a vibrant Polish women's movement. In 2010, Poland was home to a wide spectrum of NGOs and community organizations working on issues related to women, including causes such as reproductive rights, women's employment and violence against women.[29] For decades, most of these organizations operated largely outside of the public spotlight. One exception was the successful campaign organized in 2010–2011 by the Congress of Women to collect 100,000 signatures to force the Polish parliament to consider a law on gender quotas in parliamentary elections. While the end result was only a qualified success—the watered-down compromise bill the Sejm eventually passed has only slightly raised the number of women elected to national office—it has nonetheless forced political parties to field more female candidates.[30] In 2016, Polish women's activists organized the country's largest popular protests since the Solidarity strikes of the 1980s in reaction to a bill that would have banned abortion in all instances, with no exceptions for maternal health or cases of rape. Over 100,000 women and their male allies participated in a one-day strike and braved rain to march at demonstrations held in 143 locations around the country. While some PiS leaders mocked the black-clad demonstrators as "women playing dress-up," the Sejm rejected the bill.[31]

Despite the existence of local feminist organizations, many East Europeans saw gender equality as an imported concept promulgated by the EU. The *acquis* for EU accession included directives prohibiting discrimination on the basis of gender, as well as nationality, race, religion and sexual orientation; the EU has also provided funding for NGOs devoted to these issues. Yet the need to meet EU requirements has seldom been sufficient to change attitudes about the social roles of men and women. In 2008, when the Czech Republic passed an antidiscrimination act in order to comply with EU legal norms, the Czech Senate took the extraordinary step of issuing a declaration noting that it considered the antidiscrimination legislation merely a requirement of EU law. It urged the Czech government "not to consent to the adoption of further anti-discrimination measures at the EU level." In the opinion of the Czech Senate, the EU norm of equality "artificially interferes with the natural evolution of society." According to Czech legal scholar Barbara Havelková, most Czech judges, lawyers and lawmakers do not accept the idea that gender is a socially constructed category, meaning that the characteristics and roles attributed to men and women in a given society are the products of that society, rather than universal qualities that stem from male and female biology. While the idea that gender roles are determined by society rather than by nature was not controversial for EU officials or academics, it became a point of contention in 21st-century Eastern Europe.[32]

Since 2010, attacks on what rightist activists call "gender ideology" (or the idea that gender is a socially constructed category) have become more and more frequent in Eastern Europe, uniting mainstream conservatives, religious groups and far-right parties in a culture war aimed against feminism, gender equality and all those who do not fit a heterosexual norm. Eastern Europe's anti-gender campaigners claim that "genderism" endangers the heterosexual family and its traditionally gendered division of labor.[33] To overcome this threat, they have launched a variety of initiatives aimed at limiting gay rights and promoting traditional marriage. In Romania, a group called Coalition for the Family gathered three million signatures in 2016 to force a vote on a referendum for a constitutional amendment forbidding gay marriage. One of the coalition's leaders, Mihai Gheorghiu, characterized gay marriage as part of a "social and cultural revolution happening in the West" and foreign to Romania. Romanians, he said, "have the right to defend our values and way of life." Gheorghiu likened gender ideology to Communism, "when a minority thought it held the absolute truth and imposed it on others." Romanians, he said, needed to prevent this from happening again. Campaigners for the Romanian marriage referendum tried to galvanize support by marshalling homophobia, arguing that if gay marriage was legal, gay couples would be able to adopt children and "convert" them to homosexuality. The referendum failed due to low turnout, but gay marriage remained illegal in Romania.[34]

The specter of "gender ideology" was used in Bulgaria in 2018 to create opposition to the Istanbul Convention, a treaty sponsored by the Council of Europe to combat domestic violence and violence against women. The United Patriots Coalition (VMRO), a Bulgarian political party, wrongly claimed that "international lobbies" were working through the convention to require Bulgaria "to legalize a 'third gender' and introduce school programs for studying homosexuality and transvestism and create opportunities for enforcing same-sex marriages."[35] VMRO and its allies asked Bulgaria's Constitutional Court to rule on the legality of the Istanbul Convention. The court rejected the Convention's use of "gender" as incompatible with the Bulgarian constitution because it blurred the line between the biological sexes. According to the court, the Istanbul Convention espoused a dangerous "gender ideology" because it ostensibly promoted the idea that people could choose their own gender identity.[36] In 2020, Poland, which had ratified the convention in 2012, decided to withdraw from the treaty for similar reasons. Although the Istanbul Convention does not address gay rights, Zbigniew Ziobro, the Polish justice minister, claimed that it was "a feminist creation aimed at justifying gay ideology."[37]

In 2018, the Hungarian government removed the accreditation from the two gender studies programs that existed in the country, making it impossible for students to receive university degrees in this discipline. The government claimed that this was a financial decision, falsely arguing that there was no market for graduates from these programs. It also cast aspersions on gender studies as a field of academic research. According to Bence Rétvári, the political undersecretary in the Ministry of Human Resources, university subjects must have scientific foundations. Gender studies—similarly to Marxism-Leninism—can be called an ideology rather than a science, and therefore it is doubtful that it attains the scientific level expected at ELTE [the Eötvös Lórand University, the most prestigious public university in Hungary]. Moreover, the subject of the discipline goes against everything the government thinks about human beings.[38]

For Rétvári, gender was determined by biology. Since the discipline of gender studies took gender as socially constructed instead of biologically determined, it could, Rétvári suggested, be nothing more than quackery.

In Hungary, the idea that gender ideology was a form of colonialism being spread by the EU, neoliberal elites and global corporations was unwittingly underscored by an advertising campaign launched by the Coca-Cola Company in the summer of 2019. The campaign featured posters of same-sex couples drinking Coke with slogans like "love is love" and "zero sugar, zero prejudice." Right-wing commentators condemned the ads as the work of an international "homosexual lobby," and some Fidesz officials, including the party's deputy speaker, István Boldog, demanded their removal. Hungarian gay rights activist Tamás Dombos speculated that the reaction to the Coca-Cola campaign might be a test balloon on the part of Fidesz, which had previously not focused on LGBTQ issues. "The entire government propaganda is built on conflict, and they need enemies. After the EU, migrants, NGOs and even the homeless, now it may be LGBTQ people," said Dombos.[39] His theory gained some credence a few months later when Hungary unexpectedly pulled out of the annual Eurovision song contest, a pan-European event that spread to Eastern Europe in the 1990s. While no official reason was given, many speculated it was because Eurovision, long popular with Europe's gay community, was seen as "too gay."[40] Then in March 2020, the Fidesz government introduced a bill to prevent Hungarians from changing the gender listed on their birth certificates, forcing Hungarian trans people to carry IDs that did not recognize their lived identity.[41] Katalin Kobak, a Hungarian trans woman, was devastated by the news. "I couldn't believe that they could be so malicious," she said. "This is just evil."[42]

The campaign against "gender ideology" has been most vocal in Poland, where it has brought together grassroots activists, the Catholic Church and professional politicians in campaigns against sex education in schools, reproductive rights, feminism and gay rights. During its 2019 election campaign, PiS increased its agitation against what it termed "LGBT ideology." PiS party Chairman Jarosław Kaczyński characterized the LGBT movement as an import from the West that threatened the Polish nation and Polish identity.[43] As he told a crowd of supporters, "We don't have to stand under a rainbow flag." In solidarity, over 30 Polish municipalities passed resolutions against gay marriage or declaring that they were "free of LGBT ideology." Fueled by this rhetoric, violence erupted at the city of Białystok's first gay pride march in July 2019.

FIGURE 8.2   A demonstrator holds a sign saying "I am not an ideology" at a protest in support of gay rights in Kraków (Poland) on June 21, 2020. © Photo by Omar Marques/Getty Images.

Thousands of protesters surrounded a few hundred marchers, yelling slurs and throwing rotten eggs, bricks and stones. Dozens were injured in the melee. However, while the violence in Białystok grabbed headlines, it was atypical. In 2019, more LGBT pride parades were held in Poland than ever before, including in smaller towns and cities, and almost all were peaceful.[44]

In 2020, Polish President Andrzej Duda seized on anti-LGBT rhetoric as a means of energizing a reelection campaign that had been delayed due to the COVID-19 pandemic. Duda promulgated a "Family Charter" in which he promised to oppose same-sex marriage, prevent gay couples from adopting children and forbid the teaching of "LGBT ideology" in schools. In a speech on June 15, Duda claimed that LGBT ideology was more dangerous than Communism, likening it to an "ideological hurricane." "We cannot allow our family to be taken away," he declared, "we must protect it with all our strength."[45] Duda's family values platform motivated some supporters. Kamila, a 37-year-old mother from a Warsaw suburb, told a reporter,

> I voted for Andrzej Duda because he supports families … I am not one of these rainbow flag people and I don't want our children to be forced to learn about 'genderism' and these strange kinds of things—I really don't like it.

Yet while Duda was able to eke out a win, the close nature of the contest revealed the intensely polarized political climate in Poland. Barbara, a retiree who voted for Duda's opponent, Rafał Trzaskowski, declared her disgust for Duda and his party by remarking, "We want to have peace, to be governed by cultured people, not by the boorish thieves that we have now."[46]

Like populism, anti-gender activism did not originate in Eastern Europe. Similar organizations and campaigns also flourished in Western Europe, and East Europeans participated in global networks of activists devoted to anti-gender causes. Yet, while it was a global phenomenon, anti-gender activism always spoke to local concerns and took somewhat different forms in different countries or regions. In the context of post-Communist Eastern Europe, the concept of "gender ideology" crystallized fears about the loss of national identity in the wake of EU accession. The idea of gender signified a supposedly foreign culture that had infiltrated the region along with EU norms and multinational corporations. Like populism, with which its activists were often allied, the anti-gender movement provided a set of strategies for resisting this invasion and gave comfort to those who felt their way of life was under siege.[47] While it could not claim the allegiance of a stable majority of East Europeans, the anti-gender movement showed that even more than three decades after the end of Communism, many East Europeans were still uncertain about their future and their place within an increasingly globalized world.

String Bags and Secret Police Agents

In early 2002, a new museum commemorating the victims of Nazi and Communist violence opened in Budapest. It was funded by the Hungarian government, which was controlled at the time by the Fidesz party. The museum is located on one of the city's grandest boulevards, inside a building that had been closely associated with both regimes. Before World War II, it had served as the headquarters of the fascist Arrow Cross Party. During its tenure, the Arrow Cross created a prison in the basement which they used to hold and torture their opponents. After the war, the Hungarian secret police (ÁVH) took over the building. The ÁVH housed its own prisoners there, including members of the Arrow Cross and the victims of Stalinist-era political trials. In reference to this history, the museum was named the House of Terror. It has become a popular attraction in the city, visited by Hungarians and foreign tourists alike.[48]

The House of Terror is not a traditional history museum. Its goal is not to present facts about the past or to display historical artifacts in their appropriate context. Instead, its aim is to provide an immersive experience that gives the visitor an emotional impression of the past. Rather than displaying historical objects or documents in glass vitrines, the exhibition rooms in the House of Terror present dramatic and sometimes surreal tableaux of artfully arranged objects, enhanced by moody music and stage lighting. The exhibition space provides little text to explain what the visitor is seeing. Even the items on display are rarely identified, leaving it unclear if they are original objects from the period, modern reproductions of historical originals or merely fanciful bits of scenery with no direct historical antecedent. For example, the museum's basement contains what are ostensibly reconstructions of the cells used to house prisoners in the 1940s and 1950s. Visitors are invited to enter the cells to experience what it might have been like to be a prisoner there. However, the original cells were removed in the 1960s, and there were no records detailing their dimensions. What the visitor enters is neither the real thing nor a reconstruction, but a simulacrum.[49] According to museum designer Attila Ferenczffy-Kovács, the staged spectacles presented in the House of Terror conveyed the truth of the past in a way that glass cases filled with historical objects could not. By creating an atmosphere of horror and dread, the museum purports to give the visitor a sense of what the past was like.[50]

The House of Terror's lavish multimedia displays create a narrative of the past based around Hungarian victimization. According to the House of Terror, Hungary suffered from two consecutive foreign occupations, beginning with the Nazis in 1944 and continuing with the Soviets in 1945. The museum's first room, "Double Occupation," presents these occupations as two sides of the same coin. The room is dominated by a wedge-shaped wall of video screens running down its center. One side, labeled "Nazi occupation," projects images of Hitler and Nazi concentration camps. The other side, marked "Soviet occupation," contains footage of the Soviet Red Army and the siege of Budapest.[51] Both regimes, the images suggest, were primarily characterized by their use of terror and violence against the innocent Hungarian population. The ties between the two systems are emphasized further in the room "Changing Clothes," which depicts a Hungarian Arrow Cross member switching uniforms to become a member of the ÁVH, the Communist-era secret police. The exhibit suggests that the violence of both periods was the work of a small number of evil men who collaborated with foreign powers to terrorize their own innocent people.

While the museum is organized around the idea of Hungary's "double occupation," only a small fraction of the displays deal with World War II and the murder of roughly 450,000 Hungarian Jews. The vast majority of the museum is devoted to commemorating the terror of the Stalinist period, including the deportation of class enemies to the countryside, the arrest and torture of the political opposition and the persecution of the Catholic and Protestant Churches. However, because the museum is not organized chronologically and the displays do not contain dates, the exhibition gives the uninformed visitor the impression that the deportations and show trials of the Stalinist era continued unabated until 1991, when the last Soviet troops left the country. As the museum's displays tell it, Hungary's socialist state was a foreign imposition held in place by violence.[52] Terror and oppression were the essence of the Communist past. The House of Terror's perspective on Communism leaves little room for pleasant memories of vacations at Lake Balaton or listening to music at Ifipark. The true history of Communism, the museum suggests, has no place for these memories, which merely serve to hide the Communist state's true nature.[53]

When it opened, the House of Terror was criticized by a number of professional historians. Much of the criticism centered around the museum's concept of "double occupation" and its treatment of the Holocaust. The museum begins its exhibition in 1944, when the Germans invaded Hungary and installed the fascist Hungarian Arrow Cross Party in power. This choice renders the persecution of Hungarian Jews into a foreign crime, committed by the Germans and a small group of Hungarian collaborators. It ignores the fact that Hungary was a willing ally of Nazi Germany and is silent on Hungary's own history of antisemitic policies. Further, the idea of "double occupation" subsumes the experiences of Holocaust victims into the experiences of those who were persecuted by the Communist regime, erasing the particular situation of Jewish Hungarians into one common history of victimhood. While the House of Terror presents both sides of this "double occupation" as equally evil, critics claim that the museum's lopsided coverage of these two regimes, where over 80 percent of the space is devoted to the Communist era, makes the fascist dictatorship seem relatively unimportant. While the number of those killed for racial or political reasons during World War II vastly outnumbered those who lost their lives to Communist terror, the House of Terror presents socialism as the far greater enemy of innocent Hungarians.

For Mária Schmidt, the director of the House of Terror museum, these critiques were beside the point. Hungary, said Schmidt, had never properly come to terms with the crimes of Communism. When Communist rule had ended with the first free elections in 1990, former Communist leaders were mostly allowed to go about their lives as they wished. Even those who had been involved in putting down the revolution of 1956 faced no consequences for their actions. For many of those on the Hungarian right, this was a travesty. They believed that the Communist state was an illegitimate dictatorship and that its architects were criminals who needed to be held accountable. The House of Terror was not a court of law, but it did have the power to pass moral judgment on the perpetrators of Communist violence.[54] The museum contains a "Gallery of Persecutors," containing photographs of Communist officials and employees of the secret police. While most objects in the museum are not identified, these photographs are carefully labeled with the subject's full name.[55]

The Romanian Memorial Museum for the Victims of Communism and of the Resistance in the city of Sighet shares a similar approach to the past, one rooted in staunch anti-Communist sentiment.[56] Like the House of Terror, the Memorial Museum is located in a former prison that once held members of the political opposition. The museum's exhibits construct the Romanian nation as a collective victim, subsuming the stories of individuals into a larger narrative of common national oppression. For example, on the ground floor of the museum, a long hallway is papered with the pictures of hundreds of people described as the victims of socialism. But all of the faces are anonymous. The images have been chemically treated to give them a similar look and cropped to minimize distinguishing features from the setting. There is no text that reveals what brought them into conflict with the socialist state. Their ages, hometowns, professions and even their names are not revealed. Rather than representing the specifics of individual lives, the sea of faces turns all Romanians into a collective victim, suggesting that oppression and violence were the common experience of socialism.[57]

Museums like the House of Terror and Romanian Memorial Museum in Sighet offered East Europeans a way to exert control over an unruly past. These museums turned a complicated era into a simple story of oppression, populated by easily identifiable heroes and villains. In this interpretation of the past, the Communist era was characterized solely by oppression, fear and poverty. Communist governments were illegitimate regimes, imposed by foreign powers and held in place by Communist party leaders, secret police officers and their agents. These enablers were responsible for everything that had happened during the four decades of Communist rule. Ordinary people were their victims. This black and white narrative was compelling to many people across the region. While the future might be uncertain, the past was rendered legible and easy to understand.

The House of Terror and the Romanian Memorial Museum both interpret Communism in Eastern Europe through the lens of *totalitarianism*. The term "totalitarianism" typically denotes a form of dictatorship whose authority is founded on terror. As most people imagine it, a totalitarian system opposes an all-powerful state against a resisting society. A totalitarian state aims to control all aspects of its citizens' lives, rendering them incapable of independent thought or action. It runs on fear, obtaining acquiescence through its arbitrary use of violence. The term became popular in the West after the outbreak of the Cold War because it provided a means of making a moral equivalence between Communism and Nazism. By using the same category to describe both systems, analysts implied that these two ideologically opposed regimes nonetheless shared a style of rule, one that was particularly evil. While most academics have abandoned the totalitarian theories developed during the Cold War, the term is still commonly used, albeit often without a precise meaning.

The concept of totalitarianism has shaped the ways many East Europeans view the socialist era, although it can sometimes come into conflict with individual memories. In 2002, the anthropologist Maya Nadkarni was sitting in a Budapest café with her friend Vera and Vera's 19-year-old son, Ádám, talking about the newly opened House of Terror. Ádám argued that Hungarians needed a museum that would illuminate "the truth about our history" by showing how life during the Communist regime was oppressive and ruled by fear. Under Communism, Ádám claimed, everyone was under constant surveillance. As an example, Ádám offered up the collapsible string bags that most women carried with them to hold their shopping. These bags, said Ádám, were devised to allow informers to see what everyone bought. Vera laughed heartily at Ádám's idea, which he got from a young teacher who, like Ádám himself, had little personal memory of Communism. No, she said, the reason women carried string bags was a reaction to shortages. Socialist stores did not typically give away free plastic bags, and women needed to be prepared with a bag in case they wanted to buy something they saw unexpectedly in a store window. The string bags, she said, were small and convenient to carry. Ádám, however, was not convinced by his mother's protestations. For him, the string bag was clearly a sign of the ubiquity of Communist oppression.[58]

In Eastern Europe today, the concept of totalitarianism dominates the official memory of the Communist past, as consolidated within state-sponsored museums and other institutions of national memory such as government-funded research centers. The largest such research center in Eastern Europe is the Institute of National Remembrance in Poland (Instytut Pamięci Narodowej or IPN), which was created by the Polish Parliament in 1998. As part of its activities, the IPN operates the archives of the Communist-era security service and uses them to research the Polish past. In 2019, the IPN's education and research branch was the largest research center for contemporary history in Poland, employing some 200 historians.[59] It is one of Poland's largest publishers of historical works, putting out dozens of books each year, including monographs, document collections and edited volumes, many of them written or edited by its own employees. In addition to its scholarly activities, the IPN publishes educational materials for libraries and classrooms and offers training courses for school teachers. It organizes exhibitions based on its research and sponsors public lectures and film series.[60]

The IPN's official mission is to investigate the crimes committed by Poland's Nazi and Communist rulers, to commemorate their victims and to examine the courageous resistance of the Polish people to these oppressive regimes. Its charge is to investigate these issues and publicize the findings in order to promote democracy and prevent the rise of another dictatorship in Poland. This mission relies upon a totalitarian view of the Polish past. It posits a moral equivalence between Nazism and Communism, seeing both as foreign, criminal regimes standing in stark opposition to Polish society. The published historical research coming out of the IPN has tended to follow this interpretation, assuming a united Polish nation longing for freedom, menaced by club-wielding security officers or faceless bureaucrats.[61]

The IPN's charter privileges research into certain kinds of historical subjects, such as anti-Communist resistance, moments of public outrage and demonstrations against the socialist regime and the activities of the security services. The IPN does not prioritize topics related to the history of everyday life under socialism, such as the history of work, leisure, sexuality or the family. From 2000 to 2012, the IPN published 107 monographs on the socialist period. These included 29 books about Communist oppression, 10 books about armed resistance to Communism and 14 books about political opposition to Communism, but only 1 on the subject of daily life.[62]

The IPN's resources have allowed it to dominate the historical landscape in Poland. One historian, Dariusz Stola, speculated in 2012 that the IPN's budget was larger than that of all the other historical research centers in Poland combined. As Stola notes, other historians cannot blame the IPN for concentrating on the topics and using the approaches that were mandated by its mission. The problem, says Stola, is that the IPN's size, influence and dominance of the publishing landscape have had the effect of marginalizing alternative historical perspectives and methodologies.[63] While some historians working at Polish universities or the Polish Academy of Sciences have published research on the broad spectrum of life under socialism, these historians have found it hard to challenge dominant totalitarian narrative produced by the IPN in the Polish media.[64] This tension increased after PiS took over the Polish government in 2015.

The model of the IPN influenced the creation of similar state-sponsored historical research centers elsewhere, including the Nation's Memory Institute in Slovakia and the Institute for the Study of Totalitarian Regimes in the Czech Republic. While these centers all conduct academic research using archival documents, they were not founded merely to further historical knowledge, but with a moral mission. Their task was, at least in part, to determine and publicly identify those who were responsible for the evils of socialism. This impulse to divide society into heroes and villains, however, is more difficult than many have wanted to acknowledge. The papers contained in the archives of the security services are not always easy to interpret, and neither is the past itself.

This difficulty was illustrated in 2008, when Adam Hradilek, a young Czech researcher at the newly founded Institute for the Study of Totalitarian Regimes (ISTR), published a sensational article, alleging that the Nobel prize-winning author Milan Kundera was a Communist informer. Kundera became famous in the 1960s and 1970s for novels that were critical of Czechoslovakia's Communist regime, but in his youth he was a committed member of the Communist party and even wrote poems in praise of Stalin. This was already well known. But according to a document Hradilek found in the archives, in 1950 Kundera told the police the whereabouts of a man who had deserted from the Czech military, Miroslav Dvořáček. As it turned out, Dvořáček had illegally fled the country and returned as a courier for American counterintelligence. He was arrested and spent 14 years in prison. Kundera denied the allegation, but he was excoriated in the press as a Communist collaborator.[65]

For Hradilek, the story had a clear and unambiguous meaning. Turning Dvořáček into the police was an evil act, and Kundera needed to be held morally accountable for Dvořáček's imprisonment. Even Kundera accepted this moralizing interpretation; he denied he had ever contacted the police but did not claim that the act of calling them should be viewed as anything but reprehensible. For both sides, the goal was either to condemn Kundera or to exonerate him. But focusing on the question of Kundera's moral responsibility does little to help us understand the complexities of the Communist past. To do this, we would need ask different kinds of questions, as this book has done. For example, what was it that drew many educated young people toward Communism in the early 1950s? What might have led them to report suspicious strangers? A sense of patriotic duty? Or a fear of being seen as an enemy during the height of Stalinist terror? In short, we would need to consider all of the complexities of individual lives, realizing that most people cannot be easily categorized as either victims or perpetrators.[66]

Institutions like the House of Terror, the IPN and the ISTR were founded on the idea that there is one clear meaning to the history of Communism in Eastern Europe. They encourage people to remember the socialist past in simple terms, as a time of oppression and unfreedom. Yet, as this book has shown, this was not the only story of socialism. Communist governments did limit people's freedom, but they also gave some people what they considered to be a better life. After 1989, East Europeans appreciated the new freedoms they gained, but many also mourned aspects of the life they had lost. Rather than ignoring this complicated reality, we must strive to understand it.

Notes

1 Philipp Ther, *Europe Since 1989*, trans. Charlotte Hughes-Kreutzmüller (Princeton, NJ: Princeton University Press, 2016), 210–211, 221–226. The commercial can be viewed at: https://www.youtube.com/watch?v=OjXl61uKq8c (accessed July 3, 2020).

2 Valérie Gauriat, "Hungarians Debt Crisis Still Crippling Middle Class," *Euronews*, July 4, 2014, https://www.euronews.com/2014/07/04/hungarian-debt-crisis-still-crippling-middle-class (accessed July 3, 2020); Léna Pelladini-Simanyi and Zsuzsanna Vargha, "Spatializing the Future: Financial Expectations, EU Convergence and the Eastern European Forex Mortgage Crisis," *Economy and Society* 47, no. 2 (2018): 280–312.

3 István Benczes, "From Goulash Communism to Goulash Populism: The Unwanted Legacy of Hungarian Reform Socialism," *Post-Communist Economies* 28, no. 2 (2016): 157.

4 Jan-Werner Müller, *What Is Populism?* (Philadelphia: University of Pennsylvania Press, 2016), 1–5.

5 Marc F. Plattner, "Illiberal Democracy and the Struggle on the Right," *Journal of Democracy* 30, no. 1 (2019): 5–19.

6 Jacques Rupnik, "Hungary's Illiberal Turn: How Things Went Wrong," *Journal of the History of Democracy* 23, no. 3 (2012): 132–137.

7 Kim Lane Scheppele, "Hungary and the End of Politics," *The Nation*, May 26, 2014.

8 European Federation of Journalists, "New Report: Hungary Dismantles Media Freedom and Pluralism," https://europeanjournalists.org/blog/2019/12/03/new-report-hungary-dismantles-media-freedom-and-pluralism/ (accessed July 3, 2020).

9 "Fidesz holds Budapest's Józsefváros in mayoral election amidst 23 percent turnout," *Hungarian Free Press*, http://hungarianfreepress.com/2018/07/09/fidesz-holds-

budapests-jozsefvaros-in-mayoral-election-amidst-23-percent-turn-out/ (accessed July 10, 2020).

10 Casey Quackenbush, "Hungarian Prime Minister Says Europe's Migrant Crisis is a 'Poison'," *Time.com*, July 12, 2016, https://time.com/4425549/enums/ (accessed August 5, 2020).

11 "Full speech of V. Orbán: Will Europe Belong to Europeans?" *Visegrad Post*, July 24, 2017, https://visegradpost.com/en/2017/07/24/full-speech-of-v-orban-will-europe-belong-to-europeans/ (accessed July 9, 2020).

12 Franklin Foer, "Liberalism's Last Stand," *The Atlantic*, June 2019, 64–72.

13 "Hungarian passes anti-immigrant 'Stop Soros' laws," *The Guardian*, June 20, 2018, https://www.theguardian.com/world/2018/jun/20/hungary-passes-anti-immigrant-stop-soros-laws (accessed July 9, 2018).

14 Nick Thorpe, "The man who thinks Europe has been invaded," *BBC.com*, https://www.bbc.co.uk/news/resources/idt-sh/Viktor_Orban (accessed July 10, 2020).

15 Benczes, "From Goulash Communism to Goulash Populism," 158.

16 Anna Gryzmala-Busse, "Poland's Path to Illiberalism," *Current History* 117 (March 2018): 95–101.

17 Gryzmala-Busse, "Poland's Path to Illiberalism,"; Anne Applebaum, "A Warning from Europe," *The Atlantic*, October 2018, 53–63.

18 Marc Santora, "In Poland, Nationalism with a Progressive Touch Wins Voters," *New York Times*, October 10, 2019, https://www.nytimes.com/2019/10/10/world/europe/poland-election-law-and-justice-party.html (accessed July 13, 2020).

19 Santora, "In Poland."

20 "Rule of Law in Poland and Hungary has Worsened," Press release of European Parliament, January 16, 2020, https://www.europarl.europa.eu/news/en/press-room/20200109IPR69907/rule-of-law-in-poland-and-hungary-has-worsened (accessed July 15, 2020).

21 Nanette Neuwahl and Charles Kovacs, "How the EU Can Better Protect the Rule of Law in Its Member States," https://blogs.lse.ac.uk/europpblog/2020/05/08/how-the-eu-can-better-protect-the-rule-of-law-in-its-member-states/ (accessed July 15, 2020).

22 Seán Hanley and Milada Anna Vachudová, "Understanding the Illiberal Turn: Democratic Backsliding in the Czech Republic," *East European Politics* 34, no. 3 (2018): 276–296.

23 Agnieszka Graff, "Report from the Gender Trenches: War against 'Genderism' in Poland," *European Journal of Women's Studies* 21, no. 4 (2014): 431–432.

24 Sharon Wolchik, "Reproductive Policies in the Czech and Slovak Republics," in *Reproducing Gender: Politics, Publics and Everyday Life after Socialism*, ed. Susan Gal and Gail Kligman (Princeton, NJ: Princeton University Press, 2000), 77.

25 Joanna Goven, "New Parliament: Old Discourse? The Parental Leave Debate in Hungary," in Gal and Kligman, *Reproducing Gender*, 286–306.

26 Eva Fodor and Erika Kispeter, "Making the 'Reserve Army' Invisible: Lengthy Parental Leave and Women's Economic Marginalisation in Hungary," *European Journal of Women's Studies* 21, no. 4 (2014): 382–398.

27 Wolchik, "Reproductive Policies," 76; Susan Gal and Gail Kligman, *The Politics of Gender Under Socialism* (Princeton, NJ: Princeton University Press, 2000), 16.

28 Eleonora Zielińska, "Between Ideology, Politics and Common Sense: The Discourse of Reproductive Rights in Poland," in Gal and Kligman, *Reproducing Gender*, 23–57.

29 Magdalena Grabowska, "The Polish Women's Movement Between East and West: The Formation of the Polish Women's Movement Identity," Ph.D. diss, Rutgers University, 2009, 76–77.

30 Anja Vojvodić, "Lingering Legacies and Emerging Progress: Explaining Gender Quota Adoption in Central and Eastern Europe," Ph.D. diss, Rutgers University, 2020, 146–165.

31 Agnieszka Król and Paula Pustułka, "Women on Strike: Mobilizing Against Reproductive Injustice in Poland," *International Feminist Journal of Politics* 20, no. 3 (2018): 366–384.

32 Barbara Havelková, *Gender Equality in Law: Uncovering the Legacies of Czech State Socialism* (Oxford: Hart, 2017), 1–6.

33 Elżbieta Korolczuk and Agnieszka Graff, "Gender as 'Ebola from Brussels': The Anticolonial Frame and the Rise of Illiberal Populism," *Signs: Journal of Women in Culture and Society* 43, no. 4 (2018): 797–821.

34 Claudia Ciobanu, "'New World Order': The 'Natural Family' Franchise Goes Global," *Balkan Insight*, November 21, 2018, https://balkaninsight.com/2018/11/21/new-world-order-the-natural-family-franchise-goes-global-11-05-20181/ (accessed July 31, 2020).

35 "Bulgaria Court Says 'Istanbul Convention' Violates Constitution" *Balkan Insight*, July 28, 2020, https://balkaninsight.com/2018/07/27/bulgaria-s-constitutional-court-says-istanbul-convention-not-in-line-with-basic-law-07-27-2018/ (accessed July 31, 2020).

36 Bulgarian Helsinki Committee, "NGOs in Bulgaria Condemn Court Decision Rejecting Istanbul Convention," July 30, 2018, https://www.bghelsinki.org/en/news/20180730-press-istanbul-convention_EN/ (accessed July 31, 2020).

37 Ziobro made the comment in 2012, before he was Justice Minister. Marc Santora, "Poland Considers Leaving Treaty on Domestic Violence, Spurring Outcry," *New York Times*, July 27, 2020, https://www.nytimes.com/2020/07/27/world/europe/poland-domestic-violence-treaty.html (accessed July 31, 2020).

38 "The Orbán Regime Feels Threatened by Gender Studies," *Hungarian Spectrum*, August 10, 2018, https://hungarianspectrum.org/2018/08/10/the-orban-regime-feels-threatened-by-gender-studies/ (accessed May 18, 2021).

39 "Pro-LGBT Coca-Cola Adverts Spark Boycott Calls in Hungary," *The Guardian*, August 5, 2019, https://www.theguardian.com/world/2019/aug/05/pro-lgbt-coca-cola-ads-spark-boycott-calls-in-hungary (accessed August 1, 2020).

40 "Hungary pulls out of Eurovision amid rise in anti-LGBTQ+ rhetoric," *The Guardian*, November 27, 2019, https://www.theguardian.com/tv-and-radio/2019/nov/27/hungary-pulls-out-of-eurovision-amid-rise-in-anti-lgbt-rhetoric (accessed August 1, 2020).

41 The Hungarian Registry Act requires men to have male names and women to have female names; there are no gender-neutral names in Hungarian.

42 Nico Lang, "'This Is Just Evil' New Law Would Force Trans Hungarians to Out Themselves," *Vice*, May 5, 2020, https://www.vice.com/en_us/article/n7wjbg/hungary-transgender-law-id-birth-certificates-orban (accessed August 1, 2020).

43 Juliette Bretan, "Activist Signposts Polish Towns as 'LGBT-Free Zones' in Protest Against Anti-LGBT Resolutions," *Notes from Poland*, January 25, 2020, https://notesfrompoland.com/2020/01/25/activist-signposts-polish-towns-as-lgbt-free-zone-in-protest-against-anti-lgbt-resolutions/ (accessed August 3, 2020).

44 Marc Santora and Joanna Berendt, "Anti-Gay Brutality in a Polish Town Blamed on Poisonous Propaganda," *New York Times*, July 27, 2019, https://www.nytimes.com/2019/07/27/world/europe/gay-pride-march-poland-violence.html (accessed August 3, 2020); Daniel Tilles, "Poland's Anti-LGBT Campaign Explained," *Notes from Poland*, June 17, 2020, https://notesfrompoland.com/2020/06/17/polands-anti-lgbt-campaign-explained-ten-questions-and-answers/ (accessed August 4, 2020).

45 Daniel Tilles, "Polish President Condemns LGBT 'Ideology of Evil' in New Speech as EU Commissioner Issues Criticism," *Notes from Poland*, June 15, 2020, https://notesfrompoland.com/2020/06/15/polish-president-condemns-lgbt-ideology-of-evil-in-new-speech-as-eu-commissioner-issues-criticism/ (accessed August 3, 2020).

46 Christian Davies and Shaun Walker, "Poland's Presidential Election Too Close to Call as Voting Under Way," *The Guardian*, July 12, 2020, https://www.theguardian.com/world/2020/jul/12/poland-presidential-election-too-close-to-call-voting-begins-andrzej-duda-rafa-trzaskowski (accessed August 3, 2020).

47 David Paternotte and Roman Kuhar, "Disentangling and Locating the 'Global Right': Anti-Gender Campaigns in Europe," *Politics and Governance* 6, no. 3 (2018): 6–19.

48 Maya Nadkarni, *Remains of Socialism: Memory and the Futures of the Past in Postsocialist Hungary* (Ithaca, NY: Cornell University Press, 2020), 135–136.

49 Amy Sodaro, *Exhibiting Atrocity: Memorial Museums and the Politics of Past Violence* (New Brunswick, NJ: Rutgers University Press, 2018), 75–76.

50 Péter Apor, "An Epistemology of the Spectacle? Arcane Knowledge, Memory and Evidence in the Budapest House of Terror," *Rethinking History* 18, no. 3 (2014): 328–344.

51 "Double Occupation," House of Terror website, https://www.terrorhaza.hu/en/allando-kiallitas/second_floor/double-occupation (accessed December 17, 2020).

52 Apor, "An Epistemology of the Spectacle?" 335.

53 Nadkarni, *Remains of Socialism*, 134–135.

54 Sodaro, *Exhibiting Atrocity*, 66–67.

55 Nadkarni, *Remains of Socialism*, 122.

56 Gabriela Cristea and Simina Radu-Bucurenci, "Raising the Cross: Exorcising Romania's Communist Past in Museums, Memorials and Monuments," in *Past for the Eyes: East European Representations of Communism in Cinema and Museums after 1989*, ed. Oksana Sarkisova and Péter Apor (Budapest: Central European University Press, 2008), 275–305.

57 Alina Haliliuc, "Who Is a Victim of Communism: Gender and Public Memory in the Sighet Museum, Romania," *Aspasia* 7 (2013): 108–131.

58 Nadkarni, *Remains of Socialism*, 131–132.

59 Valentin Behr, "Historical Policy-Making in Post-1989 Poland: A Sociological Approach to the Narratives of Communism," *European Politics and Society* 18, no. 1 (2017): 82.

60 Dariusz Stola, "Poland's Institute of National Remembrance: A Ministry of Memory?" in *The Convolutions of Historical Politics*, ed. Alexei Miller and Maria Lipman (Budapest: Central European University Press, 2012), 45–58.

61 Stola, "Poland's Institute of National Remembrance," 56.

62 Behr, "Historical Policy-Making in Post-1989 Poland," 88–90.

63 Stola, "Poland's Institute of National Remembrance," 55–57.

64 Behr, "Historical Policy-Making in Post-1989 Poland," 91–92.

65 Aviezer Tucker, "Czech History Wars," *History Today* 59, no. 3 (2009): 43–45.

66 Muriel Blaive, "Introduction," in *Perceptions of Society in Communist Europe: Regime Archives and Popular Opinion*, ed. Muriel Blaive (New York: Bloomsbury Academic, 2019), 1–9.

INDEX

Note: *Italic* page numbers refer to figures and page numbers followed by "n" denote endnotes.